PROFITABLE PENALTIES

PINE FORGE PRESS TITLES OF RELATED INTEREST

- *Adventures in Criminal Justice Research Using SPSS for WINDOWS* by George W. Dowdall, Earl Babbie and Fred Halley
- *Crime and Everyday Life: Insights and Implications for Society* by Marcus Felson
- *Exploring Social Issues With SPSS for WINDOWS* by Joseph F. Healey
- *Race, Ethnicity and Gender in the United States* by Joseph F. Healey
- *Race, Ethnicity, Gender and Class* by Joseph F. Healey
- *Building Community: Social Science in Action* by Philip Nyden, Anne Figert, Mark Shibley, and Darryl Burroughs
- *Diversity in America* by Vincent N. Parrillo

The Pine Forge Press Series in Research Methods and Statistics
Edited by Kathleen S. Crittenden

- *Regression: A Primer* by Paul Allison
- *A Guide to Field Research* by Carol A. Bailey
- *Designing Surveys: A Guide to Decisions and Procedures* by Ron Czaja and Johnny Blair
- *Social Statistics for a Diverse Society* by Chava Frankfort-Nachmias
- *Experimental Design and the Analysis of Variance* by Robert Leik
- *How Sampling Works* by Caroline Persell and Richard Maisel
- *Program Evaluation* by George McCall
- *Investigating the Social World: The Process and Practice of Research* by Russell K. Schutt

Sociology for a New Century: A Pine Forge Press Series
Edited by Charles Ragin, Wendy Griswold, and Larry Griffin

- *Crime and Disrepute* by John Hagan

The Pine Forge Press Series in Crime
Edited by George S. Bridges, Robert D. Crutchfield, Joseph G. Weis

- Volume 1 *Crime (Readings)*
- Volume 2 *Juvenile Delinquency (Readings)*
- Volume 3 *Criminal Justice (Readings)*

PROFITABLE PENALTIES

How to Cut Both Crime Rates and Costs

DANIEL GLASER

PINE FORGE PRESS
Excellence and Innovation for Teaching

For information:

 Pine Forge Press
A Sage Publications Company
2455 Teller Road
Thousand Oaks, California 91320
(805) 499-4224
E-mail: sales@pfp.sagepub.com
http://www.sagepub.com/pineforge

SAGE Publications Ltd.
6 Bonhill Street
London EC2A 4PU
United Kingdom

SAGE Publications India Pvt. Ltd.
M-32 Market
Greater Kailash I
New Delhi 110 048 India

Printed in the United States of America

Library of Congress Cataloging-in-Publication Data

97 98 99 00 01 02 03   10 9 8 7 6 5 4 3 2 1

Glaser, Daniel.
    Profitable penalties: How to cut both crime rates and costs /
Daniel Glaser.
      p. cm.
    Includes bibliographical references (p.) and index.
    ISBN 0-7619-8534-4 (pbk.)
    1. Punishment in crime deterrence—United States. 2. Crime prevention—United States. 3. Crime—United States. I. Title.
HV9950.G58 1997
    364.6'01—dc21   97-4599

Production Editor: Michèle Lingre
Production Assistant: Denise Santoyo
Typesetter/Designer: Janelle LeMaster
Indexer: Cristina Haley
Cover Designer: Ravi Balasuriya

Contents

About the Author

Daniel Glaser is Professor Emeritus of Sociology, specializing in criminology at the University of Southern California. He is the author or editor of a dozen books and about 200 articles and is past president of the American Society of Criminology, the Illinois Academy of Criminology, and California's Association for Criminal Justice Research.

About the Publisher

Pine Forge Press is a new educational publisher, dedicated to publishing, innovative books and software throughout the social sciences. On this and any other of our publications, we welcome your comments, ideas, and suggestions. Please call or write to

> **Pine Forge Press**
> A Sage Publications Company
> 2455 Teller Road
> Thousand Oaks, CA 91320
> 805-499-4224
> Internet: sdr@pfp.sagepub.com

Visit our new World Wide Web site, your direct link to a multitude of on-line resources:

> http://www.sagepub.com/pineforge

Foreword

Profitable Penalties details my thoughts and experiences of a half century of employment and research in correctional agencies in the United States, Western Europe, and elsewhere around the world.

I wrote the book to fill a perceived gap. No broad-based books, readable to undergraduate students and the general public alike, focus on whether the vast sums we are spending to "get tough on crime," give us our money's worth by using what the best research evidence available shows are the most profitable reactions to lawbreakers.

The rallying cries merely to impose more severe punishments in hopes of thereby suppressing crime may enhance political capital and earn handsome dividends to politicians who champion this approach, but their policies also divert public funds from investments that can be more beneficial for recidivism reduction.

Profitable Penalties discusses both general principles in reacting to crime, and details pertinent to specific types of offenses. Chapter 1 explains why we invest our criminal justice system with so much importance today, and why the search for profitable penalties is so urgent. Chapter 2 describes the options, penal and nonpenal, that today's criminal justice system offers for punishing convicted criminals. Chapter 3 explains the motivations behind our punishments, the practical considerations that constrain our choices, and the underlying principles of cost-effective crime control. Most importantly, we need to ensure that the penalties meted out fit not only the crime but also the offender.

Chapters 4 through 9 examine particular types of crime, the persons most likely to commit them, and cost-effective methods for their control.

Chapter 4 deals with adolescent lawbreaking and the goals of changing possible criminal careers at their beginnings, while also achieving deterrence and retribution for the general public. Chapter 5 tell the history of our efforts to control vices and so-called "victimless" crimes and describes the methods best suited for reducing their cost to society. Chapter 6 explores the antecedents of crimes of passion and some policies for reducing the potential damage arising from conflict between individuals. Chapter 7, which is about sex crimes, draws some useful distinctions among perpetrators and discusses nonpenal punishments; the chapters also discusses criminal defenses based on pleas of insanity and incompetency. Chapter 8 deals with the large variety of lawbreaking common in most legitimate occupations, offenses that range in their separate significance from petty to enormous, but in total are much more expensive to society than most people realize. The concern of Chapter 9 is those who pursue crime for profit not just episodically, but as an established and continuous profession that has its own subculture.

The book ends with Chapter 10, which summarizes the measures we can take to ensure that our punishments are cost-effective. The most profitable penalties are the ones that reflect not only the convicted person's latest offense but also his (or her) total life history. Different kinds of correctional interventions work with different kinds of offenders, depending on their prior relationships and experiences.

In revising and sharpening these chapters, I benefited a great deal from the advice and wise counsel of those who reviewed the initial manuscript of this book, and also from Rebecca Smith, my editor, who helped me to improve the final draft.

This book is dedicated to my best friend and most helpful critic, whom I love tremendously, my wife Pearl.

1

Crime and Punishment
at Century's End

On any given day, you are likely to see or hear something in the media about crime and its victims. For instance:

- A 46-year-old woman is shot in the head during a home-invasion robbery and dies from her injuries.

- A number of new immigrants are surprised to find that the terms of their automobile lease contracts are different from the oral representations of those contracts, and the firm's owner is indicted on fraud charges.

- A teacher is struck in the head by a stray bullet, in full view of the fifth graders in his classroom, during an outside shoot-out between juvenile gang members.

- A newborn baby has two fingers shot off and her father is shot in the chest when two men in dark suits, posing as pie salesmen, open fire inside the home to which they have been admitted.

- A 12-year-old boy is sexually molested by a city employee, who is caught and prosecuted.

- Four people are methodically slaughtered by a man who is identified as a convicted felon and alleged gang member but who remains at large.

- A model is murdered and buried in a shallow grave in a national forest, and the photographer accused of her murder pleads not guilty.

Incidents like these are shocking because the victims are people just like us, going peacefully about their daily lives until they cross the paths of criminals.

Understandably, stories like these make us angry and fearful. We all cope with these strong emotions in different ways. We might carelessly ignore the dangers around us, or we might become little more than prisoners in our own homes or neighborhoods. We might buy a gun for self-protection. Or we might pressure our political representatives for more police, more prisons, greater criminal penalties. In fact, in recent years members of the public have responded in all these ways.

This book focuses on the punishments we have devised for convicted criminals. In the past few years, a number of "get tough on crime" measures have been adopted, including mandatory penalties, "three-strikes" sentencing, and expansion of the death penalty. These measures are intended to put criminals out of business and to keep more good citizens from being murdered, assaulted, robbed, and otherwise victimized. But they are expensive, especially in an era of tight government budgets. And so it is reasonable for us to ask whether we are getting our money's worth from the crime-control system we have recently been building: Are the penalties we impose profitable, in the sense that they cost-effectively achieve our goals?

Crime and the Fear of Crime

The public's response to certain crimes is dramatic. In 1993, when 12 tourists were murdered in Florida, frequent media reports about the crimes described how the victims were trapped in unfamiliar territory by vicious predators. The media advised people which areas to avoid and how to conduct themselves in public. Large numbers of Florida-bound tourists decided to avoid potential problems altogether by vacationing elsewhere. Many of the Florida victims were tourists from other countries, and so the hysteria spread worldwide. The state lost millions of dollars in canceled reservations.

But media publicity about the murders obscured some important facts. Most notably, Florida has more than 40 million tourists annually, so the prospect of a tourist being murdered was less than 0.0001%. This rate was lower than the murder risk for Florida's 13.5 million residents or for the residents of other states. In addition, the tourist murder rate has sub-

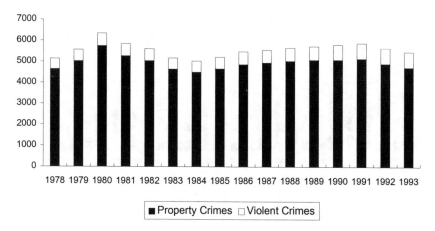

**Number of Serious Victimizing Crimes
per 100,000 U.S. Inhabitants**

■ Property Crimes □ Violent Crimes

Exhibit 1.1. Number of Serious Victimizing Crimes Known to the Police per 100,000 U.S. Inhabitants, 1978-1993

sequently declined (Moran, 1995). Obviously, we cannot judge the prevalence or seriousness of crime solely by what we read in the newspapers and newsmagazines or hear on radio and television.

Crime Rate Trends

The media and some politicians have led us to believe that crime rates have been increasing at an alarming rate. In reality, however, research shows that crime rates have fluctuated somewhat from year to year with no clear trend up or down. Although trends in crimes reported to the police do seem to differ from trends reported in a confidential survey of U.S. residents, these differences make sense in light of the ways the two types of statistics are gathered.

Crimes known to the police (see Exhibit 1.1) are compiled by the Federal Bureau of Investigation (FBI) from data supplied by local city and county police agencies under its Uniform Crime Reports (UCR) program, through which police classifications of lawbreaking have become standardized. The FBI's *index crimes* (its term for serious victimizing crimes) can be categorized, for the period covered, as follows:

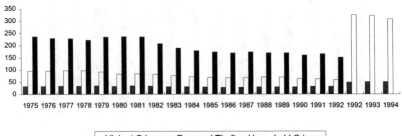

REPORTED VICTIMIZATION RATES IN THE U.S
Personal and Household Crime, 1975-1994

■ Violent Crimes □ Personal Theft ■ Household Crimes

Exhibit 1.2. Reported Victimization Rates for Personal and Household Crims in the United States, 1975-1994

- *Violent crimes:* murder and nonnegligent homicide, forcible rape, aggravated assault
- *Property crimes:* robbery, burglary, larceny-theft, motor vehicle theft

In contrast, the confidential survey of U.S. residents (see Exhibit 1.2)—now known as the National Crime Victimization Survey (NCVS)—relies on direct reports from the general populace. The U.S. Justice Department contracts for interviews every 6 months of a representative national sample of 110,000 persons 12 years old or older in 66,000 households. Randomly selected fractions of the sample are replaced periodically by new random selections from the total U.S. population. Members of the sample are asked whether in the past 6 months they were the victims of the crimes on a standardized list. For each crime that they report experiencing during this period, they are asked whether the police were notified.

Originally, the survey was known as the National Crime Survey. It had several noteworthy differences from the NCVS, which replaced it in 1992. For instance, the category "household crimes" in the National Crime Survey included

> attempted and completed crimes that do not involve personal confrontation. Examples of household crimes include burglary, motor vehicle theft, and household larceny. (Bureau of Justice Statistics, 1994, p. 134)

The questionnaires were redesigned for the NCVS by adding numerous probes regarding theft. As a result, respondents reported many more small personal losses than before, especially losses blamed on persons whom the victims knew or suspected (often a friend or relative). The distinction between personal theft and household crimes became less clear, and so the categories were combined.

NCVS crime rates are higher than crime rates known to the police because, according to the NCVS interviews, only about 36% of all victimizations are reported to the police. The police are notified in only 34% of property crimes (including, however, 78% of motor-vehicle thefts) and 42% of violent crimes, the survey indicates. Most nonreporting of crimes to the police seems to be due to the relationship between the victim and the perpetrator and some due to the victim's reluctance to get involved with the police.

Both sources of data on crime rates—the UCR and the NCVS—greatly underreport a significant portion of all crime. Experts believe that the most frequent crimes in the United States are illegal drug offenses, such as the sale, purchase, or possession of marijuana, cocaine, heroin, or other legally forbidden substances by persons other than the physicians, pharmacists, or others who are licensed to handle these drugs. Very few drug crimes are reported either to the police or to crime victimization surveyors, however. This problem is discussed in more detail in Chapter 5.

Rates of total victimizing crimes known to the police have been stable overall in recent decades, according to Exhibit 1.1, although the 10% to 14% that are crimes of violence have increased somewhat. This small increase may be due only to growth in the rates of notifying the police of violent crimes, perhaps because more crimes are committed by strangers now than formerly. The United States has become more urbanized, and therefore people know a smaller percentage of the other persons in their communities than most people once did.

Unlike the rates of crimes reported to the police, the rates of violence reported to victimization surveyors have been remarkably stable overall, as Exhibit 1.2 shows. Furthermore, the rates of personal theft and household crimes reported to the surveyors have declined, probably mainly because of demographic trends. Teenagers are not only the majority of arrestees for crimes of this type, with peak arrest rates for boys from 16 to 18 years old, but these youngsters also have the highest rates of reported victimization by these crimes. In 1960, one third of the U.S. population was under 18, but today only one fourth are that young. After about 1985, the postwar baby-boom children started reaching their thirties and forties, when crime rates diminish. A small "echo boom" in crime rates may mark the end of the 1990s and persist briefly after the year 2000, because these are the years when the offspring of the baby boomers—the so-called boomerang generation—will become teenagers and young adults. However, at the same time more people will be reaching old age, when few engage in serious crimes and few keep the hours or go to the places where victimizing crimes by others are most frequent.

Reasons for the Fear of Crime

Despite the moderate trends in crime rates in the 1990s, fear of crime has become a major source of anxiety for many people. One reason for the discrepancy is that today a larger percentage of violent attacks are by strangers and a larger percentage are by gun, both of which are more fear-provoking than the other offenses that most people have experienced. In earlier times, people were less frightened by crime because it was rarely life-endangering and it could usually be ascribed to relatives, friends, or acquaintances, whose motives were easier to discern.

Another explanation for the recent surge in the fear of crime is greater media attention to scary offenses. In addition, when politicians exploit the public's anxiety about crime to get votes, media coverage of their campaign rhetoric means all the more dramatic news stories about crime. All this attention to crime leads the public to believe that they have more to fear than ever before.

Finally, demographic trends have increased the fear of crime, despite their contributing to the decline in crime rates by reducing the proportion of youths in most communities. Older people, whose numbers are growing, are persistently the most fearful of being attacked, and they agitate most for giving criminals severer punishments. Policymakers cannot help focusing on complaints about crime from the elderly, as older persons as a group vote more regularly than others and are active and vocal on matters that concern them.

The Escalation of Penalties

The result of growing fear of crime has been a notable change in the way we punish convicted criminals. In the 1960s and 1970s, sentencing principles were multidimensional. Judges could freely choose among confinement, supervised release into the community, restitution and fines, and suspended sentences. Thus penalties varied greatly from one court to another. Punishments could be tailored to suit not only the crime but also the criminal and the prospect of reforming the offender.

In the 1980s and 1990s, as crime became a staple of the nightly news and fear of crime began to mount, governments adopted an escalating series of measures designed to stop crime. Legislators always find that their easiest and most popular response to the fear of crime is to support a law mandating higher penalties.

One dramatic consequence has been revival of the death sentence. For the first few years after the U.S. Supreme Court reinstated capital punishment in 1976, only one or two persons were executed each year in this country. But in 1985, five were executed; in 1986, 21 received punishment by death; and an irregular increase occurred thereafter. The total peaked at 38 in 1993 and has remained over 30 per year since then.

The rising number of death penalties has been far overshadowed by increases in prison terms, however. Several developments in law enforcement and corrections have contributed to the increase in prison populations. Especially important is a change in sentencing laws, which in many jurisdictions now force judges to incarcerate each person convicted of certain crimes for a *mandatory minimum prison term*, the length of which is based only or mostly on the person's current crime. Courts pay less attention than in the 1960s and 1970s to the defendant's prior, noncriminal life. Indeed, they tend to pay less attention than previously to whether an offense was the defendant's first, second, fifth, or fiftieth.

Since 1980 we have also been engaged in a largely futile intensification of the "war on drugs." By the early 1990s in most large U.S. cities, about two thirds of arrests were for drug-related crimes. Roughly a third of first-timers in state prisons are serving sentences for drug possession or sale, and many others are there for crimes committed to get money for drugs. More than 60% of federal prisoners are sentenced on drug charges. In California, although the total number of prisoners increased fourfold in the 12 years from 1980 through 1991, the number confined for drug crimes increased fifteenfold (Zimring & Hawkins, 1995, p. 162).

California's burden of prisoners rose especially after 1994, when the state passed a *three-strikes law*. Several other states followed with similar legislation. Such laws require, for a third felony conviction, prison terms of 25 years to life without parole. Some states enacted two-strike laws and one-strike laws to mandate long prison terms for a second or even first instance of a specified type of violent felony. Such rigid rules have produced some obvious injustices. In one much publicized case, the third-strike offense that evoked a sentence of life imprisonment was stealing a pizza. In another, it was stealing a pound of meat. The frequency of these sentences diminished slightly after a 1996 court decision that gave judges discretion to overlook as "strikes" some less serious felonies and those committed by a very young person or by a previously convicted felon who had since had more than 5 crime-free years. However, politicians quickly drafted laws to weaken the impact of these court rulings.

When public demands for more severe punishment coincided with widespread money shortages in state and local governments, a host of other measures were introduced. These innovations imposed harsher penalties but a briefer period of confinement than typical of imprisonment. For example, "shock incarceration" and "boot camps" spread rapidly during the 1980s and 1990s, primarily for young offenders. Shock incarceration briefly exposes impressionable young people to the harsh realities of prison and criminal life, in the hopes that they will be scared into obeying the law from then on. Boot camp incarcerates them for a relatively brief term of vigorous drill and exercise, as in basic training for military recruits. Some boot camps also provided hard work and remedial education, which are justified as increasing the postrelease employability of inmates. There have also been scattered revivals of chain gangs in the South, with much publicity, but mostly they have been used to handle a few jail inmates who are serving short sentences. Other places have removed TV sets and weight-lifting equipment from buildings where prisoners are housed. Officials assert that these much publicized innovations "get tough on crime" by making punishments harsher.

The High Cost of Getting Tough on Crime

Our crusade to get tough on crime is not without costs. New prisons and jails, new courts, and additional police are expensive. Exhibit 1.3 shows the rapid escalation in U.S. expenditures for criminal justice from 1982

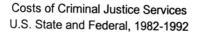

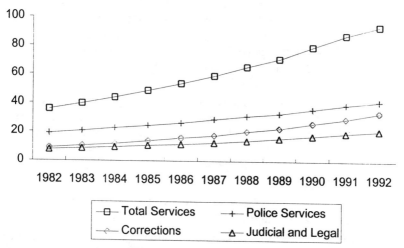

Exhibit 1.3. Total State and Federal Expenditures for Criminal Justice Services in the United States, 1982-1992 (in billions of dollars)

through 1992, a period when we were instituting many new "get tough on crime" measures.

Most of the growth in costs of all criminal justice agencies—police, courts, and corrections—comes from our increased efforts to suppress illegal drug use. From 1988 to 1992 the Bush administration spent more than $45 billion in its war on drugs, yet illegal drug imports increased, heavy users became more numerous, and seized drugs became purer—suggesting a more plentiful drug supply. In addition, billions were squandered overseas in vain efforts to stop the growth of crops that yield illegal drugs. Meanwhile, legislators kept raising penalties for drug crimes, often mandating long prison terms. These trends, continued in the Clinton era, required crash spending for prison construction by states and the federal government, a form of spending that is much more expensive than well-planned and budgeted.

Mandatory minimum sentences and three-strikes laws have also been expensive. Mathematicians of the Rand Corporation calculate that full implementation of California's three-strikes law might reduce serious crimes there by 25%—but at a cost of $5.5 billion annually ("Three Strikes," 1995). The state's entire annual budget is $61.5 billion, including income from the federal government and payments for education and welfare, so the cost for three-strikes laws seems prohibitive. The Rand study pointed out that most crime reduction attributable to the three-strikes laws would come from confining youthful offenders, for it is in the late teens and early twenties that the highest rates of conviction for felonies occur. Because life in prison for these offenders would mean paying their room and board for 50 or more years, the study concluded that

> dollar for dollar, [three-strikes laws] are not as effective in reducing violent crime as more targeted laws. They cast too wide a net and catch a lot of little fish—nonviolent offenders and older felons who no longer pose much threat to society but who are going to spend the rest of their lives in prison getting geriatric care. ("Three Strikes," 1995, p. 1)

Ironically, three-strikes laws and some of the other harsh new measures have actually impeded the ability of the criminal justice system to get tough on crime—that is, to give criminals what they justly deserve. Defendants facing life terms are much more likely to insist on a jury trial, which increases the financial difficulties of budget-strapped prosecutors and courts and exacerbates the shortage of courts and judges for civil cases. Because of the logjam, prosecutors have been charging only misdemeanors for many persons arrested on felonies, if they agree to plead guilty. Such covert bargaining defeats efforts to achieve justice.

Questions of justice have also been raised because racial minorities are disproportionately being penalized with long prison sentences for their crimes. Nearly two thirds of all prison inmates are black, Native American, or Hispanic, yet these minorities make up only about a fifth of the total U.S. population. More than 9% of all African American adult males are in jail or prison or on probation or parole, compared with not quite 2% of all white adult males (Browne, Gilliard, Snell, Stephan, & Wilson, 1996, Table 1.2). Of males in their twenties, about one in three African Americans and one in seven Latinos are under these court-ordered restraints (Ostrow, 1995). African Americans, about an eighth of the U.S. population, are nearly half of its adult prisoners; they are only a third of its probationers. Yet researchers have found that people of the same income level and neighborhood tend to commit crimes at similar rates, except for the low rates of some Asian groups (Sampson, 1987). We must therefore ask to what extent the predominance of minorities in prison is due to prejudiced police and courts and to what extent it reflects the lower incomes and inferior educations of these minorities and their segregation in slum neighborhoods.

Focusing on crime and punishment also raises some issues of social priorities. Partly to pay for the explosive rise in prison costs, states have already sharply cut funding of universities and other educational institutions. Doing so, however, jeopardizes long-run economic growth. Work technologies are changing at an exponential rate, making higher levels of knowledge mandatory for those who seek well-paying jobs. It seems impractical for a society to spend more on punishing youth than giving them an education.

The Search for Profitable Penalties

The financial and social costs of getting tough on crime would perhaps be acceptable if we knew that they were buying significant decreases in crime. Yet little attention has been devoted to determining whether the higher penalties change crime rates. What little research has been done is inconclusive. For example, evaluations of boot camp effectiveness usually find that its releasees return to crime at about the same rate as similar offenders with longer confinement in jails or prisons. Educational and drug treatment programs in the camps appear possibly to reduce future criminality, but the data that have been gathered are inadequate to test the results of these programs well (Harland, 1996, pp. 102-112; Mackenzie, Brame, McDowall, & Souryall, 1995). Also not well assessed are the diverse special programs of postrelease control and assistance given boot camp inmates (Bourque, Han, & Klein, 1996).

Similarly, it appears that efforts to establish mandatory minimum prison terms have neither achieved justice in sentencing nor protected the public from crime, for several reasons:

- Nearly all drug crimes and large fractions of property offenses, as well as almost all acts of violence within families, are never reported to the police.

- Criminals are caught and convicted for less than a 10th of their serious crimes against others and for a fraction of 1% of their illegal drug transactions (Chaiken & Chaiken, 1982; Felson, 1994, p. 9). Many surveys of high school seniors and others show that even extensive illegal drug taking generally does not result in arrest.

- A majority of those who most often commit serious crimes engage in many different types of offense (Sampson & Laub, 1993; Wolfgang, Thornberry, & Figlio, 1987). Chance alone determines whether they are caught for their worst crimes or for lesser ones. Even if they are convicted of and punished for their lesser crimes, they are in effect still getting away with more serious lawbreaking.

♦ A term in prison or jail is in itself unlikely to keep some offenders from returning to criminal activity. The likelihood of a criminal's future lawbreaking can be most accurately assessed by four factors: frequency and severity of the person's previous crimes; age at which the person became active in crime; extent of drug and alcohol use; and extent of legitimate employment in recent years (Blumstein, Cohen, Roth, & Visher, 1986). Future criminality of drug offenders is especially tied to their history of drug and alcohol use.

The lesson we should be absorbing is that despite the great costs of imprisoning people convicted of serious crimes, we have not yet succeeded in reducing crime rates, at least not to a level that justifies the expense. We need to seek ways to make our penalties more profitable— that is, legislators and judges need to consider what researchers have found about how alternative penalties, which are described in Chapter 2, affect various types of offenders. For every dollar spent on crime control, we should try to achieve the maximum result.

Note

1. Reprinted by permission of the *Los Angeles Times*.

2

Punishment Options
for Convicted Criminals

All societies have norms to foster what they regard as morally correct conduct, and all societies devise punishments that they consider appropriate for violations of these norms. The norm violations for which law, or tradition generally accepted as legal, prescribes punishment by an agency of government are called *crimes*. Usually some members of society have more influence than others in deciding what the law will define as criminal and how it will be punished. Nevertheless, most members of society consider the specification of crimes and penalties essential for the peaceful and productive operation of communities, families, commerce, and many other types of organized activity. In the United States, for example, "Equal justice under law," carved in the stone of the Supreme Court Building, is a widely accepted ideal.

The practical purpose of punishment is to prevent further violations of society's norms. Punishment of criminals serves this purpose in two ways. First, it may reduce criminals' inclination to repeat the sort of behavior that got them punished. Such repetition is called *recidivism*. Second, punishment may serve as a warning to others who contemplate violating the norms themselves.

Even the most nonviolent cultures, such as the Quakers in early America, have punished transgressors, using such passive means as shunning and ostracism. But in many societies, punishments have often been more violent than the crimes for which they were imposed. Convicted criminals were sometimes stoned to death or eviscerated in the public square. In most nations today, however, penalties are generally nonviolent. They are also extremely diverse. The principal variations are confinement, limitations on freedom in the community, monetary and community service penalties, and suspended sentences. Each has advantages and disadvantages.

This chapter discusses the traditional forms of these penalties, as well as innovative variations used in parts of the United States and in other nations. Most persons, including judges, know little about some of these variations. Nevertheless, if the goal is to make criminal penalties more profitable, these punishments are worth evaluating.

Confinement

In our society, convicted criminals can be confined in an institution for many types of crime. When people think about punishing serious crime, they most often think of confinement. The crimes for which the maximum confinement penalty is a year or less are called *misdemeanors*; those for which the convicted criminals may be confined for a year or more are called *felonies*. In the United States, felonies include the most violent crimes, such as murder and assault, but only about 20% of felonies involve violence. The rest are mostly burglaries, thefts, and drug offenses.

Adult criminals who are sentenced to a period of confinement may be locked up in one of two types of places:

- *Prisons:* operated by state and federal governments; used primarily to hold adults who have been convicted of felonies and sentenced to more than a year in confinement
- *Jails:* operated mostly by county governments; used to confine those convicted of misdemeanors for a year or less and to hold felony arrestees who are not released pending trial or between trial and sentencing

In 1980, 330,000 people were in U.S. state and federal prisons. By 1995 there were a million. Rapid growth also occurred in local jailing (and in the total number of people whose freedom in the community was limited through probation or parole), as Exhibit 2.1 shows. Altogether, well over five million U.S. adults now have their freedom restricted because of their crimes.

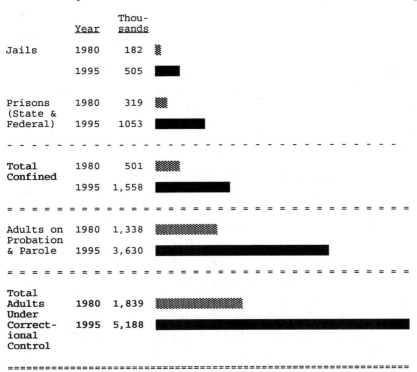

	Year	Thou-sands	
Jails	1980	182	
	1995	505	
Prisons (State & Federal)	1980	319	
	1995	1053	
Total Confined	1980	501	
	1995	1,558	
Adults on Probation & Parole	1980	1,338	
	1995	3,630	
Total Adults Under Correct-ional Control	1980	1,839	
	1995	5,188	

Sources: Beck and Gilliard, 1995; Snell, 1995; A. Miller, 1995.

Exhibit 2.1. Adult Correctional Populations in the United States, 1980 and 1995
SOURCE: Beck and Gilliard (1995); Miller (1995); Snell (1995).

Imprisonment has increased much more in some parts of the country than in others. California prison rolls rose more than fivefold, from less than 25,000 in 1980 to more than 130,000 in 1995. Texas had the highest rate of increase in prisoners and also led all states in total prisoners per 100,000 population (Shogren, 1995). The high confinement rates in these two states might have been equaled or exceeded by other states had not court orders prohibited extreme prison crowding in Alabama, Nevada, and elsewhere.

Juvenile offenders, legally defined in most states as those under 18, are processed in separate juvenile or family courts. Any confinement that these courts order is typically in a detention center, correctional camp, or training school reserved for juveniles. However, federal and state jurisdictions each specify an age range, generally from 14 to 18, in which those who have been charged with the most serious crimes or have been arrested for repeated crimes may be tried in criminal courts as adults and sent to adult prisons.

An average of about 30,000 juveniles enter local detention each year, and nearly 70,000 are in state training schools or other long-term confinement for delinquency (Snyder & Sickmund, 1995, pp. 164-165). An uncounted larger number are on formal or informal probation or warning locally, from police or from the courts. They have been warned that they will be locked up if they commit further offenses.

Juveniles are not confined for a length of time that is specified in advance. Rather, they are held for an indefinite period, depending on their behavior, but not to extend beyond their 21st birthday. In California since establishment of its Youth Authority in 1941, and in several other states thereafter under similar youth commissions, persons committing crimes before their 21st birthday may be sentenced by either a juvenile or a criminal court to a youth correctional institution until their 25th birthday. Almost all are paroled before this date, however.

Short of the death penalty (which is discussed in Chapter 6), confinement is the surest way to control a convicted criminal's behavior. Yet confinement entails the highest expenditures of any punishment method considered in this chapter. Confining criminals means not only assuming the cost of housing, feeding, and guarding them but perhaps also providing welfare for their dependents. The estimated cost of confinement per inmate currently ranges from $35,000 for penitentiary incarceration in high-wage states (where the cost of staffing prisons is high), such as New York and California, to $15,000 per year or less in prisons of the Southeastern states. This cost does not include amortization of construction costs, which run from $50,000 to $100,000 per inmate capacity for high-security, celled institutions.

Confinement is also a daunting management prospect. The care and feeding of large groups of people is never easy, and when those people are depressed, angry, or antisocial, the task is fraught with difficulty.

The Subculture of Violence

A primary concern of those who manage correctional confinement facilities is curtailment of inmate violence, against one another but especially against staff (Fleisher, 1989; R. Johnson, 1996). The personal security and the job security of wardens and guards depends on preventing violence. At worst, violence can escalate into inmate riots, which may spread rapidly, cause much destruction and injury, and even kill.

The task of curtailing violence is not easy, primarily because many prisoners come from a delinquent or deviant subculture. Much emphasized in such subcultures, especially in correctional institutions, is toughness and the need to respond with violence to any show of disrespect. One prisoner observed:

> The majority of cons try to work some game on people. They try to con them into doing something they wouldn't ordinarily do, maybe just out of laziness. If you see somebody with a little bit of weakness, you play on that weakness. (Cordilia, 1983, p. 14)

Another added:

> If someone betrays you, you can't let him get away with it. If you do, everybody else will start to pick on you. If anybody puts you down in front of other people, unless you tell him where to go, the other cons will say, "How come you let him do that to you?" If someone steals a pack of cigarettes off you, you have to be ready to kill him or at least hurt him so he can't harm you. (Cordilia, 1983, p. 20)

Serious injuries or death from conflict among inmates are common. Prisoners make lethal stabbing weapons from almost any type of metal, hard plastic, or glass, by grinding it to a sharp edge or point on concrete floors or walls.

Such violence is aided and abetted by the cliques or gangs that develop among confined offenders, especially young ones. Some of these cliques are linked to delinquent or criminal groups in the communities from which the inmates come. Such groups provide mutual aid and influence; they also engage within the institution in bullying, extortion, theft, homosexual rape, and other crimes.

Correctional institutions are especially dangerous for prisoners with minimal experience in a violent subculture, as in the case of an older juvenile charged with minor theft after repeated conflict at home and at school:

> Bobby Nestor was sent to Camp Hill correctional facility, an adult prison, to "learn a lesson." After more than 4 months of incarceration, he hung himself after being sexually assaulted by adult inmates. ("In Brief," 1995, p. 25)

It has been estimated that at least a sixth of male prisoners are raped while confined. Prison rape usually has long-term traumatic effects psychologically, and it also increases the spread of HIV and AIDS among inmates, because an appreciable number have undetected infection on admission. In 1994 the U.S. Supreme Court unanimously decreed that those raped while incarcerated may sue the prison administration for allowing or facilitating such assaults (*Farmer v. Brennan*, 92-7247), but few have done so.

Control and Discipline
Within Correctional Institutions

The administrators of correctional institutions seek to reduce the influence of their most deviant and violent prisoners, and to reduce the harm they may inflict on staff, by separating inmates into types according to their threat to order, plus their special medical, educational, or other needs. Those deemed least dangerous and most trustworthy are assigned work in front offices, work in warden's homes on prison grounds, or even duties outside the prison grounds. Those considered most dangerous are given little freedom, some never leaving their cells or small cell blocks. The federal government, and large states with many prisons, build and operate some institutions primarily for maximum security, others for medium or minimum custody, and a few as hospitals.

Prisoners were once classified primarily by senior prison officers on the basis of personal impressions, plus the inmates' crime records and prior conduct in institutions. Later, classification decisions were made by institution committees, which often called the inmate before them to consult on his or her preferences, discuss their decisions, and offer preferred placements if good conduct occurred at the initial assignment (Craddock, 1996). Today, this sorting of prisoners is increasingly influenced by classification guidelines based on statistical research on the correlates of prison adjustment and postrelease crime. Studies regularly show that predictions based on such actuarial research are usually more accurate than those based only on case impressions, even the impressions of presumed experts such as psychologists, psychiatrists, or prison staff (Glaser, 1985).

Most correctional institutions of Continental Europe, especially the older ones for adults, alleviate classification problems through their design. Architecturally, they separate prisoners and reduce their contacts with other inmates. Often each prisoner is held in a small room with a solid door that has a peephole for staff and a small locked panel for passing things in and out without unlocking the door. Where congregate rooms are used, they usually hold only 6 to 12 inmates. Each room has a bed section, plus a table-and-chair area for meals, leisure, and sometimes work or schooling. Outside yard activities generally involve the unit's residents alone.

In contrast, U.S. correctional institutions, especially those holding delinquent youths, criminalize by their architectural design, for they enhance inmates' influence on one another. Housing of juvenile offenders is usually in dormitories, many with 50 or more occupants. Adult prisoners are more often in cells, alone or with one or two others. But food, work, and recreation for all prisoners, juvenile or adult, generally are provided in large halls or yards, where scores of inmates communicate with and thus influence one another.

In the absence of a well-designed facility, administrators have two conflicting tactics available to prevent violence: (a) enforcing rules rigorously and trusting no one; (b) gaining rapport with inmates, to reduce their hostility and to be informed by them about secret crimes or plots. Rule enforcement efforts produce prisons-within-prisons. These are the disciplinary cells to which those who misbehave may be confined for days or even months. If those held in disciplinary cells are still unruly when their term is up, they may be placed naked into cells furnished only with a toilet hole in the concrete floor and completely without light most of the time. In our society, such treatment is associated with torture and other inhumane punishments. Enlightened prison administrators thus usually seek to ensure discipline by building rapport with inmates.

Staff efforts for rapport with prisoners have not always been sensitive to the norms of the prisoner subculture. Prison staff may secretly reward inmate informants, a policy that makes all prisoners suspicious of the "finks" or "stool pigeons" among them. Some modern institutions, however, have elected inmate councils to help maintain order, plan recreation, and air complaints. Another approach assigns all or most prisoners to group counseling sessions that are labeled "therapy" but that discuss mainly how to get along in prison (Glaser, 1995, pp. 74-82).

In the Netherlands, other methods are used to maintain rapport between staff and inmates. For example, an effort is made to keep the same staff continuously at each of the residential units and to keep both the institutions and these units small. This practice fosters personal relationships between inmates and officers. The staff, well trained in human relations at a special school in The Hague, do not punish individual misbehavior as much as hold each inmate group responsible for the conduct of all its members. They teach groups to develop legitimate behavior norms collectively. The Dutch also encourage prison visits by approved outsiders and grant inmates brief releases before full freedom, which test readiness for a noncriminal life. Although Dutch practices seem to be converging with those of more punitive countries (van Swaaningen & de Jonge, 1995), they are still distinctive.

More important, the Dutch methods are unusually effective in reducing criminality. The Netherlands has only about 25 prisoners per 100,000 adults, as compared to about 50 in Sweden, over 80 in Germany, and more than 500 in the United States (Browne et al., 1996, Table 1.5; Steenhuis, Tigges, & Esser, 1983).

Limitations on Freedom in the Community

Compared to confinement, supervised release of a convicted criminal to the community costs the government much less. The main expense is the salaries of case workers, each of whom may supervise many releasees at a time without the need for weapons and other security measures. Additional expense may be incurred for special monitoring devices and facilities to which releasees report, but again, these expenses are low compared with the expense of correctional confinement facilities and equipment.

The two key methods used to limit the freedom of convicted criminals in the community are often confused:

- *Probation:* a sentence to a period of supervised release, as the initial penalty ordered by a court after it finds a defendant guilty
- *Parole:* a supervised release from a confinement sentence, beginning after a portion of that sentence has been served, which is authorized by an independent parole board rather than by the sentencing court

Although probation and parole incapacitate less than confinement does, they do restrain releasees' activities. The rules usually require living in an approved residence; either employment, diligent job search, school attendance, or some combination; avoidance of known criminals; regular hours at home; no alcohol or drugs; no other crimes. A probationer, parolee, or other supervised releasee may be tested for drugs or for breath alcohol on randomly scheduled dates, with little or no advance notice.

Special requirements may also be imposed for some individuals, such as an obligation to get treatment for addiction, to make regular payments to victims of their crimes or to the government, to avoid contact with particular named persons, and to perform services for victims or for the community.

Judges have much discretion to designate other conditions of probation, and they are often quite imaginative. For example, in Lynn and New Bedford, Massachusetts, judges collaborated with English professors, probation officers, and others to develop a literature program for probationers, as an alternative to jailing. These offenders must be sufficiently literate, agree to complete the program, and have no conviction for a violent offense. They attend a weekly class for which they are assigned fiction readings and asked to interpret their own problems, such as family conflicts, in comparison to those of the fictional characters. Their final assignment is to prepare a program for themselves that considers their skills, education, financial resources, and personal goals. Participants are reported to have low recidivism rates, and a few continue in other English courses ("Busting Books," 1994).

Supervision of Probationers and Parolees

Probation and parole are unlikely to be viewed as punishment or to prevent recidivism unless someone oversees the convicted criminal. Therefore, supervision officers are assigned to each releasee, to counsel and assist but also to monitor and to arrest or have the police arrest the releasee for serious rule violations. In some states and for the federal government, the same officers supervise both probationers and parolees in their districts. In most of the United States, however, probation is administered by the county government in conjunction with local courts; parole is handled only by the state.

Probationers and parolees are classified according to the level of supervision deemed justifiable given their likelihood of recidivating, the probable seriousness of their new crimes if they recidivate, their need for assistance, and the available supervision staff. Classification decisions are often based on standardized rating forms, especially one called Client Management Classification Guidelines, which itemize the age, criminal record, and other pertinent attributes of each offender and then score each item. Completing such forms adds about 90 minutes to an officer's initial interview with a releasee but indicates an optimum mode of supervision.

The procedure cuts parole revocation and new offense rates enough to make the time profitable (Eisenberg & Markley, 1987; Harris, 1994).

Although supervisors who are assigned those releasees deemed most dangerous or most in need of special aid receive fewer cases, since the 1970s the average caseloads of U.S. probation and parole officers have generally increased. Formerly 50 or 60 cases were supervised by each officer, but some now get up to several hundred or even a thousand cases. The burden greatly reduces supervisors' ability to provide surveillance or assistance. In Los Angeles County, for example, which claims to have the world's largest probation department, two thirds of the probationers are in caseloads of 1,000 and report only by mail, monthly (Petersilia, 1996). The remaining third requires extensive effort, as the following account describes:

> She is 16, pregnant and fears for her life. Gang members are threatening her because they believe she ratted on one of their own who's now jailed for rape. She's no longer in school, too scared to leave home. Only instead of telling the police, she's telling her former probation officer, Robbie Robinson. It's a brief encounter, but it sets off a week of activity for this full-time Los Angeles County deputy probation officer. At breakneck speed, he works the case, meeting gang members in jail and at home, talking with attorneys, police, parents and counselors.
>
> Robinson cuts through that angry straight-ahead stare of youths. With one teenager at Juvenile Hall: "You owe me boy, you hear? You'd better straighten up or you're going to juvenile probation camp."
>
> With a second: "I know the influence you have on the street. I know you intimidate people, and I just can't let this go on."
>
> And with a third: "I'm going to give you another chance, son. I'm going to let you go home, but I'm going to check on you and I'm going to keep making sure you don't mess up again."
>
> After Robinson says he will help the frightened girl huddled on her living room couch, her eyes fill with tears. "I'm thankful God sent him to me."
>
> Robinson's caseload currently includes about 50 people—mostly teenagers—ranging in age from 13 to 25. Some are the sons and daughters of parents already on probation. Most are repeat offenders. He knows all about them, their parents and siblings, cousins, aunts and uncles, their gang nicknames, and their friends.
>
> "My function is to work the streets to become aware of what's going on, to defuse situations and detain the worst elements," he says. "My whole focus is to understand these kids and the problems they are having. I believe in giving them chances . . . but I will lock them up." (abbreviated from Shuster, 1996)[1]

The job of actually supervising probationers gets much less priority in local offices than the job of preparing the presentence investigations that guide judges in penalty decisions. This imbalance occurs because job-threatening reactions against an officer are less likely to be based on lax supervision than on presentence reports that are late or impress a judge poorly. One of the best studies of a juvenile court's functioning quotes one of its probation officers as saying:

> Basically, the probation system operates on the "squeaky wheel" principle—if the schools are bugging you about a kid, or the parents are bugging you about a kid, then you're going to be on the kid, and whatever you do, you're going to do a lot of it. The kid may be out doing all sorts of things, but if he's not being complained about, then nothing's going to happen, because we're a reactive system. (Jacobs, 1990, p. 111)

Probation and parole are commonly viewed as endangering the public because the convicted lawbreakers are not confined. However, these conditional releases usually protect the public by facilitating prompt arrest of recidivators. Prisoners released unconditionally at the end of their sentence are free to go wherever they please. If they resume a life of crime, officials tend not to know as quickly as they know about the activities of most probationers and parolees. In the event of a violation of the terms of release, a court hearing is held for a probationer or a board hearing for a parolee. The result of the hearing may be incarceration or more restrictions under which the release may continue.

The ability to punish recidivism is very important, but supervisory powers may be abused. Probationers and parolees are often imprisoned for rule infractions that would not get other persons incarcerated. Their "technical violations" may be unauthorized absence from home, work, or school or failure to mail in monthly reports or to take drug tests. Persons on probation or parole for a felony may also be put in prison for misdemeanors, such as drunken or disorderly conduct, that for others would result only in a fine or brief jailing. Some releasees flee to avoid such overzealous monitoring of their conduct.

Ironically, excessive penalties for minor rule violations and supervision so visible as to stigmatize a parolee or probationer at home or on the job may impede reformation. Because an emphasis on rule enforcement often prevents effective counseling or role modeling, some experts have urged that postrelease assistance be the responsibility of different persons from those charged with surveillance or drug testing (Conrad,

1981). This separation occasionally occurs but probably should be more frequent.

Alternatives to Traditional
Probation and Parole

In response to dramatic reports of heinous offenses by some parolees, 15 states and the federal government have abolished parole. However, they have overlooked the equally vicious crimes and higher recidivism rates of persons released from prison without parole. Moreover, where parole has been curbed, judges have become more creative in the penalties they impose in order to fit the punishment to the criminal. The result, at least in California, was chaotic diversity in punishments (Holt, 1995). Penalties for similar cases are usually made more consistent by having one parole board review all the sentences from many courts.

In other places where parole has been officially ended, judges have begun imposing more "split sentences," a prison term followed by a probation sentence, thus ensuring post-prison supervision similar to parole. Prison administrators may also give parole-like releases, instead of unconditional discharges, when offenders are let out of prison. "Good time," taken off sentences if offenders behave properly while in prison, is calculated at standard rates, such as 3 days per month during the first year or first several years of confinement and often a larger number of days per month for later years of long sentences. "Good time" releases resemble parole in that they may be canceled for postrelease offenses or for such serious rule infractions as failing to make required reports, failing to appear for a drug test, or testing positively for illegal drugs.

Most people are unaware of the many other variations that have been developed. See Exhibit 2.2 for a summary of the advantages and disadvantages of the following:

• *Intensive Probation or Parole Supervision (IPS).* This is increasingly used for what are deemed to be high-risk or high-need cases. In IPS, each officer may have a caseload of only 15 to 25 offenders, or a team of five officers may supervise about a hundred releasees. IPS has been shown to be much more economical and at least as reformative as confinement, particularly for juveniles (Burton & Butts, 1990; Mair, Lloyd, New, & Sibbit, 1995; Petersilia & Turner, 1993). A frequent condition of IPS is house arrest or home confinement, requiring that the offender stay at home when not at work, school, or some other approved place.

- *Electronic Monitoring.* This augments house arrest by use of a device attached to the ankle or wrist of a probationer or parolee. The device signals a supervision office if the offender leaves home when she or he is supposed to remain there. Supervision offices also receive an alarm if the anklet or bracelet is cut off. Such surveillance reduces recidivism rates, as compared either to jailing or to less intensive supervision, when used for offenders with little prior criminality but with a poor work record and the habit of much carousing in leisure hours (Baumer & Mendelsohn, 1992; Glaser & Watts, 1992; Lilly, Ball, Curry, & Smith, 1992).

- *Electronic Paging.* Electronic paging converts IPS to intensive reporting. In Miami, for example, a probationer who tests positively for illicit drugs is placed in anti-drug abuse education sessions and tested more frequently but is also required to page a probation officer before moving from one location to another and on arriving at home. If the officer does not phone back within 15 minutes, the probationer must phone the officer's answering machine to report, in a standard format, the time and nature of the move. By reviewing these messages and responding by phone or by visits and community inquiries, the officer learns more about the supervised person and has greater influence at less cost than with other forms of IPS (Freburger & Almon, 1994).

- *Halfway Houses* (often called "community correctional centers" or "work furlough centers"). These residences provide a degree of restriction intermediate between that of prison and of probation or parole. Prison inmates are usually placed in halfway houses near their home community a few weeks before the date of their parole or discharge from prison, but occasionally courts order that an entire sentence be served in a halfway house. Some halfway houses are run contractually by private or non-governmental organizations; others are owned or rented and administered by the state. A halfway house may be a freestanding building in a residential area or a wing or floor of a large establishment for transients, such as a YMCA hotel. Residents leave halfway houses daily to seek or to hold jobs or to attend school. Those with incomes are charged for room and board. Before full release, residents are allowed a gradually increased amount of time for home visiting and outside recreation. However, if they return late, drunk, or drugged or otherwise misbehave, their restrictions may be increased. They may even be sent to jail or prison. Absconding from the house may be prosecuted as the crime of escape from legal custody, as with prison escapes, for which a new prison sentence can be imposed.

Type	Methods of Incapacitation	Advantages	Disadvantages
Jailing or imprisonment	Secure confinement	Prevents new crimes in the community	Costly, and may increase recidivism
Probation	Enforcing conduct rules by surveillance; for rule violations it may add severer penalties, even its replacement by a confinement sentence.	Avoids costs and criminalization of confinement; may assist in reformation; aids arrest of recidivists.	Surveillance is often too lax, too petty, or too stigmatizing; policing role may impede its aid role.
Parole	Same as above, but violation penalty may also be to complete the term of confinement from which paroled.	Same as above; also tests readiness for release and for early end to sentence.	Same as above, but parole boards often are more politicized than most courts.
House Arrest and Electronic Monitoring	Confines offender to home when not at work or other approved place; usually is part of probation, with some violation penalties.	Same as above, but reduces out-of-home carousing; builds family bonds, helps probationer save money.	Responses to alarms often lax; sometimes monitor can be evaded; its severity may foster absconding.
Electronic Paging	Gets communication with officer at every move of probationer within the local area.	Same as above, but may provide more control at less cost.	Requires more officer time per case than any of above types.
Halfway House	Keeps offenders in confinement when they are not at work or other approved place.	Greater incapacitation than all the above except jail or prison; makes release more gradual.	Criminalization of some by others; costlier than all the above except jail or prison.
Group Home	Each home holds only a few offenders, and in family atmosphere; they attend local schools, churches, scouts, etc.	Less criminalization that other correctional types of housing; desirable if own home lacks good influences.	Utilization is limited by officials' fear of residents' misconduct.
Day Reporting Center	Offenders come to them in hours when not at school, work, or other approved place, if their home supervisor must be away from home; may also give temporary residence for a few.	Cheaper and less criminalizing than residential places; some give classes and antidrug programs or other services.	Do not insulate some youths enough from problems in their homes or communities.

Exhibit 2.2. Punishments That Limit Freedom

Periodic Detention	Same as above, but imposed mostly on weekends, and has its offenders do community service or nonprofit-agency work, under government supervisors.	Cheaper and less criminalizing than confinement; reformative work provides good social influences.	Must start with only low-risk cases to be accepted in the neighborhood.
Blended Sentences	For older juveniles (e.g., 13-15) after very serious crimes; begins in juvenile facility but its long term is finished in adult corrections.	Presumed less criminalizing than starting a juvenile in an adult correctional agency.	Tried only in Minnesota, Connecticut, and a few other states; not yet well assessed.
Informal or Unofficial Probation or Warning	Release with oral admonition and warning by police, prosecutor, or judge of penalties if new misconduct occurs.	No stigma of official record; cheaper than any of the others above.	Usually no surveillance or assistance is provided; often duration is not made clear.

Exhibit 2.2. Continued

• *Group Homes.* These are residences inhabited by persons whom the state deems good parent figures and whom it pays to shelter a few youngsters lacking adequate family relationships. These juveniles then attend local schools, scout troops, churches, and other appropriate area organizations. They are supposed to be treated by the home operators as their own children. Jerome Miller (1991) points out that state-run halfway houses tend to acquire the rigid regimentation of an institution that views youths as "delinquents suited for incarceration," but group home residents are more often viewed as "adolescents in need of caring supervision" (p. 165). Miller reduced recidivism rates of Massachusetts delinquents by closing all that state's correctional institutions for juveniles and contracting with social work organizations to establish group homes for youths who needed substitute families.

• *Day Reporting Centers (DRCs).* These are called "attendance centers" in Britain and Australia. They are places to which offenders are required to report when not in school or at an approved job or when supervisory parent figures must be away from home. Some centers also have temporary living quarters for youths without satisfactory homes. Some, notably Portland, Oregon's "Our New Beginnings" for women, are for specialized categories of adults. Most American DRCs are open only 5 days per week and serve fewer than 100 offenders at any time. An average of 19 hours attendance per week is required. Total costs are around $20 per day per person, with about one staff member for every 7 attendees. The centers provide antidrug classes, courses on applying for and holding jobs, and other instruction, as well as individual and group counseling. Many attendees would otherwise be incarcerated at greater cost. Those who conform to the rules are rewarded by graduated decreases in surveillance and drug testing, but they are subject to night telephone calls at home and calls at work to check on their whereabouts. More than half of those committed to DRCs are arrested for a new offense or for rule violations, especially nonattendance, during their first half year there (Diggs & Pieper, 1994; Parent, Byrne, Tsarfaty, Valade, & Esselman, 1995; Robinson, 1992).

• *Periodic Detention (PD).* Periodic detention has been in use in New Zealand since 1962, where convicted persons may be required to report for community work for up to 9 hours on any day or up to 15 hours per week, for periods of up to a year. The work is usually done on weekends, primarily for community organizations to which the Department of Justice contributes funding for administration. Now more than four times as many New Zealand offenders are on PD as in prison (Eskridge & Newbold, 1993).

• *Blended Sentences.* This type of sentencing was developed in Minnesota, Connecticut, and other states for juveniles who commit heinous crimes, such as murdering their mother or raping their sister. Although the perpetrator is a child, perhaps 12 or 15 years old, the public often demands that he or she be tried in the criminal courts as an adult and, if found guilty, be sent to prison for a long term instead of to the limited duration of control—to age 21 or 25—of youth institutions. Under blended sentences, the juvenile court maintains power over the individual for the full duration of correctional controls, but it may specify that when the maximum age for juvenile confinement is reached, the offender begins a sentence as an adult, such as a term in prison or on adult probation.

• *Informal Probation.* This is imposed on many offenders, especially juveniles, by an official telling them that charges will not be processed if they commit no further offenses, conform to probation rules, or, in some cases, obey special requirements, such as avoiding certain places or persons. Often informal probation has no time limit. These unofficial conditional releases are made by police, prosecutors, probation officers, and judges. Usually the releasees are not routinely monitored.

Probation and parole in all their forms are almost always much cheaper than prison, but their costs are extremely diverse, depending on how much surveillance or assistance is given to releasees. In contrast, prisons spare society the potential cost of new crimes that many—perhaps most—inmates would commit if not locked up. But prison sentences may be a net loss for society for inmates who would recidivate at lower rates if released into the community under supervision.

Payback Penalties

Another type of punishment that may cost less than confinement is the imposition of penalties that require offenders to compensate crime victims, the community as a whole, or the government for the costs of the crimes. Restitution and fines, the two main types of payback penalty, cost the government nothing or even add to its income.

Restitution

Restitution, an old type of legal penalty, requires the offender to give valuables or services to the victim. Formerly it was even used for murder, with the offender and his or her family forced to give wealth or services to the victim's kin. It was used especially if the criminal's prior status was high and the victim's low. The underlying expectation that a privileged offender owes the victims something seems evident in the O. J. Simpson case. The families of the victims sued for damages in a civil trial following the celebrity's acquittal in the highly publicized 1995 criminal trial.

Unofficially, restitution is still common in the United States and elsewhere, as the basis for out-of-court agreements in criminal complaints. The defendant agrees to make restitution payments in exchange for charges being withdrawn.

Restitution is officially used in Continental Europe and in the many countries elsewhere that copied the German, French, or Spanish legal system (Japan, Vietnam, and most of Latin America, respectively). When courts sentence convicted persons, they also routinely order payments to victims and sometimes services such as cleaning or repairing to remove the effects of the offense. In English-speaking nations, however, victims usually must sue the offender in a civil court for payment of any criminally inflicted injuries or losses. This time-consuming and expensive process is usually not worthwhile, because most offenders are poor and cannot realistically pay damages.

Increasingly, however, courts in the United States and in other nations with the British court system add some type of restitution proviso to probation sentences. For example, the releasee may be required to make monthly or weekly payments, either directly to the victim or to a government office for victim compensation. Alternatively or in addition, offenders may be ordered to do a specified number of hours of unpaid community service, such as cleaning parks or providing help to handicapped persons, or they must complete specified tasks, such as painting over graffiti.

In the Netherlands, particularly in Rotterdam, a well-developed system of restitution for juveniles, known as *Halt*, is commonly used. Even for minor offenses, delinquents are asked to help decide on an appropriate reparation to the community or to their victims. For lesser offenses, a prosecutor may approve their plans and impose 20 to 40 hours of work, but a judge must approve for serious crimes and may impose up to 100 hours of work. Research shows that *Halt* reduces both officially known and self-reported rates of subsequent offenses (van der Laan, 1993).

Some creativity is also being applied in the United States. Newspapers in April 1995 reported on "Project Payback" in Florida, a restitution program for adjudicated delinquents whose crimes caused expenses for their victims. The offenders are first given a $4\frac{1}{2}$-hour course in work ethics. Each then starts a part-time job arranged by a board representing the prosecutor and the local Chamber of Commerce. About three fourths of each youth's wages are paid to the victims until full restitution is made. Initial evaluations of this program are very favorable, as it appears to gratify victims, offenders, and the offenders' parents.

Fines

The cost of fines as a punishment is probably the lowest of any method. Fines usually bring money to the government in excess of the cost of administering them. And they do deter: Most auto drivers, for example, limit their illegal parking or illicit driving behavior when appreciable fines are highly probable. Persons convicted in Los Angeles municipal courts, most for misdemeanors, have less recidivism following such penalties than do similar offenders who are sentenced to probation or jail with no required monetary payment (Glaser & Gordon, 1990b; Gordon & Glaser, 1991).

Included as "fines" here are all purely monetary penalties, which may have other names. They include required contributions to a state fund for helping crime victims or achieving some other purpose, or they may be called "court costs" or "costs of probation services." An example is the fee imposed in some jurisdictions to cover the use of electronic monitoring:

> Two-thirds of using agencies [responding to a survey] impose fees on offenders; . . . they average $200 per month, which is often sufficient to cover the cost of the monitoring but not the total cost of supervision. Sliding scales are often used to avoid discrimination against impoverished offenders. (Renzema, 1992)

Court staff total a probationer's fines, restitution, and other levies and calculate ostensibly affordable monthly or weekly installments. Offenders are unlikely to know which payments go for each of their obligations, and usually the total is designated as for "fines."

But fines are often considered unfair, because they are more easily paid by an affluent than by a poor offender. To overcome the inequities, *day fines* were introduced in the 1920s by Finland, which was soon joined by the rest of Scandinavia and eventually by more than a dozen other nations in Europe and elsewhere. Day fines attempt to equalize the burden of monetary penalties by requiring that each lawbreaker pay a specified number of days' income. A collection office, often part of the government's income tax service rather than part of the court, determines what the amount should be. It estimates the individual's average daily income and deducts a certain amount for dependents and for necessities. As a result, a poor person who is fined 10 days' income pays much less than a rich one with the same fine. Day fines were established in New York's Richmond County (Staten Island) and Arizona's Maricopa County (Phoenix) with initial assistance from the staff of the Russell Sage Foundation. Other localities in the United States have also planned for use of these penalties (Hillsman, 1992).

Suspended Sentences

After a trial, when the sentence (such as a prison term or a fine) is announced, the judge may suspend this penalty. A sentence is suspended on condition that the defendant either commit no further crime or conform to other requirements during a specified period. Thus a suspended sentence resembles informal probation. Prosecutors are to notify the court of any violations of the requirements by the defendant, in which case the judge, after a hearing, can order the imposition of the sentence previously suspended.

Suspended sentences have a serious drawback, as British legal scholar Nigel Walker (1971) pointed out:

> By pronouncing a suspended sentence the sentencer must to a great extent deny freedom of choice to a later court if the offender is reconvicted. . . . By the time of his reconviction the offender's circumstances may be so different that the automatic imposition of the suspended sentence would be objectionable. . . . For example, . . . a short prison sentence would not be excessive punishment for an unmarried thief without a job; but if by the time it has to be imposed he has acquired a job and a family, it would be excessive to incarcerate him. . . .
>
> If the second court has complete discretion in its choice of sentence the effectiveness of the threat will be diminished. (pp. 84-85)

Suspending sentences seems to be a more common practice in much of Europe than in most of the United States, but there are few studies of its prevalence and consequences.

Conclusion

Legal penalties for criminals vary widely, although the majority of penalties in use today fall into four categories: confinement, limitations on freedom in the community, payback penalties, and suspended sentences. In general, confinement is the most costly punishment, and payback penalties are the least costly. A number of practical issues affect the expense of imposing each type of punishment.

This chapter has only begun to address the issue of the effectiveness of criminal penalties. Before we can fully ascertain their profitability, we have to identify our goals in punishing criminals. Legislators seek to make the punishments for specific crimes sufficiently severe to be generally regarded as just deserts for those offenses. To maximize society's profits from its penalties, however, we should allow judges, parole boards, and correctional officials considerable freedom to specify the details of initial punishments, as well as to change those details on the basis of each offender's subsequent conduct and circumstances. The reasons for such diversity are the concern of the next chapter.

Note

1. Used by permission of the *Los Angeles Times*.

3

The Objectives of Punishment

Sometimes it seems that nobody is satisfied with our criminal justice system. Crime victims often feel that the lawbreakers who assaulted them or who stole their possessions were treated too leniently by the courts. Society in general often concurs. As for convicted offenders, although they may admit their guilt, they frequently complain that their punishment was too harsh. Some law-abiding citizens agree.

The problem is one of divergent purposes. People have different ideas about what criminal penalties are supposed to accomplish. Some are influenced by such emotional and social goals as revenge and shaming; others consider the practicalities of trying to control and change offenders' behavior. This chapter discusses several types of objectives, penalties for achieving those goals, and ways to alleviate practical problems.

Goals in Punishing Criminals

As Chapter 2 indicated, persons who break important norms impede society's smooth operation. Governments punish such rule breaking in an effort to communicate the importance of the rules and to discourage their violation. In prescribing penalties for particular offenses, an effort is made to achieve *just deserts*, which is a proportionality between the seriousness of the wrongdoing and the severity of its punishment. Thus, a prison term is not imposed as the punishment for a parking violation, and a small fine is not considered adequate as the penalty for committing a murder.

The motives behind the law's penalties for crime are not always simple. The legislators, judges, and correctional officials who determine actual punishments have multiple objectives. Also, their decisions are influenced by the public's prevailing attitudes—which change from time to time and vary from place to place—toward different types of criminals. Exhibit 3.1 lists the major goals behind society's punishments and shows how those goals may be attained in the U.S. criminal justice system.

Revenge

Most people believe that lawbreakers should be made to "pay for their crimes" by suffering. Victims, in particular, tend to equate justice with achieving revenge. Legal philosophers prefer the less passionate term *retribution*, but Susan Jacoby (1983, p. 4) aptly calls this term only a euphemism for "revenge."

In societies with an informal system of justice, families and friends of victims seek private vengeance, which often causes long and deadly feuds. Such feuds are prominent in classic tales, such as Shakespeare's *Romeo and Juliet*, which tells of the tragic love affair of two children from feuding families in a period when the powers of formal justice agencies were less developed than they are now. Private vengeance-seeking by victims and their families and friends occurs in real life as well. The recent genocidal ethnic cleansing in Bosnia and Rwanda reflect longstanding, bitter feuds between ethnic groups.

Punishments by governments evolved as efforts to end such private vengeance-seeking. As Susan Jacoby (1983) points out:

> Stripped of moralizing, law exists not only to restrain retribution but to mete it out . . . on behalf of individuals whose rights have been violated as well as in the interests of society as a whole. . . . A society that is unable to convince individuals of its ability to exact atonement for injury is a society that runs a constant risk of having its members revert to the wilder forms of justice. (pp. 10-11)

A dramatic example of wild justice as a consequence of inadequate official revenge occurred in Los Angeles in 1992. The most destructive riot in U.S. history was precipitated by a court's failure to convict any of the police officers whom almost everyone in the area had seen, on a televised video-tape, excessively beating Rodney King.

Courts formerly imposed physical pain, hard labor, or solitary confinement on culprits as the public's revenge, but most contemporary experts on sentencing and prison administration decry the deliberate infliction of

Goal	Methods of Attainment
Revenge	Imposing severe punishments
Deterrence	Applying punishments with speed and certainty; tracking offenders, monitoring their behavior, and testing them for alcohol and drugs
Incapacitation	Imposing confinement, community surveillance, and electronic monitoring to control offenders' behavior
Anticriminal Enculturation	Classifying and separating inmates, promoting good staff-inmate relations, encouraging noncriminal visitors, providing law-abiding role models
Retraining	Providing academic and vocational instruction and employment during confinement; providing postrelease aid and personal counseling
Restitution	Requiring that offenders pay victims or perform community services
Reintegrative Shaming	Condemning the offense but accepting the offender's apology, and granting public respect

Exhibit 3.1. Ways of Attaining the Goals of Punishment

pain as a goal of criminal justice. More recently, law professors who have greatly influenced sentencing policies (e.g., Singer, 1979; von Hirsch, 1976/1986, 1993) emphasize making penalties—society's revenge—proportional in severity to the "reprehensibleness" and harm of the offense. The public expects penalties for serious crimes to be difficult experiences, at least by denial of liberty and luxuries. The courts inflict social pain on convicted criminals by taking away their freedom or money (or both) or by threatening to do so if the offense is repeated. Officials risk their jobs if the pleasures they allow prisoners are alleged to be too lavish.

Deterrence

Punishment for a crime usually aims to make the offender conclude that repeating the offense is not worth the risk of more punishment. This effect, if achieved, is called "individual," "specific," or "special" deterrence. A related goal is to make noncriminals fear the penalty, hence persist in not breaking the law. This effect is called "general deterrence."

For noncriminals, fear of the disgrace of arrest usually suffices to deter, regardless of subsequent punishment. Thus, general deterrence of nonoffenders is usually accomplished by any penalty sufficient to deter offenders. But when no punishment seems likely for a particular sort of behavior, general deterrence can quickly diminish, and much of the usually non-criminal population may then violate the law. During the 1992 Los Angeles riots, when television showed the police merely standing by while rioters looted stores, people of diverse incomes and all ethnicities got into cars and trucks to rush for tens of miles from all directions to join in the looting.

For criminals, the key factor in deterrence is the expectation that committing the offense will result in a significant punishment. Those who demand tougher penalties are likely to argue that severer punishments will more strongly deter crime. However, they are generally seeking mostly to get greater revenge for crime's victims. Statistical evidence shows that if customary penalties are already severe enough to make crime unprofitable for the criminal, then increasing the certainty and promptness of arrest and punishment is much more likely to deter recidivism than increasing the severity of the prescribed penalties.

One study, using Denmark's very complete criminal records, followed up on all males born there from 1944 through 1947 and living there for the next 26 years. The statistics showed that the higher the percentage of arrests that were followed by government penalties, the lower were subsequent arrest rates; that different types of penalties had similar effects in reducing recidivism; and that, after prior penalties, if no punishment followed new arrests, subsequent arrest rates rose (Brennan & Mednick, 1994). Similar results were found in American studies (Paternoster, 1989; Smith & Gartin, 1989), but they varied somewhat with the type of offense and offender.

Recidivism also depends heavily on individual circumstances. For example, a defendant's total life history has more effect on recidivism than the nature of the last crime committed (Blumstein, Farrington, & Moitra, 1985; Jenkins & Brown, 1988; LeBlanc & Frechette, 1989). Another important factor is what happens to ex-prisoners following release. Most releasees seem to make an initial effort to "go straight" when they get out, but long-run follow-ups show that a majority eventually drift back into crime (Blumstein et al., 1985; Kitchener, Schmidt, & Glaser, 1977; Sampson & Laub, 1993). In the moments of frustration that are especially common for most releasees, who are often unemployed and afflicted with costly vices, they recall numerous crimes that "they got away with." Also, much lawbreaking is committed in a state of intoxication, excitement, anger, or sexual passion that impedes thinking about the risks. Finally, the simplicity of life in confinement has great appeal for some, such as this prisoner:

A lot of guys really want to stay in prison to get away from the hassles on the outside. . . . Some guys eat better in here than on the outside. . . . In prison you eat good, get to bed early, relax, get exercise when you feel like it. In the street, it's very different. You have responsibilities, job problems, everything goes up and down, your mind is filled with responsibility. In prison, I'm relaxed. (Cordilia, 1983, p. 5)

Incapacitation

Locking up offenders has the obvious goal of rendering them unable to commit crimes in the community. This goal is usually well achieved by confining convicted criminals in jails and prisons, because less than 1% of inmates escape, and most who do escape are soon caught. Incapacitation in the community by probation or parole, without full-time confinement, less completely stops crime. However, probation and parole are usually much cheaper and less criminalizing than imprisonment, and hence on balance they may be profitable for many cases. Thus probation and parole are more frequently used than incarceration.

The value of probation is that, for persons with little or no prior criminal record, it deters recidivism but is generally neither as criminalizing as confinement nor as dangerous to the public as unconditional or unsupervised release. Yet some judges reduce probation's effectiveness by "piling up" more rules, fines, restitution obligations, and community service duties than offenders with little resources or successful work experience can possibly satisfy. Although a lengthy list of conditions for probation might be considered appropriate as just deserts for an offense, it makes probation violations much more likely. Both the offenders and their supervisors, and often the judges, admit the high probability of probation violations when the terms are too severe.

For probation to be reformative and profitable, probation penalties must be based on careful assessment of the offender's behavior prospects. This assessment may be informed by guidelines grounded in statistical research on past probation outcomes for persons of similar background and in comparable postrelease settings. More and better studies with this focus are needed to help judges choose among fines, restitution payments, public service duties, and the curbs to freedom in the community described in Chapter 2 (such as regular or intensive supervision, residence in a halfway house or group home, electronic monitoring or paging, etc.).

All such decisions should be subject to revision on the basis of supervision reports.

Most crimes are committed by two or more associates. Such group lawbreaking especially prevails among youthful offenders, particularly those under 18, who compose more than a fourth of arrestees for serious crimes. Youths, even more than adults, seek popularity among peers, boast cockily of successes, rationalize failures, and befriend those who seem supportive of them. Through such interaction among young law-breakers, crime-oriented ways of speech, thought, and behavior are readily adopted by all, creating a delinquent or criminal subculture. *Criminalization*, which is the development of criminal thinking and behavior habits, can occur in lone offenders who are successful in crime, but it is especially promoted by acquisition of a criminal subculture from one's associates.

Criminalization is most likely when youngsters start lawbreaking at an early age and have little successful experience in school, work, or other legitimate pursuits in law-abiding social circles. It occurs especially when their closest friends are their partners in crime, when they live in high-crime neighborhoods, and when they have little close contact with law-abiding adults at home. These conditions tend to *enculturate* youngsters into crime. Conversely, youths experiencing only activities, talk, and social contacts that support conformity to the law are enculturated into anti-criminality.

Reformation is the process of replacing criminal with anticriminal enculturation. (The word *rehabilitation* is sometimes used instead of *reformation*, although rehabilitation more commonly refers to the medical process of curing someone of a mental or physical disability under medical supervision. Similarly, the term *socialization* is often used to refer to what is here, and in much anthropology literature, called *enculturation*.) A reformative penalty disengages an offender from a criminal social world and promotes strong bonds with anticriminal individuals and groups. A major challenge in sentencing and corrections is to achieve this objective simultaneously with achieving just desert, deterrence, and other goals.

To reduce recidivism by sentenced offenders, judges and correctional officials should aim to maximize reformative enculturation and minimize criminalizing enculturation. Attaining these goals requires an understanding of how offenders are influenced by others. Ulla Bondeson's (1989) *Prisoners in Prison Societies* is a study of confinement experiences and attitudes of prisoners and of their postrelease records. Bondeson studied 13 Swedish institutions—some for juveniles, some for adults, and a few of each for females only—that differ in their architecture and in their emphasis on psychological treatment. She found that in all these places, the longer persons were confined, the more they acquired a pro-criminal subculture, including distinctive criminal vocabulary and rationalizations for crime, as well as higher postrelease recidivism rates. Criminalization was most rapid and extensive in juvenile facilities and in those for females. The facilities with the most psychotherapy also showed greater criminalization, probably because they have the most group confinement and group activities for inmates, hence greater influence of inmates on one another. The most beneficial aspects of confinement, especially for youthful inmates, were vocational and academic education and work experience.

Retraining

The knowledge, skills, attitudes, and personal contacts needed to get and hold legitimate jobs and to adjust well in conventional social settings are often referred to as "social capital." Most persons in government custody for serious offenses are undercapitalized, for they have poor school and job records and inadequate bonds with law-abiding persons. Retraining aims to instill in offenders the skills and ideas needed to achieve self-sufficiency in a law-abiding life. For this purpose, prisoners often are given academic education, vocational instruction, counseling, psychotherapy, or simply work experience.

At academic schools in correctional institutions, the local school district usually issues diplomas or certificates that are based on the standard curricula and tests used in public schools and that do not show the correctional institution as the place of instruction. Most classes are at the elementary or high school level. To supplement such efforts, the American Correctional Association has initiated in 12 jails and prisons a program of "Direct Educational Television for Corrections," to make prisoners' TV more instructive ("DETC Teaches," 1996). Research demonstrates that receiving a high school diploma, or markedly raising the highest grade completed, is associated with reduced recidivism rates (Gerber & Fritsch, 1995; Maguin & Loeber, 1996). It has also been shown that prison education programs are economical simply because they keep inmates preoccupied, thereby reducing the number of guards needed to maintain security (DiIulio, 1991, pp. 118-123; Worth, 1995).

A few inmates get college courses, either by correspondence, by release to attend a nearby college, or by extension courses offered in the prison by local college faculty. The largest evaluation of college education for prisoners, more than 25 years ago, concluded that it paid for itself by increasing students' later earnings and tax payments, especially for the few who completed degrees. But in-prison college education had no overall impact on recidivism rates, perhaps because many inmates have unrealistic expectations of how much and how soon their college work can boost postrelease income. A few may also seek education to help them develop greater verbal sophistication for perpetrating frauds. In sum, college studies did not raise the percentage who refrained from crime, but they enhanced the income of those who did refrain (Seashore, Haberfield, Irwin, & Baker, 1976).

The 1990s brought a wave of state and federal reaction against education for prisoners. Federal Pell Grants, which in the 1993-1994 school year paid college and trade-school costs for about four million poor students, including 23,000 in prison, were banned for prisoners by a Congressional amendment to the 1994 Federal Crime Bill. Governor George Pataki of New York terminated state support for inmate higher education. Fortunately for the one quarter of New York prisoners who read below the fifth-grade level when admitted, elementary school classes were retained (Kunen, 1995).

Work training, and the experience of useful work, may also be a reformative part of prison life, but it has had a spotty history in U.S. prisons. Before the Great Depression of the 1930s, American prisons were beehives of industry, with factories comparable to those outside. Most denim work clothes and school chairs in the United States were prison-made, as were many other goods. But in the 1930s, when so many law-abiding people were unemployed, unions and businesses lobbied successfully to bar prison-made goods from interstate commerce. Today, however, federal prisons and some state prisons again operate fairly large industrial plants within their walls and provide much vocational training.

Governments once widely sold prisoners' labor to private firms. Although this practice is still common in many nations, protests against it by unions and unemployed persons in the United States led to inmates being allowed to work only for the prison itself or for other government agencies. Thus, license plates, mail bags, and government office furniture are generally made in prisons, but even such "state-use" employment is often restricted due to the lobbying and the campaign contributions of private firms that want this business. Still, a 1979 law permitted the U.S. Department of Justice to authorize inmate employment in "joint ventures" of private businesses and prisons in seven states. This provision was expanded in 1984, and 32 correctional agencies had received federal permission for such joint ventures by March 1993 (Dwyer & McNally, 1993; Sexton, 1995).

Prisoners usually earn a low wage for the work they do, seldom exceeding $200 per month and often closer to $20 or $30 per month. Inmates usually receive the higher pay levels for industry assignments and skilled jobs, but sometimes nothing is paid to prisoners who do other work, especially unskilled kitchen, laundry, or janitorial tasks. With any pay, plus limited sums allowed from outside sources, convicts may make purchases from the institution commissary, send gifts or money to relatives, and save for postrelease freedom.

Many prisons also encourage and facilitate inmate art and handicrafts. This activity keeps prisoners occupied and fosters self-esteem. Sometimes the creations are sold to the public in a shop at the prison, giving the inmates some income. Of course, like everything else at these institutions, staff must check carefully to assure that no weapons or other contraband items are produced.

In the 1990s, several states instituted diverse other types of prisoner employment—including, mainly in the South, work in chain gangs. Arizona enacted a law requiring that each able-bodied prisoner engage in hard labor at least 40 hours per week, at 10 cents per hour (*Los Angeles Times*, Dec. 7, 1995). But these initiatives were meant more to publicize politicians' claims to be "tough on criminals" than to accomplish much work (Booth, 1995).

Restitution

Restitution (sometimes called *reparation*) is not only a specific type of penalty, as discussed in Chapter 2, but is also an abstract goal in sentencing. It is related to the goal of retribution, and both contribute to our sense of achieving justice. However, restitution is oriented toward restoring conditions as they existed prior to a crime, if feasible, rather than simply gaining revenge by making the offender suffer.

Restitution by returning stolen property, repaying money taken (even if by small weekly or monthly installments), or repairing damage done (e.g., painting over graffiti) helps to change the self-concept and self-esteem of the offender. It also improves his or her reputation in law-abiding social circles. These effects may explain why the *Halt* program in the Netherlands and Project Payback in Florida, described in Chapter 2, reduce recidivism. One important study found that when juvenile delinquents pay reparation directly to their victims, recidivism is lower than after any other type of punishment or combination of penalties for similar offenders (Schneider, Griffith, & Schneider, 1982).

Shaming

Police and courts alone cannot make all of society conform to the law. The main factor keeping most people noncriminal is not their fear of arrest and punishment but their consciences, their beliefs about what conduct is right and what is wrong. Families, churches, schools, and many other organizations try to instill such moral beliefs. The criminal law, by declaring which acts are officially deemed wrong and the penalties for each, also shapes consciences.

One of the most influential persons in the history of sociology, France's Emile Durkheim (1893/1947/1984), provocatively asserted that punishment of a criminal

> does not serve, or serves only very incidentally, to correct the guilty person or to scare off any possible imitators. . . . Its real function is to maintain the common conscience in all its vigor. . . . This conscience must be conspicuously reinforced the moment it meets with opposition. The sole means of doing so is to express the unanimous aversion that the crime continues to evoke, and this is done by an official act that inflicts suffering upon the wrongdoer. . . . Such suffering is not a gratuitous cruelty. It is a sign indicating that the sentiments of the collectivity are still unchanged, that the communion of minds sharing the same beliefs remains absolute. (Durkheim, 1893/1947/1984, p. 108)[1]

A court's process of convicting and sentencing is what Harold Garfinkel (1956) aptly called a "degradation ceremony." By declaring someone delinquent or criminal, a court defines that person as of lower character, thereby reinforcing to society the idea that what the person did is wrong. Those sharing such moral beliefs have consciences that make them ashamed to perform this act.

Shaming a person for committing a crime, Australia's John Braithwaite (1989) points out, can either promote or prevent that person's recidivism. If shaming so stigmatizes the offender that he or she is alienated from law-abiding social circles, and if it also fosters bonds with others who share a criminal subculture, it promotes recidivism. But if shaming is done in a way that labels as unacceptable the deed but not the person, especially if the offender apologizes, it may be *reintegrative*, strengthening the law-breaker's bonds with family, noncriminal friends, church, or other sources of moral beliefs (see also Makkai & Braithwaite, 1994). Reintegrative experiences promote a conscience that rejects the idea of committing a crime.

Japan and Switzerland, Braithwaite points out, are the only technologically advanced nations without a large increase in crime rates since World War II. Both promote strong ties between the individual and the family and community and try to reintegrate offenders into these groups after their crimes. Switzerland is governed by a highly decentralized democracy of town meetings, in which family and community ties are especially strong. These ties are mobilized to reintegrate offenders. Japanese culture greatly emphasizes apologies to the victims of crimes or accidents and other expressions of repentance and contrition. In Japan, for example, if an airplane crashes, the airline's president and subordinate employees publicly apologize to the victims or their relatives, attend funerals, pay reparations, or even resign from their jobs. In contrast, on lawyers' advice, U.S. airlines bar or limit employee contact with victims or their kin and sidestep admissions of fault. Interestingly, Japan has the lowest overall crime rate of technologically advanced nations; Switzerland has one of the lowest (van Dijk & Mayhew, 1993). And the United States has one of the highest, especially for homicides. The lesson should be clear for anyone seeking profitable penalties for criminal acts.

Practical Considerations

Choices in an ideal world would often differ greatly from the choices forced on us by reality. At century's end, the reality of U.S. society is a severe crimp in government resources for pursuing social goals. The national debt quadrupled from 1980 to 1992, and although deficit spending has slowed, it has not yet stopped. Elected politicians have endorsed balanced budgets but have not shown how they would achieve them before well into the 21st century, if at all. Thus sensitized to financial conditions and prospects, legislators and policymakers tend to evaluate any proposal for change in social programs in hard-nosed, practical terms. Two inescapable considerations in devising profitable penalties are thus

Practical Concern	Methods of Attainment
Convenience	Keeping convicts contented; routinizing staff's work
Economy	Charging for correctional services; using nonconfinement penalties

Exhibit 3.2. Practical Concerns in Punishing Criminals

the ease or convenience of administering them under budget constraints and the economical allocation of limited resources. Exhibit 3.2 summarizes how these administrative objectives can be achieved.

Convenience

At every level of any organization, employees want their jobs to be comfortable, secure, and satisfying. This generalization is readily confirmed in all components of our criminal justice system. For best results, therefore, any new proposals for criminal penalties should try to avoid making life significantly more difficult or dangerous for police, courts, or correctional agency staff and officials.

In an era when the incarceration of felons has become so popular, the convenience of prison employees in particular is a critical issue. As indicated in Chapter 2, prison officials give institutional order and security top priority, because riots and other publicized violence are dangerous in themselves and also evoke demands for change of personnel. Officials of U.S. prisons have developed a somewhat standard system—using negative reactions to inmate misconduct, rewards for good behavior, and decent food and recreation—to satisfy staff needs for routine and to maintain order among prisoners.

To keep inmates orderly, it is essential to provide activities and diversions that reduce the boredom of being locked up. Education and work programs serve this purpose, as do more conveniently supplied diversions like athletics, music, television, movies, playing cards, and board games (chess, checkers, etc.). Institution management is easiest if such diversions are made available to the maximum extent compatible with security. Inmates of all ages are likely to devote most of their extensive free time to them.

The most popular self-improvement activity among prisoners is body-building, because it helps keep them busy and feeling more secure during correctional confinement. In correctional institutions, especially those for males, a main preoccupation of most residents is to put up a front of being as tough as the others, to avoid being pushed around, robbed, injured, or homosexually raped. Yet during the 1990s, governors or legislatures of several states banned bodybuilding equipment with the charge that such activities promote violent crimes. They also ended some of the other recreational and educational opportunities that had been given to inmates.

Unfortunately, many of these decisions have been made on the basis of emotion and not fact. Many of those responsible for the design of prison facilities and programs attach little importance to research on ways to improve the prospects of inmate reformation, perhaps because they give top priority to public perceptions of the institution and to administrators' convenience and security. The danger is that the measures for maintaining order and security can become so routinized as to make officials complacent about monitoring inmate and staff conduct and morale, even though success in prison and jail management has often been shown to depend on avoiding complacency (DiIulio, 1991, chap. 1). When institutional order is achieved, administrators also tend to become indifferent to the larger goal of reducing recidivism, as do legislators and governors who seek votes by stressing only their promotion of harsh penalties.

Economy

Incarceration—whether in jail or prison—is usually the most effective way to achieve revenge and incapacitation, but it is also the most criminalizing penalty, especially for unadvanced offenders. It is also the most expensive method. The cost of imprisonment runs from about $15,000 to well over $50,000 per inmate per year, with even higher net costs for places with maximum security or psychiatric treatment but lower net costs when prisoners live and work in forestry camps or on prison farms. This figure does not include prison construction costs, which for high security prisons total $50,000 to more than $100,000 per cell, usually funded by bonds paid off only gradually. Like a home mortgage, more is paid in interest than on principal. These economic facts partly explain the efforts to use other ways to punish criminals.

Ordinary probation and parole usually cost no more than 1/10th as much as confinement, and intensive supervision costs a quarter or a fifth as much, depending on how intensive it is. In addition, in a growing number of jurisdictions, probationers must pay for their supervision. The fee is set relatively high for those who can afford it but is cut or waived for those who cannot (Finn & Parent, 1993). Restitution, fines (including day fines), and community service penalties create only the costs of their administration and thus normally yield net benefits for the jurisdiction. When these alternative punishments are equal to or more effective than confinement for reducing recidivism and are acceptable for other goals, such as revenge or deterrence, they are clearly more profitable than incarceration.

For persons not much involved in lawbreaking, using expensive incarceration facilities, especially county jails, is a false economy. Many destitute persons seek emergency food and shelter by short stays in jail. They commit a petty offense for sustenance, in some places with apparent police and court collusion in locking them up. Also, jails and juvenile detention facilities receive many persons who are clearly more mentally ill than criminal. Both these patterns increased in the 1990s, when homelessness rose and mental hospital funds were cut but too little growth occurred in shelters and other free services for the homeless.

In an increasing number of jurisdictions, private correctional services are replacing those operated by governments, especially for juveniles. Defense attorneys hired by affluent parents of children in trouble with the law often get court approval to hire private individuals or social service organizations to prepare presentence studies on the accused children and to supervise them on their release.

Several states and the federal government contract with private firms to run some prisons and halfway houses, and a few counties have such arrangements for jails, juvenile detention, or probation. These are controversial arrangements at first, but often they become well accepted because they are believed to save money and to improve services (Bowman, Haim, & Seidenstat, 1993; Logan, 1990; McDonald, 1990). Such claims have been disputed (Shichor, 1995). However, if privately operated establishments are regarded as competitors, rather than as full replacements for all government-run facilities, private facilities provide a useful "yardstick" for measuring the quality and efficiency of public administration.

Seven Principles of Cost-Effective Punishment

Profitable penalties are those that achieve the goals of punishment and the practical considerations of convenience and economy. But, using the four main types of punishment described in Chapter 2—confinement, limits on freedom in the community, payback penalties, and suspended sentences—how can those objectives be attained? Research shows that observance of the seven principles described here will help criminal justice professionals and policy makers design more cost-effective penalties for lawbreaking.

Penalties are most likely to be profitable when all politically acceptable punishments are identified for each type of crime and criminal and then courts are given sentencing guidelines based on research rather than on fear of crime.

Prior to the 1970s, judges in many states and in federal courts had more latitude in sentencing than they generally do today. Within the upper and lower limits authorized by law, judges could order widely varied periods of incarceration for individuals convicted of the same type of crime. Alternatively, the law in several states prescribed widely separated minimum and a maximum penalties for each crime (such as 1 to 20 years in prison or 5 years to life) and let the parole board determine the actual release date after the minimum had been served (see Glaser, 1996).

Since the 1970s, however, complaints of bias and inconsistency in court and parole board decisions have gradually led the federal courts and about 20 states to adopt *sentencing guidelines*. Several also have guidelines for parole. These guidelines specify a very limited range of penalties that the judge can order for each case, based on the offense, the offender's age, and the offender's prior criminal record. States differ in the weight the guidelines give to various factors and in the discretion they still give judges to fix penalties within the guideline limits.

The guidelines' impact in the federal system and in some states has recently been eroded by laws mandating severe penalties for many types of crimes, especially drug offenses. Ten years in prison are mandated for certain drug offenses, regardless of the offender's prior record and regardless of imprisonment's cost or the prospect that other penalties would be more reformative for a particular individual. Federal courts and courts of half the states, including California and New York, now allow judges relatively little sentencing latitude. They permit only one kind of punishment, or a very small range of penalties, for each type of crime. These mandatory sentences evoke much covert bargaining by prosecutors to change charges to lesser offenses on condition that the offender plead guilty or inform on others (Tonry, 1995b).

To ensure that penalties are profitable, sentencing and parole guidelines should be developed in all jurisdictions to reflect research on the range of punishments the public will accept for each major type of crime and for different kinds of offenders (e.g., first offenders or recidivists). The guide-lines should also reflect research on the likely costs and effects of a particular penalty for offenders who differ on such recidivism predictors as prior criminal record, employment history, and alcohol or drug use.

First offenders' recidivism rates are usually reduced more by a formal finding of guilt and a nonconfinement penalty than by either informal release or a confinement penalty.

Research in many places has repeatedly supported this principle. Joan McCord (1985) traced the criminal records of 506 Boston-area male juve-niles for the 30 years following their selection during the 1930s by teachers and others who predicted the juveniles would have high prospects of delinquency. The ones who subsequently committed crimes had lower recidivism rates following their first offense if they got a formal penalty in court than if released informally. Similarly, first offenders found delin-quent by juvenile courts in Illinois and Pennsylvania had less recidivism if released on probation than if confined. This conclusion applied regard-less of the juvenile's gender, race, or age (Brown, Miller, & Jenkins, 1988; Wooldredge, 1988). In Denmark, any definite punishment following arrest was found to reduce rearrest rates (Brennan & Mednick, 1994).

McCord (1985) refers to a clear official warning and release as "a light touch of the law." The implication is that a little penalty goes further toward reforming a lawbreaker than either a lot (confinement with other criminals) or none (indulgent release). The reformative effects of light but formal penalties may be due less to their creating fear of a severer penalty next time than to reintegrative shaming by the offender's family or by other accepting and respected persons:

Public shaming puts pressure on parents, teachers and others to ensure that they engage in private shaming.

Within the family, as the child grows, social control shifts from external to internal controls (that is, conscience); . . . this is precisely why families are more effective agents of social control than police forces. (Braithwaite, 1989, pp. 82-83)

Subtle and often inadvertent criminalization occurs when penalties promote interaction and identification among offenders.

These subtleties were revealed by the unanticipated results of an ex-periment that tried to reduce the stigma of being identified as a criminal for juveniles referred to the police on minor charges. An experimental group of juveniles who were not arrested were instead required to go regularly to a counseling center. Ironically, visiting the center associated them with other offenders, which seemed to give them a more pervasive neighborhood reputation as delinquents. In the end, the experimental group had higher recidivism rates than did randomly selected youngsters who were formally warned and then released (Klein, 1995, pp. 43-49).

The criminalizing effects of segregating and labeling offenders often occur when lawbreakers are sent to community centers reserved for tutoring, counseling, or providing other services to offenders. However, when these services are offered at places where nonoffenders also receive them, they are less likely to have unintended, criminalizing consequences.

Many police, probation officers, and courts are astute in using unofficial probation for minor offenses, especially by juveniles. They formally warn but release an arrestee who has little or no prior offense record and seems remorseful. But they release in this fashion only if confident that parents, employers, or other persons deemed responsible accept the releasee and give assurance of appropriate further monitoring or discipline. This sort of credible warning to unadvanced offenders interrupts their crime sprees and helps reintegrate them into anticriminal groups.

For advanced criminals, counseling tends to be most effective if done individually by ex-offenders of their own background, instead of by officials or even trained counselors of a different background, provided the counseling is extensive. An example of such an effort, which seems to have reduced crime rates over its more than 50-year life span, is the Chicago Area Projects, a group of organizations in high crime neighborhoods. They mobilized anticriminal residents of slum neighborhoods to collaborate in giving lawbreakers, including both youths and older persons newly released from prison, friendship and support in moving from criminal to noncriminal social worlds (Schlossman, Zellman, Shavelson, Sedlak, & Cobb, 1984). In New York state prisons, the treatment program for drug-addicted inmates that most clearly reduced recidivism rates was staffed entirely by ex-addicts, who made the drug-addicted inmates assume responsibilities and who enhanced privileges for doing so but withdrew privileges for misconduct (Lipton, 1996).

The optimal use of ex-offenders, or of others with backgrounds similar to those of offenders in correctional programs, is to bridge the cultural differences between offenders and professionals by forming teams that include some professionally trained persons. Some years ago in Los

Angeles, in a program called "RODEO: Reduction of Delinquency by Expanding Opportunities," well-selected "community workers" shared juvenile caseloads with probation officers. The community workers, mostly ex-probationers or former welfare mothers in the slums, usually were better than the professionals in investigating the homes of the accused youths and in helping heads of households cope with their problems. The community workers also staffed a small community center linked to the program. The professionals were more skilled than the community workers in reporting to the court, but community workers were encouraged to enhance their education to qualify for professional openings. RODEO reduced recidivism, but drastic fund-cutting and some resistance by professionals to such unorthodoxy ended this program (Cocks, 1968; Rushen & Hunter, 1970).

Appreciable and certificated improvements in offenders' academic education and vocational training reduce their recidivism rates.

As documented earlier in this chapter, school deficiencies are especially predictive of criminal conduct. Most persistent offenders need reeducation. If instruction is individualized by personal attention, particularly if aided by programmed texts and computers, considerable progress can be made. These students then obtain much gratification from their success in school.

Evaluative research shows that job training, and work in prison, can reduce recidivism rates if it is appreciable and in a field with good job potential (e.g., machinist, welder, carpenter); no such postrelease benefits follow from less-skilled institutional maintenance work (e.g., janitor, shoe repair) (Gerber & Fritsch, 1995; McKee, 1972, 1978, 1985; Saylor & Gaes, 1992). McKee (1972) showed in a study of California prisons that 1,000 hours or more of training in mechanical trades pays for itself within 18 months after parole; its cost is exceeded by the increases it produces in a releasee's income tax payments. He compared trainees' earnings in this postrelease period, as reported for Social Security credit, with earnings of similar inmates released without such training. His analysis likely underestimates the differential in postrelease benefits, because it omits the added tax payments after 18 months out of prison, the probable lower welfare payments received by the trained releasees and their dependents as compared to the untrained, and cost savings to potential victims and the state from less recidivism.

Skilled trade training in correctional institutions can enhance significantly a releasee's chances of postrelease success in legitimate jobs. But
this training must be extensive, include work experience, and fit postrelease job possibilities. Academic and vocational training for convicts can
thus be highly profitable. Yet because little appropriate economic analysis
is made of such training, it is often cut from budgets by short-sighted
politicians, as is evaluation research.

*Work experience in correctional institutions and postrelease assistance that keeps
paroleesfrom being unemployed yield public benefits worth more than their cost,
because of the releasees' greater earnings and tax payments and their lower
recidivism and need for welfare.*

Beginning in 1978, California gave prisoners unemployment insurance
credit of $2.30 per hour for work at prison jobs (at which they actually
were paid only 20 cents per hour), plus $2.30 (then the minimum hourly
wage in the United States) for participation in prison vocational training.
If their total credit was the $1,500 then required of all unemployment
insurance applicants (652 hours in prison at $2.30), and if they were
unemployed during their first year out, they could apply for "FI" (former
inmate) insurance at regular unemployment insurance offices. Like others,
they had to look for work, as shown by their undertaking job interviews;
earnings of less than $25 per week were not deducted from unemployment
compensation.

Statistical analysis demonstrated that California prisoners who were
paid this unemployment compensation had lower arrest rates in their first
year out than unpaid similar releasees (Rauma & Berk, 1987). We do not
know how much these lower arrest rates were due to the abilities gained
from work and training in prison and how much to the financial aid the
unemployment insurance benefits provided after release. Unfortunately,
the legislature did not renew funding for this program after the 1980s,
despite its profitability in terms of lower crime rates.

Of course, a released prisoner without funds or a job can apply for
welfare assistance like any other destitute person, as some do. Most
unemployed releasees, however, are reported to get subsistence mainly
from family, which creates strains at home if they are destitute too long
and seems to contribute to their relapse to crime.

*Good-conduct modeling by staff at confinement institutions, their maturity-
promoting relationships with inmates, behavior modification programs, and inmate*

contacts with the opposite gender and with noncriminal outsiders all reduce recidivism rates.

To aid inmate reformation, the Dutch Ministry of Justice provides human relations training at its national correctional staff school in The Hague. Trainees role-play interaction with inmates while being videotaped, and the tapes are reviewed in class. This training emphasizes the need to make inmates responsible for democratic management of their small group units.

In the United States, many correctional institutions have thousands of inmates and most have hundreds. Their replacement by smaller prisons is unlikely, but they can be subdivided into smaller units. Smaller units typically improve staff-inmate contacts, which are often more important to the staff's job satisfaction than their pay or other objective benefits (Hepburn, 1989). Smaller units also impede gang formation, facilitate prisoner reformation, and enhance security. Incarceration in smaller units is less criminalizing than confinement where inmates must always be with many others in dormitories, yards, and other unstructured settings. Robert Levinson (1980), a leader in decentralizing federal prisons, asserts:

> The establishment of mini-institutions—semi-autonomous units— within a large prison has repeatedly demonstrated that this organizational structure results in a more smoothly functioning, safer, more humane, and (there is reason to believe) more rehabilitative institution. . . . It reduces the depersonalizing aspects of prison life. It establishes subgroups within both the inmate and the staff populations, which can productively interact with each other. (p. 51)

In the absence of small units, inmates are preoccupied with maintaining separations from others. They seek what Hans Toch (1977) calls "niches," places where they are relatively free to do as they wish, safe from attack or theft, surrounded by a few supportive friends, and living and working in predictable circumstances. Inmates assess their work, housing, and recreation mainly by these conditions. Self-improvement opportunities, even assignments that increase prospects of parole, are often declined to get or retain good niches. Compartmentalized confinement units increase safe niches.

To reduce brutalization and hence criminalization, designers of correctional institutions for juveniles should avoid using harsh technology, such as concertina wire with razor edges, to subdue aggressive inmates. The punishment cells at many adult institutions have a similar effect. Recalcitrant prisoners may be kept isolated for days in complete darkness, without toilet facilities and sometimes also cuffed hand and foot. Such methods seriously impair staff-inmate relationships (Miller, 1991, pp. 75-79; see also Hamm, 1993).

Research shows that criminalization and recidivism are also reduced and reformation is enhanced, especially for young offenders, when a unit's correctional personnel have the qualities of good coaches. Their goal should be to help their charges develop the skills and character traits needed for legitimate lifestyles when free, as well as to adjust better to life in confinement. In a controlled experiment in Washington state, nearly 200 institutionalized boys were randomly assigned to behavior modeling groups, discussion groups, or a control group. The youths in behavior modeling groups attended 14 weekly 1-hour sessions, with specially trained teachers who were graduate students in psychology, to observe demonstrations of desired behavior and then to rehearse it. The boys in discussion groups only talked about how to behave. The lessons in both groups centered on how to take problems to teachers or other adults, how to apply for a job, and in general, how to defer immediate pleasure for long-run satisfaction. The control group got none of this instruction. A 5-year follow-up demonstrated that the boys in both the modeling and discussion groups had significantly less recidivism than those in the control group (Sarason, 1978). More attention should be given to extending this research and to applying its findings.

Group counseling is not always effective, however. In nondirective group counseling, especially in institutions, offenders tend to rationalize the past and fantasize about the future. Discussions on a law-abiding life among those with little or no successful experience at it can be a case of the blind leading the blind. Furthermore, like talk sessions that occur informally when offenders are alone, discussions in nondirective group counseling are too often dominated by the most articulate and aggressively pro-criminal participants, who are preoccupied with deploring their mistreatment, blaming and denigrating the justice system or its officials, and stifling any who disagree with them. In those groups in which staff actively attempt to draw out all views, counseling sessions may reveal and reduce maladjustment to institutional life or supervision practices, but the participants seldom provide much insight into avoiding further difficulty with the law. Individual counseling and conventional work experience are much more conducive to achieving a noncriminal life.

"Co-ed" correctional institutions, those holding both females and males, have long existed for juveniles in some Southern states, but the first modern one for adults in the United States was opened by the federal prison system in 1971 at Ft. Worth, Texas. Others now exist elsewhere. Each gender has its own housing units, but they eat, work, attend school, and have some recreation together, with close surveillance to limit physical contacts. A dramatic feature of co-ed places, to anyone familiar with the ambience in one-sex institutions, is the great improvement of language and manners. "Co-correction," as officials call it, prepares inmates for proper postrelease conduct with the opposite sex, but its dimensions are limited because about 95% of prisoners are males.

Visits to prisoners by family and friends, including conjugal visits with spouses in private rooms where sex is permitted, have repeatedly been shown to result in less violence within the prison and to lower recidivism rates (Ellis, Grasmick, & Gilman, 1974; Goetting, 1982). Visits by representatives of other types of organizations can also be important sources of anticriminal enculturation and provide postrelease contacts. For example, most large prisons now have inmate Alcoholics Anonymous chapters to which outside chapters send speakers and listeners. Much prison visiting is also done by religious groups, including both conventional denominations and deviant cults. Many prisoners welcome their visits and correspondence. Religious and other organizations in several states help inmates' relatives travel to visit at remote prisons. Toastmasters, bridge clubs, chess clubs, and other hobby groups also often visit similar groups in prisons. They all give inmates an opportunity to interact during confinement with persons of conventional background and ease postrelease entry into these groups.

Correctional programs are most profitable if, for those unadvanced in crime, they are entirely in the community and, for more experienced criminals, they include postinstitution controls and assistance.

When they curb recidivism as well as or better than other penalties, fines are obviously the most profitable penalties. Restitution also compensates the public and reduces recidivism for many offenders. For many crimes, fines and restitution may also suffice as revenge. Making them conditions of probation is usually an effective way of enforcing them.

Almost all states and the federal prison system have developed gradual transitions from incarceration to freedom. Work release and school release permit selected inmates to leave the institution each morning for a job or class in a nearby town. Some prisons grant such releases quite liberally, and others restrict them to a few of the safest inmates; however, all are limited by the availability of nearby schools or employers receptive to releasees.

Furloughs from prison for a few days of freedom not long before the expected date of full release permit inmates to visit their families and to make arrangements for postrelease life. From 97% to more than 99% of furlough recipients return to their institutions on schedule or only slightly late. More important, extensive statistical studies in Massachusetts and in the federal prison system show that prisoners of the same risk category (as classified mostly by prior criminal record), whether low-risk or high-risk, consistently have lower recidivism rates with furloughs before their final release (Eichenlaub, 1992; LeClair & Guarino-Ghezzi, 1991).

Inmates released unconditionally from correctional institutions tend to return to the lifestyles and settings in which their lawbreaking occurred, usually have inadequate funds on release, and soon spend them. Probation and parole can prevent the obvious consequences by monitoring offenders and providing some assistance if needed. When officers become aware of a probationer's or parolee's misconduct, they can promptly order arrest or take other corrective action. They are especially likely to know of rule violations quickly if supervision is intensive. On the other hand, because unconditionally released lawbreakers are not required to stay in one residence or keep regular hours and are not monitored, their new crime sprees are not nearly as likely to be ended quickly. Yet when a parolee or probationer is intercepted for committing a much publicized new crime, journalists—as well as politicians of the party not in power—are eager to blame the concept of conditional release; they seldom note that, overall, probationers and parolees have lower recidivism rates than prisoners released unconditionally at the end of their confinement sentences.

Punishments That Fit

Everyone convicted of a crime may be called a criminal, but this label covers contrasting types of persons who commit diverse kinds of crimes and have different rates of persistence in lawbreaking. These variations raise issues for courts in sentencing and for others in administering sentences. Distinguishing among the various types of crimes and criminals helps society apportion its resources more efficiently while still achieving just deserts.

The remaining chapters address this issue of profitability in penalties for particular types of offenders. The facts are based on scientific research, and limitations of the research conducted thus far are identified—two practices that have too often been missing in the public debate on anti-crime policies. The fear of crime, rather than actual crime, has all too often determined penalties.

Chapter 4 is concerned with the lawbreaking that accompanies the growth of children into adults. Arrest rates peak during the erratic period of maturation called "adolescence" and remain high during early adult-hood. Although only 37% of the U.S. population is between the ages of 16 and 40, this age range includes 77% of arrestees (Maguire & Pastore, 1995, Table 4.4). Adolescents are also the most diverse in their crimes. The most profitable penalties for youth offenses are those that keep adolescents from becoming enculturated as criminals. Even greater savings for society are achieved by maintaining home and community conditions that keep youngsters from ever beginning serious crime.

Chapter 5 examines why our hugely expensive war on drugs has achieved so little and fosters so much other crime. Less costly demand-reduction policies could reduce society's burden from trafficking in and use of these substances. This chapter draws instructive parallels in the histories of criminal law regarding three other compulsive types of indul-gence: alcohol, gambling, and sex.

The crimes that most disturb the public, those that express rage by violence, are the focus of Chapter 6. After discussing prevailing explana-tions for such crimes, the chapter considers profitable penalties and other prevention efforts. The issues discussed here include gun control and capital punishment.

Sex crimes, the concern of Chapter 7, express lust and other passions that are not well understood. In addition to forcible rape, which usually mixes lust with anger, these offenses include sexual activity with children and the deliberate exhibition of genitals to others in public places. Also discussed here is the plea of not guilty by reason of insanity, which is frequently entered in both these offenses and in ostensibly nonsexual crimes of rage.

By far the costliest crimes to society, in terms of both money and physical injury, occur in legitimate occupations and businesses. In recent years, the public's dollar loss from the felonies that sent officials of brokerages, savings and loan organizations, and banks to prison have far exceeded the total loot from ordinary theft, burglary, and robbery. So-called white-collar offenders, discussed in Chapter 8, are most profitably given penalties that differ from those protecting the public from street criminals.

Ways to protect us from professional criminals are the concern of Chapter 9. The primary emphasis for these offenders should be long confinement, but our use of this penalty is limited by appropriate concerns for justice.

Chapter 10 winds up the book by integrating and augmenting the conclusions of the prior chapters. It also discusses other measures to impede crime, such as physical and social arrangements of housing and new types of policing. In the end, it should be obvious that the most profitable penalties are not necessarily the harshest. We can achieve our diverse crime-control objectives by taking the long view and applying our resources judiciously.

Conclusion

Many feel that the current level of crime in our society is unacceptable, and they have called for more and severer penalties for lawbreaking. But as a society, we have many urgent tasks requiring the expenditure of public funds—crime control being only one. We must therefore seek the most profitable, cost-effective methods for punishing those who break society's rules.

Profitable penalties are those that meet two large-scale objectives:

• *Justice:* The punishment must suffice as just desert for the offense, which means that the public must deem it to be neither too slight nor too severe for the harm done by the crime. To be fair, the punishment must also be consistent with penalties imposed on different persons found guilty of similar lawbreaking.

• *Efficiency:* The penalties must minimize public costs while maximizing achievement of the goals of punishment. The costs obviously include short-run, direct expenditures for things like housing and feeding prisoners and for supervising probationers. Less obviously, they include long-run and indirect expenditures, such as support for the children of those who are imprisoned; opportunity costs, like the loss of tax income from someone whose life has been destroyed by the stigma of crime and punishment; and social costs, such as recidivism by those who have been hardened by a prison sentence or who have learned new criminal skills in prison.

As a society develops a system of criminal punishments, the effort to attain justice and efficiency is modulated by the seven social goals of punishment: revenge, deterrence, incapacitation, anticriminal enculturation, retraining, restitution, and reintegrative shaming. Practical considerations, including convenience and economy in administering punishment, also enter the equation. In the end, the most profitable approach seems to be a system of penalties that the public finds acceptable and that are tailored to fit both the crime and the criminal.

Note

1. The French term *conscience* can be correctly translated into English as *conscience* or as *consciousness*, depending on its context. The above formulation relies mostly on Halls's 1984 translation but changes his "consciousness" to Simpson's "conscience," as more appropriate here.

4

Reducing Childhood
Transition Crime

It was once easier to grow up. Today, to get good jobs as adults, children need more years in school than they did even a few decades ago. Thus children's economic dependence on adults, and parental authority over children, is prolonged. Children repeatedly resist this authority, in various ways, from infancy on.

Much lawbreaking expresses this juvenile rebelliousness. Many youths see crimes as short cuts to the imagined independence and excitement of adulthood. Some of the crimes are minor—joyriding, petty shoplifting, small-scale vandalism. But some of it is surprisingly sophisticated and destructive. Although society is most concerned with preventing and punishing the serious crimes committed by youths, it also has a stake in stopping lesser crimes, for they are often the first steps on the road to serious criminalization.

Crime Rates During Adolescence

The last stage of childhood, adolescence, begins at puberty but ends only with achievement of a stable social and economic independence from parents or parent substitutes. Adolescents rapidly cease to be children physically, but as long as they are financially dependent on parental figures, they are unlikely to be given all the rights and privileges of adults. The duration of adolescence now begins earlier than it did a century ago, because a diet higher in fat and protein brings on the physical signs of puberty—such as menstruation, the growth of pubic hair, and voice change—earlier than before. In most homes, adolescence also ends at an older age than in previous eras, for changes in technology keep altering the requirements for satisfying employment. Therefore, most youths stay in school longer and enter the job market later than did prior generations.

The highest U.S. arrest rates for serious crimes are of young persons with difficulty in the transition to adulthood. Arrests for theft, burglary, robbery, and drugs peak from the late teens into the early twenties (Elliott, 1994; Steffensmeier & Allan, 1995; Steffensmeier, Allan, Harer, & Streifel, 1989). This age pattern for offenders and their victims also prevails in other technologically developed nations (Farrington, 1986).

Half or more of American adult males usually admit in surveys that, during their adolescence or early adulthood, they committed crimes that could have gotten them severe penalties if they had been caught and prosecuted (Gabor, 1994). Apparently most U.S. males, at some time, commit vandalism; breaking and entering; car theft; shoplifting; theft from schools, from libraries, or from employers; use of an illegal drug; or driving when legally drunk. They usually are not caught, or at least are not arrested, booked, or prosecuted for these crimes.

Most arrestees are boys, and their offenses usually differ from those of girls, although both often shoplift and use illegal drugs. However, girls usually reach physical maturity earlier than boys, and when sexually developed, they are treated as adults by males of a wide age range. Therefore, sexual promiscuity gives some girls a shortcut to a sense of adulthood and an escape from conflicts at home or school. Police and courts handling juvenile cases generally deal with girls for what they infer is sexual misconduct, although they are likely to label it and other misconduct by the catch-all term "incorrigibility."

It is estimated that annually in the United States nearly a half million juveniles run away from home or from juvenile detention for at least overnight, and another 125,000 are expelled from their homes or abandoned. About half of these have no place to stay. About half—not necessarily the same half—commit no crimes when away. Runaways originate everywhere but go disproportionately to our sunbelt states, from Florida to California. Most are between 13 and 15 at departure, but younger ones usually soon return home on their own. More 16- and 17-year-olds stay away, especially if ejected or abandoned (Brennan, Huizinga, & Elliott, 1978; Finkelhor, Hotaling, & Sedlak, 1990). Runaways of both genders often sell sex. In a 1990 address to the American Psychological Association,

Marjorie Robinson asserted that a third of homeless teenage girls survive by prostitution.

Half the serious juvenile offenses known to police in an area are traced to the 5% or 6% of young males who are most often arrested (Wolfgang, Thornberry, & Figlio, 1987). These boys typically start criminal activity at an early age and pursue it intensively thereafter. They also tend to be the least specialized of all criminals in their subsequent offenses. They mix thefts, rapes, burglaries, robberies, drug crimes, and other deviance with little planning and also have high rates of tardiness, auto accidents, drunkenness, sexual promiscuity, impulsive marriages, and diagnoses as mentally ill (Lerman, 1991). One general theory ascribes such criminality to slowness in developing self-control (Gottfredson & Hirschi, 1990). This theory is best supported by data on persons in custody, for their low self-control also increases their prospects of being caught.

Most youth offenders, however, engage only in *adolescence-limited criminality*, which diminishes with age unless they are long socially segregated in crime. A follow-up study of British youth found that

> by age 32 the work records of the adolescence-limiteds were indistinguishable from the never-convicted and substantially better than those of the chronic offenders. The adolescence-limited also seem to have established better relationships with their spouses than the chronics. The . . . adolescence-limiteds, however . . . continued to drink heavily and use drugs, get into fights, and commit criminal acts (according to self-reports). (Nagin, Farrington, & Moffitt, 1995, p. 111)

Many persons who commit ordinary offenses while young and then cease also engage at a later age in whatever illegal practices are common in their legitimate occupation, profession, or business (discussed in Chapter 8).

The National Youth Study concluded from follow-up data on a young sample that one can predict with 95% to 98% accuracy that "if an individual never commits minor delinquent acts, that individual will almost never commit Index Offenses" (Elliott, Huizinga, & Menard, 1989, p. 188). Index crimes are the most serious in the FBI's statistics—homicide, rape, assault, robbery, burglary, theft, and arson. Arrest rates for these crimes decline most rapidly after age 25.

Causal Factors in Adolescent Lawbreaking

Humans and other animals are playful when young. Eager for excitement, they engage in what psychologists call "stimulation seeking," usually ascribed to hormonal changes. Youths seek legitimate thrills in sports and vehicle racing, criminal thrills in stealing and vandalizing for the sheer excitement of getting away with it, or trying drugs and sex in search of pleasures.

Much youth conduct that adults consider delinquent is more aptly called defiant, for youths try to act in ways that make them feel "grown up" and independent of adults. Many of them persist in rebelling against authority well into their twenties, thirties, or older; they also resume adolescent attitudes and behavior when under stress later in life.

Any handicap to a successful school record or other types of legitimate success (sports, jobs, etc.), increases a youth's prospects of finding a sense of accomplishment in illegal acts. Several other social factors also play a role in adolescent lawbreaking, most notably family environment, socioeconomic variables, youth subcultures, and street gangs.

Family Relationships

Among the best predictors that children will become seriously involved in crime are either intense conflicts with or indifference from their parents or parent substitutes. Positive relationships with parents help children learn adult standards of conduct and ensure that children are appropriately rewarded or punished for the things they do. Children in large families, especially if not first-born, have above-average arrest rates, presumably because they have fewer contacts with parents. Juveniles are also likely to have above-average crime rates if their parents are criminals, have intense marital discord, or discipline their children too harshly, too leniently, or too inconsistently (Loeber & Southamer-Loeber, 1986).

The National Youth Study's follow-up of a large sample of American youths showed that maltreatment in childhood is predictive of later delinquency. The more severe the maltreatment, the more serious are the victim's subsequent offenses (Smith & Thornberry, 1995). A British study reached nearly the same conclusions (Farrington, 1995).

With girls more often than with boys, it is the parents who ask the police to pick up their youngsters. But some children of both genders wisely avoid their homes, as the parents or their replacements criminally abuse them or throw them out. Jill Rosenbaum (1989), studying repeatedly incarcerated women as juveniles and as adults, found that most were reared with much violence, crime, and lack of warmth at home. She asks why, under these circumstances, courts so often insist that a daughter must be with her mother.

The few youths who engage in "life-persistent anti-social behavior" appear to have both biological and social handicaps (Moffitt, 1993). Among the biological handicaps associated statistically with higher than average juvenile arrest rates are low intelligence, dyslexia, instability of mood or attention, and sluggish reactions of the nervous system either to pain or to its cessation (Raine, 1993; White, Moffitt, Earls, Robins, & Silva, 1990). Such traits may be genetic, but some are also fostered by various perinatal complications or poor nutrition of pregnant women or of infants. They may be exacerbated by deficient child supervision and bad conduct models later. Yet none of these handicaps are always or nearly always followed by above-average crime rates.

As for social handicaps, Joan McCord (1983), in a follow-up study of about 500 males who in early adolescence were deemed predelinquent, found that those with criminal fathers were likely also to commit crimes. If they did not, they usually had strong sources of anticriminal influence, such as warm and competent mothers and residence in low-crime neighborhoods.

Thus it seems that nature interacts with nurture and experience in developing both criminal and legitimate conduct; there are no purely "born" criminals. Longitudinal studies of child development conclude that several factors—such as poor parenting, birth defects, and poverty— are predictive of delinquency. The studies also conclude that these factors are multiplicative in their impact: Having two such handicaps may be four times as predictive of later arrests as only one, and having three or more further raises risks (Yoshikawa, 1994). However, these handicaps can be ameliorated by a supportive family or other social group with noncriminal values. Indeed, a theory ascribing crime to the lack of social support in legitimate pursuits has been about as well confirmed by research as the theory ascribing crime to low self-control (Cullen, 1994).

Socioeconomic Variables

Ethnicity, social class, and neighborhood have a great effect on youth criminality. The most dire effects of such variables fall on those at the bottom of the social ladder. Poverty is an obvious motivator for certain types of crime. One study of homeless youth concludes: "Consistently, hunger causes theft of food, problems of hunger and shelter lead to serious theft, and problems of shelter and unemployment produce prostitution" (McCarthy & Hagan, 1992). Unfortunately, we have almost as many homeless families—usually a mother with one or more children—as separately homeless adults (Seltser & Miller, 1993). Thus the effects of poverty may be enhanced by the lack of a stable family life.

A disproportionate share of youth crime occurs in slums, which are poor neighborhoods of crowded and dilapidated old dwellings mixed with newer commercial and industrial structures. Crowded slum housing makes the streets the children's main play space. Because vice and crime are pursued more openly in slums than in better housing areas, slum children are much exposed to lawbreaking (Stark, 1987; Wilson, 1987).

New immigrants often settle in slums, for there they find the least objection to their unfamiliar ways or to the crowding that reduces rent. But the new settlers encounter prejudice if their speech or appearance contrast with that of more established residents, and such differences also handicap immigrant children in school. Given the importance of youthful success in noncriminal pursuits, we should perhaps not be surprised that the offspring of almost every nationality or racial group had above-average arrest rates when it first settled in the slums. That is why our jail and prison inmates were mostly young Irish from about 1880 to World War I, Italian and Polish in the 1920s and 1930s, thereafter increasingly African Americans, but now in many areas predominantly Latino. Whenever an immigrant group with the highest arrest rates improves its economic status and moves to better neighborhoods, its arrest rates decline, but usually the group that replaces it in the slums then has the highest rates.

In Los Angeles County, the most rapidly growing and most multiethnic megalopolis in the United States, Leo Schuerman and Solomon Kobrin (1986) showed that neighborhoods tend to deteriorate physically before they get high crime rates, but once these rates rise, their deterioration accelerates. Predictors of a rise in crime rates in an area include subdivision of dwellings to house more families, increased proportions of broken families and unattached individuals, plus a rising ratio of children to adults. As neighborhoods acquire these features, residents who can move do so, leaving multiproblem families more concentrated there.

Data from more than 500 British cities also demonstrate that the urban areas with highest crime rates have high proportions of residents who are poor, recent immigrants, or transient; who live in broken homes, who are without friends, or who have unsupervised teenage children; and who participate little in community organizations (Sampson & Groves, 1989). Such conditions are worst in overly urbanized developing countries, from the least technologically advanced in Africa to those of industrialized Latin America, notably Brazil.

The high rates of violent crime and incarceration of urban African Americans in the past half century are fully explained by their racial segregation in slum ghettos, generations of deficient education, and family disorganization (Sampson & Wilson, 1995). These persistent problems result from our history of slavery and continued inequality in education and job opportunities. Crime rates drop sharply for those African Americans who, despite discrimination and other handicaps, succeed in obtaining an education, improving their employment, and moving from the slums.

Children of poor Chinese, Japanese, and Korean immigrants who settle in U.S. slums are exceptions to the rule that youngsters of new ethnic groups have high delinquency rates. These Asian-ancestry youths usually have very low crime rates even when they face much prejudice. They resist criminogenic slum influences because their family bonds are strong, children collaborate with adults in small-business tasks, they participate extensively in religious and fraternal organizations, and both the home and the community intensively promote academic excellence.

Groups with a commitment to religion also have low delinquency rates. Within these groups, moreover, crime rates are lowest for those juveniles who are most committed to religion (Stark, Kent, & Doyle, 1982).

Youth Subcultures

Youths having much communication with one another but little with adults develop their own subcultures. Young and old have contrasting tastes in music, dancing, slang, dress, and other matters. Peer and parental influences on a child's conduct often compete, but when parents or other adults become less available, peer impact tends to strengthen.

Especially conducive to high juvenile crime rates today is the fact that children of all ages, but particularly adolescents, are more segregated than ever from adults. In the United States, most mothers with preteen children have or seek full-time jobs outside the home. A quarter of U.S. children live in homes without a father, a rate that has quadrupled since 1950 (*Los Angeles Times*, Apr. 24, 1995). The number of childhood years spent in in mother-only families, hence likely to be deficient in contacts with adults, is a good predictor for dropping out of high school (Wojtkiewicz, 1993).

In 1979 researchers asked a representative sample of Illinois adults to recall how often, when they were 17, they were not with parents on weekday afternoons, at dinner, in an auto after dark, during daytime on Saturdays, and after 11 p.m. on weekends (Felson & Gottfredson, 1984). Grouping the sample by the decade in which they were 17, from before 1940 to the 1970s, the researchers found that each successive group increased the proportion of their activities taking place always or mostly away from their parents. Over those decades, such separation increased most at dinner and in autos after dark. Thus adolescents increasingly lived in a world of their own. The trend continues today. Such separation is also reported for Britain (Riley, 1987).

Street Gangs

Children usually engage in leisure activities in pairs, trios, or larger groups. Their friends tend to replace their families as sources of behavior standards and self-concepts. They boast to one another of their prowess at various feats and dare each other to take chances or be derided as "chicken." Therefore, many youngsters do reckless things in groups that they would not venture alone.

Most juvenile and young adult crime is committed with associates. Solo offenders usually start lawbreaking at a later age and persist at it more briefly than do co-offenders (Reiss & Farrington, 1991; Warr, 1993).

People of all ages grasp the best of whatever company they can get, rather than be lonely. Travis Hirschi's (1969) questionnaires in public schools showed that students who admit delinquency do not rate their friends as favorably as nondelinquents rate theirs. Nevertheless, the delinquent friends do provide support. Unfortunately, youths, like all of us, tend to conform to expectations in the groups where they are accepted and respected.

Street gangs develop when youths with weak anticriminal social bonds become cohesive in their activities away from home. They are especially likely to cohere closely with other youths when they are unified in their conflict with adult figures or with other identifiable youth groups.

Gangs give youths a collective identity. They invent gang names, apparel, tattoos, hairstyles, demeanor, language, and graffiti that express disdain for established authority and flaunt claims of superiority. What the law and most adults define as "bad," they call "good" and even make "bad" a compliment. Crime for them is an appealing and exciting way to feel independent, because this view of illegal behavior is enthusiastically expressed by their friends (Katz, 1988). Such activities promote a sense of group independence, bravery, and power.

The efforts of individuals and gangs to advertise themselves by their tattoos and graffiti are also associated with youth crime. Tattoos and graffiti have styles and symbols with special meanings in gang subcultures. Ferrell (1993) reports the "rush" of pride that graffiti creators get because of their work's illegality, the pressure to finish it quickly to avoid being caught, and the competition to do it well (by their standards). He also views their design preferences politically, as an anarchistic rebellion against established aesthetic standards. But residents and owners of homes and businesses in gang areas deplore the declining value of their property, the cost of removing these displays, and the prospect of rapid further physical deterioration and street crime in heavily tagged neighborhoods.

Crime among gang members extends beyond theft and vandalism. Assault and even murder are higher in gang areas than elsewhere. Gangs usually try to dominate other youths in their neighborhoods through intimidation and violence, and they war with each other for territory. Gang members engage in endless talk of past violence and of the gang's heroes and villains. These intergang feuds often continue for years. They are often deadly, but they help many youths to achieve or defend their personal honor and sense of competence.

The greatest rise in killings in the United States has recently been of 16-year-olds; murder rates were steady for those 24 to 30 years old and dropped for those over 30 (National Institute of Justice, 1995b). Much of the increase can be attributed to gang wars. In our largest cities, hundreds of deaths are now annually ascribed to gun battles between youth gangs. In "drive by" shootings, gang members often fire only in the general direction of their rivals. They may therefore hit innocent bystanders, including infants or old people inside homes.

Street gang members are not all juveniles. The average age of defendants in gang-related murders in Los Angeles is 19. Both teenagers and youths in their twenties or older who get little respect at home, school, work, church, or other socially approved settings are likely to value gang companions who welcome them. Their crime rates have been shown to be higher when in a gang than before or after (Thornberry, Krohn, Lizotte, & Chard-Wierschein, 1993).

Ways to Prevent Criminality in Youngsters

Most serious lawbreaking by older teenagers and young adults evolves from the experiences and conduct patterns of an earlier age. Therefore, the sooner in the lives of its children that a society applies the wisdom, time, and resources needed to prevent lawbreaking, the greater are the later benefits. The following suggestions are cost-effective ways to prevent adolescents from committing crimes because they focus on developmental experiences instead of trying to correct criminal behavior once it occurs.

Enhancing the Positive Influence of Parents and Teachers

Adolescents gain a sense of independence not only by "getting away with" crimes but also by successfully performing legitimate adult roles, such as getting and holding jobs, buying their own clothing (even if they pay for it from allowances that their parents give them), driving cars, and so on. The challenge in curbing youth crime is to channel into legitimate conduct the eagerness of children and young adults to feel fully grown.

Parents, teachers, and other adults who deal with children must remember that rearing children to be considerate and law-abiding requires not only penalizing them for misconduct but also

- ◆ Creating integrative rather than stigmatizing shame
- ◆ Seeing that children get gratification from good behavior

Those who reprimand or otherwise punish children should try to make clear that they are against the misconduct, not its perpetrator (Braithwaite, 1989). But researchers find that parents and teachers err by persisting too long in withholding praise and reward for subsequent good conduct. For example, children who steal are scolded and punished about as often as children who do not, but the stealers less regularly get approval when they behave well (Patterson, 1980). The lowest delinquency rates occur if parental punishment is highly contingent on the child's behavior and is consistent but is not excessively harsh (Wells & Rankin, 1988).

One manifestation of excessive punishment is childhood bullying. Bullies in preschool and elementary school tended to get harsh and inconsistent punishment at home and subsequently to have above-average arrest rates (Farrington, 1993; Olweus, Block, & Raske-Yarrow, 1986). In a rigorous effort to reduce bullying, 458 Seattle first graders (ages 6 and 7) in eight schools were randomly assigned to experimental or control classes. In this program, called "Catch 'em Being Good," parents and teachers of experimental students were trained to notice and reward desirable behavior, give clear instructions and explanations, and teach children ways to resolve conflicts. Assessed 18 months later, when the children were in other classes, the experimental boys were significantly less aggressive than the controls; experimental girls were not less aggressive but were less nervous, depressed, and self-destructive than their controls (Hawkins, Von Cleve, & Catalano, 1991).

Adolescents tend to have less social competence and to do poorly in high school if their parental figures are either highly permissive, being indifferent to what their children do, or highly authoritarian, insisting that their children do exactly as told and not try to discuss the rules. The most socially competent children have parents or parent substitutes who encourage them to consider all alternatives well but who allow them—within reason—to make their own decisions. This optimum parenting style is confusingly called *authoritative* (a term coined by Baumrind, 1978; cf. Wright & Wright, 1995), as distinct from "authoritarian." It might best be called *maturative*, however, defined by Webster as "conducing to maturity."

Simple involvement with parents also helps prevent adolescent criminalization. Comparison of drug-addicted and nonaddicted siblings in a New York slum indicated that close involvement with law-abiding parents or other adults "insulates" the nonaddicted offspring from the criminality of their streets and of their own siblings; addicted siblings were much more often in conflict with parents and seldom at home (Glaser, Lander, & Abbott, 1971). Thus, even youths in the same household may contrast in what have classically been called "differential association" causes of crime: a higher frequency, priority, intimacy, and intensity of pro-criminal over anticriminal social bonds (Sutherland & Cressey, 1978).

Low parental education levels and occupational status are statistically associated with above average delinquency rates, except in families with parenting practices that experts rate as "good" (Larzelere & Patterson, 1990). However, special training programs for parents can help reduce the delinquency of high-risk children (Hawkins, Catalano, Jones, & Fine, 1987). Indeed, a U.S. government review of research reported:

> Prevention strategies that help families develop good family management practices—including providing clear expectations and consistent

discipline to children—can work with high-risk and dysfunctional families. Home visitation programs that offer intensive support to mothers at risk of abusing their newborns have produced a 75% reduction in cases of child abuse and neglect, thus breaking a violent cycle in which the abused too often grow up to become violent offenders. (Office of Juvenile Justice and Delinquency Prevention [OJJDP], 1995, p. 2)

Therefore, a major goal in youth crime prevention should be to provide widespread education and training on parenthood. We require training, testing, and licensing to drive a car but none to rear children. In actuality, we will probably never have tests and licenses for parenting, but the classes in child rearing offered by many high schools may have delinquency prevention value.

Improving Adolescent Social Skills and Community Friendships

In one landmark study, adolescents carried a pad with a short questionnaire that they were supposed to answer at random times, in response to a beeper they carried. The questions asked what they were doing, where, with whom, and what mood they were in when buzzed. They most often described their mood favorably when they were with friends. It was then that they most frequently checked that they felt "free," "wild," and "sociable" and least often "self-conscious" and "concentrating." Many were also happiest while engaged in long phone chats with friends, listening to music with friends, or shooting basketballs. Work proved to be as pleasant as play for the teenagers in the study, but only if it produced gratifying feedback on accomplishments and especially if the work involved others. The study's directors concluded:

> Friendship, like anything else, can be cultivated or handled ineptly. . . . Runaway normless behavior . . . from peer interactions, reflects a lack of skills, an inability to deal creatively with its openness. Teens who cannot enjoy playing basketball turn to breaking windows; teens who can't cope with losses turn to cocaine; teens who have nothing to say to a friend turn to more risky sexual involvement. The skills of friendship . . . are . . . of mutually defining a set of boundaries, staying within them—and simultaneously having a good time. If the amount of time American adolescents spend among themselves provides a lasting benefit, it is the opportunity to learn this competence. (Csikszentmihalyi & Larson, 1984, p. 175)

Children can also develop social skills by becoming involved in community activities. Schools, churches, and other structures are used by area residents of different ages for beneficial recreation and instruction in late afternoons, evenings, and weekends. "Beacon Centers" in New York City school buildings—which provide tutoring, employment training, counseling, a variety of recreational activities, and especially opportunities for students to bond more closely with teachers and other adults—may be a major factor in that city's declining crime rate (McGillis, 1996).

Another method of demonstrating community cohesiveness is to institute curfews. Curfew laws, now prevailing in most of our largest cities, forbid persons under a particular age (e.g., 15, 16, 17, or 18) to be on the streets without adult escort during specified hours (e.g., 11 p.m. to 6 a.m. on weekdays and 12 a.m. to 5 a.m. on weekends). Most curfew laws make exceptions for traveling to and from work or for attending school, religious, or other supervised activities. Assessments of curfew laws have been diverse in quality, but most claim that enforcement of these laws curbs juvenile delinquency (Office of Juvenile Justice and Delinquency Prevention [OJJDP], 1996).

Reducing the Cohesiveness of Street Gangs

In high-crime-rate areas where gangs take over parks, schoolgrounds, and other recreational space, residents may need police help to get secure access to these places. Community policing (discussed in Chapter 10), with decentralized, small police stations and police-sponsored neighborhood-watch organizations, are especially useful. Without such efforts in areas where the greatest fear of crime prevails, the most law-abiding persons will isolate themselves or move away. These conditions foster physical deterioration of buildings, more fear among those who remain, and further area decline (Skogan, 1990).

One type of intervention in gangs that was much promoted for more than 20 years after World War II and is still advocated by some has been repeatedly shown by rigorous large-scale research to achieve no overall reduction in delinquency rates. This alleged remedy is the employment of "streetworkers" who "hang out" with gang boys, give them athletic equipment, take them to professional ball games, get them a storefront or other building space for a clubhouse, and equip it with pool and Ping-Pong tables. Their objective is to change gangs into law-abiding social and athletic clubs, but this attention attracts less-delinquent juveniles to gangs still dominated by the most criminalized members, thereby increasing their segregation from conventional adults. Streetworkers often can mediate inter-gang quarrels and reduce their violence, but the key to making gangs less criminogenic is to make them less cohesive (Klein, 1995, pp. 44-49).

A better approach, therefore, is to attract gang members individually into more constructive types of local organizations that have cohesive bonding between juvenile members and law-abiding adults. This effort is often aided by "lighted schoolhouses" or other community centers that are available after regular school hours, to provide supervised meeting and recreation places that offset home and community deficiencies. A federal review of research summarized the findings on this sort of approach:

> Nine out of 10 juveniles involved in gangs for 3 or more years reported committing serious crimes, compared with only 3 out of 10 nongang youth in positive peer pressure environments. . . . Boys and Girls Clubs of America target high-risk youth in 64 public housing complexes across the Nation, and their programs have helped reduce the juvenile crime rate in these areas by 13 percent. (OJJDP, 1995, p. 2)

Interventions not planned as antigang efforts eventually get most gang members out of lawbreaking and into a fairly law-abiding adulthood, especially if these events occur before the members acquire prison records. Conversion of criminal youths to law-abiding citizens is routinely achieved by employers, spouses, and churches. In recent decades, in some minority slum neighborhoods, it has been accomplished by political action groups absorbing individual youths and involving them with adults in demonstrations or lobbying. A more than 30-year follow-up of Boston juvenile delinquents shows that lasting marriages and employment are the best paths to noncriminal adult lives (Sampson & Laub, 1990). It also found that military service frequently provides "a turning point in the lives of disadvantaged men" (Sampson & Laub, 1996).

Crime prevention grows, and gangs are weakened, whenever a wide spectrum of youths, including some with poor conduct records, build bonds with law-abiding adults through collaborative activities. We should promote more of these activities, beginning in early childhood.

Reducing the Negative Impacts of Family Dependence on Welfare

We extol family unity, yet our welfare laws have broken up many families and thereby reduced children's bonds with law-abiding adults.

Aid for Families with Dependent Children (AFDC), our largest welfare program, reduced family poverty but often had negative effects on household relationships. In about half the states most clearly, and in others to a lesser extent, when a father living with his spouse and one or more children has low or irregular earnings, he can best help the rest of the family get a greater or more dependable income by leaving home. The economic benefits of getting rid of the father may be greatest when the mother or children have large medical costs (qualifying them for Medicaid in addition) or when the father has costly vices such as alcohol, drugs, or gambling that have absorbed what little family income there is.

Most welfare payments barely cover the cost of an urban household's rent plus utilities. Food stamps pay for only about three fourths of food costs. Additional income exceeding $25 per month is supposed to be deducted from welfare payments, but confidential interviews with recipients indicate that almost all get some unreported economic aid from friends or relatives, or they "hustle" additional income. This hustling may be part-time housecleaning, baby-sitting, or other odd jobs, as well as begging, peddling, theft, prostitution, or drug selling. Such income is not reported to the government and therefore cannot be deducted from welfare payments. Because social workers realize that people cannot survive on welfare alone, most probe only extra income that seems clearly too high (Edin & Lein, 1996; Tonry, 1995a, pp. 12-17).

During the second half of the 1990s, a series of state and national efforts (referred to as "workfare") have been undertaken to reform welfare by getting its recipients into self-supporting jobs. Yet welfare recipients are disinclined to give up their benefits unless their earnings securely reach or exceed minimum wage levels. Achieving such pay levels is difficult, however, partly because unemployment becomes a way of life among those with little work experience, low education, and long failure at job search. The age of children does not increase a mother's ability to replace welfare with a job, but her education and work experience do. An employed slum resident observed of her welfare-receiving neighbors, possibly stereotyping numerous cases unjustly,

> Many of them don't know how to get up on time, ready their kids for school, or adhere to a bus schedule. They don't know how to speak grammatically in the workplace, follow directions or control their temper. They have never had to squeeze grocery shopping and housecleaning into odd hours at night or on weekends, or help their youngsters with homework when they are bone weary from a day of work. . . .

> It's hard once you get in the slum of AFDC to motivate yourself because just sitting at home feels good. But once you start working, that's a must. (Gross, 1996, Part B, p. 1)[1]

Such habits make some welfare recipients unlikely candidates for successful employment. Without the "social capital" of good work habits, hopelessness often prevails in job seeking (Engbersen, Schayt, Timmer, & van Wearden, 1993; Rank, 1994).

Several places (e.g., in Wisconsin and in Riverside County in California) have shown that the number of welfare recipients is reducible, and that within a year net savings are greatest if almost all aid recipients are helped to start any jobs they can handle rather than staying exclusively in skill-training classes. Jobs are subsidized if necessary, and child care is provided if needed. Participants get slight pay raises for persistent good conduct, and they are penalized for misbehavior. This work experience helps people develop the habits required for successful employment. As their work qualifications improve, their search for unsubsidized better jobs is also facilitated. The benefits of good workfare programs more than exceed their costs not only by cutting welfare payments but also by enhancing payment of income and other taxes (Gueron & Pauly, 1991; K. Harris, 1993). The 1996 welfare reform act was promoted as a means of expanding the workforce and reducing long dependence on welfare. How well it will accomplish these objectives remains to be seen.

Collecting Full Support for Offspring
of Divorced or Separated Parents

About half of marriages now end in divorce, and about a third of births are to unwed women. No-fault divorces prevail in all our states. In a passion to end their ties, parents often split without legally obligating the fathers to provide adequate child support, and many fathers do not make whatever payments are ordered or agreed upon. Also, many unmarried women with children are unable to prove paternity, as courts demand before ordering child support payments.

First Lady Hillary Rodham Clinton (1996) observed:

> With divorce as easy as it is, and its consequences so hard, people with children need to ask themselves whether they have given a marriage their best shot and what more they can do to make it work before they call it quits.

For this reason, I am ambivalent about no-fault divorce with no waiting period when children are involved. We should consider returning to mandatory "cooling off" periods, with education and counseling for partners. (p. 43)

More than half the children of divorced parents live in female-headed homes on incomes below the poverty level. Women head 9 of 10 welfare households. These conditions mainly damage the innocents, the children. Children with no fathers in the home may suffer not only from poverty but also from insufficient adult supervision and behavior modeling.

We could benefit from studying the practices of Scandinavian and other nations that guarantee affordable and adequate care for all children, regardless of whether or not the parents can pay for it. The state forces any parent with resources to contribute to child support but picks up the slack when he or she cannot (Weitzman, 1985).

Making Teenage Motherhood Less a Source of Poverty and Neglect

About 40% of U.S. females now become pregnant before age 20, a higher proportion than exists in any other developed nation. Most of these girls are poor. Some who are in conflict with parents welcome pregnancy as a means to independence, because it makes them eligible for their own welfare checks and apartments. But early pregnancy usually curtails the mother's schooling and reduces her later employability, both of which reduce her economic standing and thereby increase the chances that her child will become involved in childhood-transition and later crime.

Regulations in some states now ban welfare payments directly to juvenile mothers; instead, the parents or other designated adults are appointed as trustees to receive the funds. But high risk of unwed pregnancy continues among women in their twenties and thirties.

Teenage pregnancies can be reduced by giving high school girls easy access to clinics that provide birth control advice and aid. Such clinics are now not as controversial as formerly, because they also combat the spread of AIDS.

When social service agencies minimize the child-rearing problems of very poor mothers, they prevent higher future costs to society from crimes by the children as adolescents and adults. Sweden, Denmark, France, and Britain all have higher rates of unwed motherhood than does the United

States, but their welfare payments are closer to the recipients' living costs. This policy may be one factor in their lower crime rates.

Reducing Racial, Ethnic, Religious, and Class Segregation

Discrimination against a racial, ethnic, or religious group in any type of activity creates a vicious cycle, because it impairs opportunities in other activities. This fact was recognized by the U.S. Supreme Court in its landmark 1954 school desegregation case. *Brown v. Board of Education* found that placing African Americans in separate schools, even if these seem to be of equal quality, gives the students inferior prospects in later pursuits because of the bias and prejudice of others.

When members of ethnic and racial groups are segregated from the rest of society, their differences in speech and other elements of culture are preserved. The differences in speech are particularly likely to impair their access to employment, to nonsegregated housing, and to political office. Each of these types of impediment helps perpetuate the others, for they all slow a group's assimilation into the larger society.

Attacking any type of group segregation is beneficial. If segregation declines in any single setting or activity—for example, housing, schools, jobs, politics, clubs, restaurants, recreation, or marriages—its decline becomes more probable (but not necessarily immediate) in the other settings or activities.

Such movement toward equality and desegregation is usually most rapid if it is mandated. Although inter-group conflict may intensify when people of different ethnic or racial ancestry first mix, their interaction as equals tends ultimately to erode prejudice. Collaboration with persons of different races or nationalities fosters greater recognition that "you meet all kinds" within each group. Desegregation is a slow process, but it can be hastened by teaching, preaching, and law.

Yet efforts to desegregate schools since 1954 have often been disappointing. Busing slum children for hours to schools in more affluent neighborhoods is not only resented by those at their destinations but also resisted by those bused and their families as too stressful physically and psychologically. Some scholastic achievement gains and greater social, employment, and residential desegregation probably can be credited to busing, but it has also fostered much white flight to the suburbs. When whites depart, they leave behind schools that are even more segregated.

Desegregation is more successful with magnet schools that draw students with specialized interests or abilities from many or all of a city's neighborhoods—especially if magnet schools are in minority or ethnically mixed areas to which others come. Magnet schools promote personal interaction across racial and ethnic lines because of their students' common interests. They also increase scholastic achievement (Rossel, 1990).

Efforts to desegregate neighborhoods, by race and by class, are another way to promote school integration. However, we have a history in the United States, since Franklin D. Roosevelt's New Deal, of providing low-cost public housing for slum dwellers only in huge "projects." Members of poor ethnic groups are concentrated in the projects, and any residents who improve their family income are forced to leave. Because this policy concentrates multiproblem families in the projects, they have high rates of crime, vice, and mental illness. Buildings then deteriorate so much that many have to be destroyed, especially the high-rise ones.

Some progress has been made in reducing segregation and other housing handicaps for poor people by requiring new public and private housing developments to be smaller and more scattered, with units diverse in cost. Under "Title 8" and "Gautreaux" programs (the first named for a section of housing law and the latter after a woman who won a suit against Chicago's racial segregation), the federal government gives housing vouchers to poor people to help them pay for residence in areas where rents are somewhat higher than they can afford on their own. Such desegregation reduces delinquency by increasing the success of welfare mothers and fathers in getting better jobs and by encouraging the mingling of all types of children at school and play.

In Los Angeles and many other U.S. cities, much racial desegregation occurred in the 1990s because the poorest new population, which was Hispanic (from Mexico, Central America, and the Caribbean) crowded into older African American ghettos. More ghetto residents then moved, and they were able to scatter widely into previously all-Anglo residential areas.

Reducing Homelessness

Another trend of the 1990s was a great increase in what Blau (1992) aptly called "the visible poor"—the homeless. Estimates of their total number vary greatly, as all censuses are incomplete. But Blau points out that in polls asking urban residents if they saw homeless persons or encountered begging on the previous day, the proportion who did rose from year to year. It now exceeds two thirds of survey respondents.

The main cause for increased homelessness is the rapid shift in the U.S. labor market from unskilled to skilled and professional employment. Low-skilled manufacturing is done increasingly by machines or overseas. Much homelessness results from migrations within the United States by displaced workers expecting better jobs elsewhere, whose hopes prove to be warranted only briefly, if at all, at their new locations, while their expenses prove greater than they expected. The incomes of Americans on welfare or in unskilled jobs are often inadequate to pay the cost of available housing plus utilities. And with greater mobility, more financially distressed persons are not near any relatives who could house them.

An appreciable minority of the homeless—there is little agreement on its size—are mentally ill and in former decades would have been hospitalized. More effective medications and other changes in treatment have reduced mental hospital populations by about three fourths from their 1950s peak of more than half a million. But many of the mentally ill cease to get or to take medicines.

Formerly the homeless were mostly alcoholic men in skid rows, and many still are. But now about an eighth are single women, and a third are mothers with their children (Blau, 1992; Hombs, 1994; Timmer, Eitzen, & Talley, 1994). The effects of homelessness are especially onerous for these children, because they then lack proper schooling and are exposed to family stress, idleness, and street criminals. Homeless young people are especially likely to engage in crime.

Reducing homelessness would thus help to diminish overall crime rates. The U.S. government attacks homelessness by creating welfare "safety nets" for the very poor and by developing "workfare" that promotes their economic independence. However, about a quarter of the homeless have part- or full-time employment; they simply have long periods when they are unable to accumulate enough funds to make a down payment for rent. The homeless avoid many shelters established for them, especially if the shelters consist of numerous cots in a dormitory, because of the theft and violence that occur there. Jencks (1994) urges constructing buildings to guarantee safe shelter for all, such as small single rooms rented for only a few dollars daily and free vouchers issued to those who lack even such rent.

Making Schools Less Criminogenic

Persistent difficulties in school are among the most accurate fore-casters of future arrests. Low grades, misconduct in class, and extensive truancy indicate a high probability of more serious offenses later. Poor school achievement is more predictive of arrest before age 18 than are race or social class (Jensen, 1976), and attachment to school is a better predictor of nondelinquency than is attachment to family (Wiatrowski, Griswold, & Roberts, 1981). The following eight policies can reduce student law-breaking.

Make schools smaller, and reduce the number of different teachers for each child

Today's youths spend more years in school than did prior generations, but they usually have weaker bonds with teachers because they have a different teacher for each subject. Delinquency rates of junior and senior high schools do not vary as much with class size as with the number of different teachers the average student has (Gottfredson & Gottfredson, 1985).

Student crime rates are also lower in smaller schools and in smaller classes (U.S. Department of Health, Education and Welfare, 1978). Smaller schools give students more contact with children of diverse ages in other grades, and also with their teachers. These features help prepare them for the age mixing of adulthood.

Some large schools reduce the handicaps of size by restructuring class assignments to increase bonds among students and teachers. Thus, Santa Monica divides its ninth grade into groups of 120, assigning all in each group the same English, math, and science teachers. Students are only mixed with those of other groups in classes for more specialized subjects that have low enrollments.

Shorten summer vacations, and lengthen the school year

Year-round schooling with shorter vacations, now widely adopted to relieve overcrowding without building more schools, reduces loss of learning during summer vacations. This loss is greatest for children living with little-educated adults, where reading rarely occurs at home (Coleman, 1982). It is also greatest for poor children (Entwistle & Alexander, 1992).

The longer school year and shorter vacations in Japan and in several other developed countries contribute to their higher academic achievement and lower crime rates compared with those of the United States. In 1992, the annual Gallup poll for the Phi Delta Kappa educational fraternity found for the first time that a majority of Americans favor a 210-day school calendar over the current average 180-day year. Among supporters of a longer year, 59% favored 3-week vacations at different times of the year— the pattern in other developed nations—instead of our long summer breaks. The traditional U.S. vacation pattern began when most students were needed to work on family farms (*Los Angeles Times*, Aug. 28, 1992).

Avoid extreme segregation of students by ability

Students of low ability learn more and have less delinquency if they attend classes with others of diverse ability and are not separated into "track" systems that keep those of each ability level always apart (Gamoran & Mare, 1989; Oakes, 1985, 1990). Similarly, children with scant knowledge of English learn best with bilingual teachers but are handicapped by too much separation from children of other backgrounds.

Magnet schools integrate ethnic and racial groups by separating students according to their specialized topical interests—such as music, mathematics, or English—rather than by ability. Being less talented than classmates does not increase the likelihood of lawbreaking as much as does absence of students who are good scholastic models and have appealing interests. Even with students of mixed ability in most classes, schools can still provide some separate classes of advanced-level instruction for those who can handle it, alternative special topic classes that appeal to others, and remedial instruction for those who need it.

The earlier that remedial instruction is provided, the fewer the students who are assigned to each teacher; and the less stigmatizing that remedial instruction is, the more effective it can be. Programmed teaching using books or computers that let children advance at their own speed, and giving remedial instruction when they make mistakes or praise when they are correct, reduce delinquency (Hackler & Hagan, 1975).

A problem of many schools, especially in Southern California, is that children of new migrants must be admitted at all times of the year. Because these new students have very diverse levels of prior education, they are placed in a grade primarily by date of birth rather than by test scores or English fluency. Schoolchildren are routinely promoted at the end of each term regardless of classroom performance or extent of absence from school. Graduating students purely by age, without remedial programs to correct their scholastic deficiencies, perpetuates their handicaps.

It has been shown repeatedly that school misconduct is reduced when teachers form academic teams for students of mixed ability, grade teams of students as a group for cooperative projects, and have students collectively participate with adults in disciplinary and some other decisions (Kimbrough, 1986). Schools also have lower crime rates if they emphasize education over recreation and athletics, and test academic progress often (Rutter, Maughan, Mortimore, & Ouston, 1979).

Provide "Head Start" type supplementary food and tutoring programs in preschools, elementary schools, and even middle and high schools, as well as in public housing projects with many children

Such services begin at preschools in some poor neighborhoods, and may be extended to higher grade levels by "Follow Through" programs. For very poor children, free lunches and even free breakfasts improve learning and conduct. This feeding not only offsets nutritional deficiencies at home, but fosters school attendance and increases personal bonds of children with adults at school. Students should share with adults the responsibilities and rewards for minimizing the food waste that often occurs because of poor administration, food prejudices, or defiant delinquency.

Psychologists have proved with rats, and infer for humans, that early learning enrichment permanently increases the thickness of the cerebral cortex, hence the ability to learn. That is why good preschool education may be among the most profitable public investments. A study in the 1980s of children who had been in a Head Start program in Ypsilanti, Michigan, during the early 1960s compared their subsequent conduct with that of similar children not in the program. Headstarters had about a 50% higher rate of high school graduation and current employment than the comparison group, about a 50% lower arrest rate, and about half as high a percentage on welfare. From these differences, an early evaluation concluded that within 20 years the government saved $7 for every $1 spent on Head Start (Berrueta-Clement, Schweinhart, Barnett, & Weikhard, 1987). More recent, shorter follow-ups also find them predominantly profitable (Currie & Thomas, 1995). However, because local programs are of diverse and often unstable quality, their benefits and costs, hence profit or loss, should be assessed frequently.

Promote police-school collaboration against truancy

Laxity on school truancy promotes criminal conduct; efforts to combat truancy reduce criminality. San Jose, California, under the leadership of Dr. Joseph McNamara (its police chief until his move to the Hoover Foundation), found that police questioning of juveniles on the streets or in parks during school hours not only curbed truancy, but also greatly cut daytime burglary and shoplifting rates. "Attendance counselors," formerly called "truant officers," or other school employees or volunteers, should check with homes about absentee students.

An ordinance requiring a truant to appear promptly with a parent or guardian in traffic court was enacted in 1995 by the Los Angeles City Council. The court can fine either or both parties, impose community service as a penalty, and revoke the truant's driver's license. It was reportedly effective in reducing truancy for the few cases in which it was applied, but police give low priority to truancy.

School uniforms, increasingly adopted in the United States, reduce student concerns about apparel. In addition, a requirement for wearing uniforms has been shown in Japan to reduce truancy rates. Young people in school uniforms are identifiable and shamed as truants if they are found away from school during class hours (Tanioka & Glaser, 1991).

Have police help teach classes on the law

Research shows that juvenile lawbreaking can be reduced by conducting classes in which teachers and police officers instruct elementary or higher-grade students on understanding and respecting the law and criminal justice agencies. But such classes have this crime-reducing effect only if the teachers and officers are trained to elicit discussion from all students, not just the least delinquent and brightest (Office of Juvenile Justice and Delinquency Prevention, 1985).

Provide students with tangible rewards for high or improved performance, and for earning a diploma

Cleveland, Ohio's, "Scholarship in Escrow" program is a "blue chip" investment in both crime prevention and the productivity of future workers. It motivates inner-city students in Grades 7 through 12 to stay in school and learn well by placing funds in an interest-bearing bank account for their later college costs: $10 for every C earned, $20 for every B, and $40 for every A (Huff, 1989).

Delinquency of high school students does not reduce their later job attainment as much as failure to graduate does (Monk-Turner, 1989). Therefore, at all grades, academic efforts should be made more gratifying for underachievers so they will be motivated to graduate. Often neighborhood adults, such as retired persons, can be helpful as volunteer teacher aides or as tutors for slower-learning students. Student behavior in Los Angeles was demonstrably improved by programs that included training of teachers and volunteers to give positive reinforcement for any gains in learning by academically deficient students; tutoring of these students by parents and student leaders; "school watch" volunteer guards against delinquency on campus; and efforts to increase school pride. Such programs not only furthered student academic achievement, but reduced annual expenses for repairing school vandalism enough to more than pay for their cost (Mayer & Butterworth, 1981).

A Rand Corporation cost-benefit analysis compared four methods of crime reduction in California: providing home visits and day care for delinquent students; training parents to monitor their children's school performance, and to reward or punish them appropriately; giving students cash payments for good school conduct and graduation; and intensive probation supervision. By far the most profitable was the program of payment to students. Students in a control group, who were not paid, had three times the arrest rate of those paid (Greenwood, Model, Rydell, & Chiesa, 1996).

Do not expel students without trying first to investigate complaints about them thoroughly and fairly, to try to settle them without expulsion; however, do what is needed to prevent misconduct that seriously and persistently disrupts others

Arrest rates of children in the United States rise most rapidly around age 13, when youngsters experience the emotional turmoil of puberty and the stress of starting junior high. The rates peak at 16 or 17, near the end of compulsory schooling, when those who are most delinquent either drop out or are expelled. In Britain soon after World War II, when the age limit of compulsory schooling was raised one year at a time from 13 to 16 over a period of several years, the peak age of arrest always went up by a year following each rise in the required schooling age (McKissack, 1967, 1973). The implication is that involuntary school enrollment promotes crime, as is also suggested by the drop in crime rates during summer vacations.

The earlier a schoolgirl expects to marry, studies show, the likelier she is to rebel against school authorities and be involved in delinquency (Bowker & Klein, 1983; Stinchcombe, 1969). American and British studies find that arrest rates of male delinquents decrease after they drop out of school, but only if they are then employed or marry a nondelinquent girl, or both, thus acquiring adult rather than adolescent roles; otherwise, their arrest rates increase (Farrington, Gallaher, Morley, St. Ledger, & West, 1986).

Jackson Toby (1983) proposes that compulsory schooling end at age 15, not only because youth crime rates are lowest in states with this limit, but because departure of the least motivated students makes it easier for the others to learn. Often misbehaving students are transferred to special schools that emphasize vocational training combined with part-time employment. This practice frequently improves problem students' adjustment and their transition from school to full-time jobs.

Learning in many schools is impeded by teachers who placate difficult students by allowing too much play and not motivating enough work. Schools should be assessed often by their students' test scores, jobs, and arrests.

In too many cases expulsion, rather than a less criminalizing penalty, is hastily ordered as an easy reaction by one irritated or prejudiced assistant principal or other functionary dealing with misconduct. Decisions on a child's expulsion or compulsory transfer should be made collectively and reluctantly by several school personnel, including those who know the student best, because such an act may create a permanent handicap.

Anyone not in school, at any age, who seeks and qualifies for further education through high school or even college should have access to it at reasonable cost. There should also be opportunities for dropouts to take the General Educational Development (GED) examinations that give those who pass a high school diploma. Half those taking it are between 18 and 24, but many are much older, including 10% over 40, Toby and Armor (1992) report. They add: "Attempting to coerce unwilling adolescents to remain in school for their own good does not seem to work. . . . GED programs have the built-in advantage of targeting people who . . . have come to realize that they need more education" (p. 90). GEDs often help school dropouts get stable jobs and have prevented or terminated many careers in lawbreaking.

Giving Students Maturative
Job Experience With Adults

Programs designed to encourage students to stay in school and apprenticeship programs help graduates avoid the dead-end jobs most available to adolescents. Delinquent students generally get work with little future, such as in fast-food sales or delivery, rather than jobs that lead to secure careers (Cusson, 1983). In both legal and illegal activities, delinquent students focus on quick rewards rather than on longer benefits. They also change jobs more often than nondelinquents.

Although some studies report that high school students with jobs have higher rates of lawbreaking than those not working, Denise Gottfredson (1985) found that those who are already delinquent are the ones who most often seek jobs. When she compared working with nonworking students of similar prior conduct records, age, and other traits, she found that those with jobs did not have higher subsequent delinquency rates than similar nonworkers. Also, employed students had as much commitment to finishing school as others.

Work experience, particularly at subsidized jobs for impoverished school-age youths during school vacations, can much enhance preparation for conventional adulthood (Williams & Kornblum, 1985). Yet such experience is hard to acquire for youths. During the early 1990s, when the *Monthly Labor Review* estimated 5.5% unemployment rates in the United States, its estimates were 15.5% unemployment for youth and 31.1% for minority youth (Hagan & Peterson, 1995, p. 2).

However, the highest unemployment rates reported for teenagers (in some areas more than 50% for those in minority groups during an economic recession) are misleading. Such percentages apply only to seekers of full-time work, but these are usually the least competent teenagers. Most others are still in school (including those with part-time jobs) or are in the armed forces, hence are not counted as in the job market when calculating unemployment rates. Youthful part-time workers usually have the best employment qualifications in their age group (Mare, Winship, & Kubitschek, 1984).

For the adolescents unsuccessful in finding work, joblessness leads to crime, and crime leads to more joblessness (Farrington et al., 1986; Thornberry & Christenson, 1984). Arrest rates for 18- to 24-year-olds are linked to poor-quality jobs as well as to unemployment (Allan & Steffensmeier, 1989).

Youths who do poorly in school, lack jobs, and "hang out" mainly with similar youths, fail to develop the habits of punctuality, sustained attention, dispassionate speech, polite listening, and respect for authority needed at jobs. Mark Wiederanders (1981), following up California Youth Authority parolees, found that tardiness, poor communication, inattention, and disrespectful demeanor—not poor work skills—were the main causes of their job losses.

Classrooms, and, especially, student-run extra-curricular organizations (such as student councils and clubs) that assign formal roles and responsibilities to every member and are run by democratic procedures, prepare youngsters for upward mobility when they enter corporate or government employment. Athletic teams run by authoritarian coaches adapt students to rigid discipline when in subordinate roles, but are not nearly as good as are more democratic student groups in preparing youths for adult success (Loeb, 1973; Otto, 1976).

Optimum work preparation for youths includes on-the-job training with more experienced workers as models of diligence. Such programs have been subsidized by some employers and by government funding, but inadequately. Upgrading the nation's labor force through good work-training and apprenticeship programs reduces crime, cuts welfare costs, and raises national productivity, from which the entire country profits.

The government can also cut crime by being the employer of last resort for youth. This seems to have been the effect of the Civilian Conservation Corps during the Great Depression of the 1930s, when youth unemployment was not as linked with high crime rates as it is today (Pandiani, 1982). This program has been renewed on a much smaller scale in federal and state job corps for youths. The Los Angeles Times ("Building New Lives," June 16, 1991) estimated that every dollar invested in the Job Corps saved $1.46 by lowering welfare costs, increasing taxes paid, and reducing crime.

Subsidized work or training, still insufficient in today's age of rapid technological change and corporate downsizing, should always be available to young people as a safety net. It should pay a minimum starting wage, but have monetary incentives to reward good performance. Such experience prepares youths for better regular jobs. Our traditional alternative is giving them welfare or, even worse, leaving them penniless and homeless, which makes them idle and gradually reduces their competence for work. Although adolescence ends when steady jobs and marriage thrust youths into adult roles, many without adequate early work experience then have high rates of unemployment, underemployment, and divorce because they persist in or revert to adolescent lifestyles. The more adequately their childhood and adolescence prepare them for legitimate adult conduct, the lower will be their criminality.

Coordination of Juvenile and Criminal Courts

Children who commit crimes in the United States may be the concern of either of two justice systems, one for juveniles and one for adults, as

Chapter 2 indicated. Until the start of this century, most parts of the world had courts only for adults. Children under age 7 who did criminal acts, even murdered, were not charged with crimes, but those 7 or older could be tried and punished as adults.

This age boundary gradually rose to 12 but became less rigid after "juvenile courts" opened, the first in Chicago in 1899. The rest of the United States and most other countries now also have juvenile courts, but in Scandinavia, the Netherlands, and some other nations, decisions on child offenders are instead made by boards of social workers (Klein, 1984). Juveniles are most often defined legally as persons under 18 years old, but this age limit is lower in some states. Also, youths a few years younger than this limit can be sent to adult courts if charged with very serious or repeated crimes.

In criminal courts under our "adversary system" of trial proce-dure, the government, represented by a prosecutor, presents charges "against" the accused, who is represented by a defense attorney. The judge referees the trial as a contest between prosecution and defense, then decides on the outcome—guilt or innocence—unless this task has been given to a jury. Finally, the judge specifies the sentence to be imposed, within the range of punishments permitted by law (except in the few cases, mostly involving a death penalty, where a jury decides on the sentence).

In juvenile courts as originally conceived, the government acts "on behalf of" rather than "against" a child. Neither prosecutors nor defense attorneys are present; the only lawyer present is the judge, who is assisted by a probation officer. This officer receives complaints about the child from the police or others, investigates them, and reports to the judge, often advising on how the case should be handled.

The Sixth Amendment to the U.S. Constitution gives adults the right to a public trial. For most criminal court sessions, anyone may attend if orderly and if space permits. All interested parties are likely to be present, as well as strangers, especially in a much publicized case.

In contrast, privacy is required for juvenile court hearings. Only the judge, one or more clerks and bailiffs, the child, its parents or guardians, and a probation officer are likely to be present in every case; a police officer or other complainant, plus prosecution and defense lawyers, frequently participate, but often one or both of these lawyers do not. Those without legitimate roles in the hearings are barred.

A juvenile court hearing may be conducted for acts that would not be crimes if done by an adult. These acts are called *juvenile status offenses* (or just "status offenses"). They include such behavior as truancy from school, running away from home, or other persistent defiance of adult authority ("incorrigibility"). After passing the juvenile age limit, usually 18, one may defy parents or teachers, and leave home or school, without fear of the law.

A juvenile court judge decides whether the complaints against a child are justified, and then rules *in loco parentis* (in place of the parents) on what should be done in the interest of the child, as though the state were the parent (*parens patriae*). The judge may order penalties for the child but also is expected to assess the parenting the child receives. The judge may order the child placed in another home or in a juvenile confinement place operated by (or for) the county or state.

Although a conviction in criminal court legally labels the defendant a "criminal," the juvenile court does not convict; instead, it "adjudicates" whether or not a child is "delinquent." A judge who finds a child's home situation deplorable and wants to change it, may declare a child delinquent not so much because of the child's misconduct, as because a delinquency finding is necessary to give the judge authority to change the home. Many juvenile courts are called "family courts" because they also have authority to punish parents for mistreating or neglecting children, and to handle other types of family problems.

Criminal court proceedings are formal, with information elicited mainly by lawyers questioning witnesses. The opposing lawyer may object to a question or to the response it evokes as biased, unfounded, irrelevant, or otherwise unfair. The judge must then rule on its acceptability. In contrast, juvenile court proceedings were initially intended to be informal: The judge usually asked all parties separately to tell their stories, and questioned them until satisfied that available information sufficed for a decision on behalf of the child.

The original ideal of such a family-like atmosphere in juvenile court is usually unrealized now, especially in big cities with many cases. Judges in most counties are rotated to the juvenile court from adult courts, and they retain adult court procedures, which are more limited to obtaining information on guilt. They do not, as in the ideal juvenile court, take time to build rapport with the child, the parents, and others involved.

Because both adult and juvenile courts are often quite busy, their officials presume that the charges are valid, and they try to reach decisions quickly, by plea bargaining. Some court officials may be prejudiced—or simply indifferent—toward accused persons, especially those who are poor or of minorities, and may discourage adequate defense participation.

The U.S. Supreme Court in the 1950s and 1960s, under Chief Justice Earl Warren, increased requirements for acceptable evidence in both juvenile and criminal courts. The Court's rulings allowed any juvenile court to have defense attorneys and formal procedures. These reforms are diversely applied. Many juvenile courts have prosecutors present but not defense attorneys. Indeed, the latter seem to be resented by judges; children with lawyers tend to get harsher penalties than are imposed in similar cases when no defense counsel is present (Feld, 1989, 1993).

A widespread juvenile court innovation uses juveniles as juries to try other juveniles, and sometimes also in roles of judge, prosecutor, or defense attorney. They are supervised by a judge, rule only on less serious lawbreaking, and are often drawn from law-related classes in the schools. It is reported that laws in 25 states make juvenile juries permissible, and they are also used informally elsewhere (Williamson, Chalk, & Knepper, 1993). Service as a juror presumably commits a juvenile to oppose lawbreaking, just as helping another alcoholic when in A.A. commits the helper to maintain sobriety. Benefit from juvenile juries may be greatest when the jurors have backgrounds like those of the accused, but are not themselves recent offenders, and are not friends or relatives of those tried.

In 1974, the U.S. Juvenile Justice and Delinquency Prevention Act banned federal funds for juvenile correctional programs to states that confined anyone for juvenile status offenses. The states then ended court control for such conduct, but police still detain runaways and other status offenders until an appropriate residence is arranged. Usually they become aware of the running away only when they can make other charges, such as theft, drug use, vandalism, or disorderly conduct. Therefore, when police cannot arrest for status offenses, runaways are held on criminal charges more likely to result in confinement (Schneider, 1984). Also, more runaways and incorrigibles are now referred to civil courts, to be made wards of the state by being declared mentally ill (Schwartz, Jackson-Beeck, & Anderson, 1984).

Criminal court records are accessible to the public, on proper application, but juvenile court records originally were not. In many jurisdictions, juvenile offenders were never fingerprinted, thus creating uncertainty as to their identities. These policies were established to avoid stigmatizing adults by allowing anyone to know about their childhood misconduct. But not knowing about prior juvenile crimes when sentencing young adults is a handicap, especially as arrest rates peak at the borderline between

juvenile and adult court jurisdiction, 16 to 18. Because extensive criminality in childhood is one of the best predictors of later recidivism and of the
level of security needed to control offenders after their arrest or sentencing, most states have changed these practices, but some have not. There is
also inconsistency within states in the prevalence of these practices, in the
frequency of waivers of older teenage offenders from juvenile to criminal
courts, and in the effects of all of these policies on the severity of penalties
that youngsters receive (National Institute of Justice, 1995b; Podkopacz &
Feld, 1996).

One may guard against lifetime stigma but still make the juvenile
record available when it is important for protecting the public, by adopt-
ing a principle widespread in other nations: Whenever a person is convicted of a serious crime, even before age 18, specify a duration of time,
varying in length with the seriousness of the offense, at the end of which
the absence of any new crime conviction will result in the current offense
record being destroyed; if a new offense occurs within this period, however, allow reporting of the prior crime to the court that sentences for the
new offense. For example, Canada's 1982 Young Offenders' Act instructs
that when a person under 18 completes the punishment for a crime in
which the most severe permissible penalty is 6 months' confinement, and
commits no further offenses in the next 2 years, this record is to be
destroyed; for more serious crimes, 5 years must elapse. Several Western
European nations have similar provisions for expunging prior criminal
histories after a crime-free period, for both juveniles and adults.

Acting in what is supposed to be the best interests of both the child and
the public, the juvenile court may assume control of a child's life until age
21. It may order confinement in a county or state institution for juveniles,
placement in a foster home, release on probation, payment of restitution,
other alternative penalties, or a combination of them in a specified sequence. If the court receives complaints about new misdeeds by someone
under 21 whom it has already declared delinquent, it may hold a review
hearing and change its penalties.

If an older juvenile is charged with murder (even when as young as 14),
or with repetition of robbery, burglary, or other felonies, juvenile courts
may waive their jurisdiction and transfer the case to a criminal court. This
procedure is followed partly because juvenile court penalties must end
when the defendant reaches age 21. But because such waivers are made
inconsistently by independent and arbitrary rulings of many separate

judges, it has been urged that standardized guidelines be adopted to regulate them (Krisberg & Austin, 1993, pp. 4-6).

Counties and states have correctional facilities for juveniles separate from those for adults. Instead of being held in jails, children are held in detention centers or probation camps, and instead of prisons they go to training schools or similar places with other names, some designed for very secure confinement. Many officers who supervise juvenile probationers or parolees get no adult cases. It is presumed, not always correctly, that teaching and counseling are emphasized more in juvenile than in adult correctional programs.

As reported in Chapter 2, several states blur the borderline between juvenile and adult corrections by having a Youth Authority, Youth Commission, or similar agency that receives both juvenile and young adult offenders, typically those charged with crimes committed before age 21. It may control them until age 25. Usually, as in California, it can receive these youths from either juvenile or criminal courts, and it has more flexibility in dealing with them than does the adult correctional system. For example, it may parole at any time its board decides is best. Contrastingly, prisons for adults must usually impose some minimum length of confinement before parole eligibility occurs, and in many states parole has been eliminated or reduced.

Profitable Penalties for Youth Offenders

What sentencing and correctional practices are optimal for youngsters? From this book's perspective, what are needed when imposing penalties in all courts, and for offenders of any age, are guidelines that pursue the multiple goals discussed in Chapter 3. Profitable penalties for youths therefore require

- The juvenile court's attention to the offender's life history, personal attributes, and current circumstances
- The criminal court's focus on just deserts in setting upper and lower limits to penalties for each type of crime, but with a wide range between limits to allow for variations in the current offenses, and in the prior lives of offenders

◆   Correctional practices that apply and expand research findings on
     maximizing both reformation and society's long-run public protection

Penalties for adolescent offenders are quite diverse, and a number of
states and localities have managed to achieve good results with innovative
programs. For instance, because correctional institutions, especially large
ones, are so criminalizing for young persons, Massachusetts in 1972 closed
its traditional large facilities for juveniles. Instead, it supervises young
offenders in their own homes, foster homes, forestry work camps, board-
ing schools, or group homes (Miller, 1991). This action was copied by
Vermont, Utah, and other states, but some states instead send more youths
to prison.

For their worst-risk cases, and especially for youngsters who have
already been confined for violence and have recidivated, even states that
closed their large institutions for juveniles retain small units of secure
confinement. About 10% of the Massachusetts juveniles who formerly
would be in large institutions are now held in group homes constructed
for tight custody, in which they get instruction, work, and recreation. They
receive longer confinement than others receive, but not in large units, and
with conditional trial releases before full freedom is granted.

A rigorous evaluation found that youths' recidivism rates in Massachusetts were the lowest of any comparable correctional population, were
achieved without transfer of serious violent offenders to adult corrections,
and cost less than the programs for similar offenders in other states
(Krisberg & Austin, 1993, chap. 5). In 1993, R. Harris could report:

> Only 55 of every 100,000 youngsters in Massachusetts are in custody,
> contrasted with more than 450 of every 100,000 in California. . . .
> [I]n Massachusetts only 23% of those committed to the state's youth
> services programs are incarcerated as repeat offenders—contrasted with
> 63% for the California Youth Authority. And . . . the cost of running the
> system is nearly half the national average. (A1)[2]

The Los Angeles Department of Probation sends some juveniles for
training in fairly secure "camps." Studying this program, Mark Lipsey
(1984) showed that prospects of recidivism are so low for unadvanced
offenders, even if they are released soon after arrest, and so high for those
with the most prior criminality, regardless of brief county programs, that

expensive retraining programs like this one in Los Angeles yield crime-reductive benefits in excess of costs only for a middle-risk group of offenders.

Fortunately, many imaginative interventions in the community are effective and are neither too risky nor too costly. Some were discussed in Chapter 2. These new programs show that even just deserts for very serious offenses can be achieved without confining youth offenders in ways that separate them from law-abiding adults for a long period of time. For example, Judge Nancy Dusek-Gomez of Springfield, Massachusetts, gained statewide publicity in 1990 by sentencing a high school senior who stole $14,000 worth of baseball cards to 1 year in jail, but suspended that sentence on condition that he graduate in that school year and pay restitution. She aptly pointed out that his prospects of employment and nonrecidivism would be much better this way than if he were incarcerated.

Some juvenile courts use prehearing home detention for arrestees with serious charges whose cases have not yet been resolved. Home detention avoids confining them in idleness with the more criminalized youths who are present in county detention. In San Diego, and in Jackson County, Kentucky, detainees and their parents sign a contract specifying that the youths will attend school, be at home after a curfew time, notify their parents of their whereabouts at all other times, abstain from drugs, and avoid "companions and places that 'might lead to trouble.' " These contracts state that if the rules are violated, the juvenile may be put in the detention home, and the parents may be charged with contempt of court or with contributing to the delinquency of a minor. Officers check on the juveniles, and the courts react to reported violations. Such programs save money and reduce the risk of criminalization in detention facilities (Ball, Huff, & Lilly, 1988, chap. 2).

In Cuyahoga County's (Cleveland) Home Detention Project, caseworkers make unscheduled daily visits to check on released juveniles at school, home, or elsewhere. They also contact teachers, parents, and other relevant adults, recording their information, actions, and impressions. The number of staff contacts with a youth was the only statistically significant predictor of nonrecidivism that researchers found. Caseworkers claimed that their greatest success was with boys who were not much involved with drugs but who were previously in state youth correctional institutions. Some of these youths said that without this close monitoring, and the knowledge that rule breaking would return them to the institution, they would neither concentrate on school work nor avoid further delinquency. The program claims to have saved a half million dollars or more annually, compared to the cost of confinement, but it served mostly white youths and was not assessed very rigorously (Ball et al., 1988, chap. 3).

Several of our states and some foreign countries, notably Japan, find that staff influences on young lawbreakers can be reformative if the youngsters do hard physical work outside of traditional institutions. For this purpose, Japanese correctional institutions operate remote and relatively small farms, forestry camps, and fishing ships. These are instructive for the inmates and profitable for the government if the offenders do useful work and are trained to do it well. Some private organizations in the United States contract to provide such services, notably Associated Marine Institutes in Florida, VisionQuest in the Southwest, and Outward Bound in many parts of the country. A few are given bonuses by county or state governments for demonstrably reducing recidivism rates (Garrett, 1985; Greenwood, 1986). It is noteworthy that most live-in staff of some of these private programs, especially VisionQuest, are only a few years older than their wards. Young staff are the most enthusiastic and charismatic, but they tend to "burn out" after a few years of living with delinquents, and they are then replaced (Greenwood, 1987).

Despite strong beginnings in the reform of penalties for youth offenders, notably in the California Youth Authority (Palmer, 1994), more adequate theory and research are needed on matching young offenders and correctional policies reliably in order to most profitably minimize their recidivism.

Conclusion

In the journey from childhood to adulthood, young people reach many turning points, some toward crime and some toward noncriminal autonomy. Family, neighborhood, and school conditions all affect delinquency. Given the diversity of influences, diverse types of prevention efforts and penalties for youth offenses—deterrence, enculturation, incapacitation, retraining, restitution, and shaming—may all be effective.

For best results, coordination of juvenile and adult courts is required, which would permit wiser sentencing of adults through shared case records. However, reintegration of youthful offenders into mainstream society is enhanced by retaining the option of expunging the records of prior offenses after long crime-free periods.

Wise spending to prevent childhood-transition criminality is the most profitable of all anticrime investments, because it is from early lawbreaking that most later criminality evolves. A dollar spent wisely to prevent crimes by children usually saves the public many dollars by reducing the need for expensive incapacitation and reform efforts later. It also reduces the costs and pains suffered by crime victims.

Notes

---

1. Reprinted by permission of the *Los Angeles Times*.
2. Reprinted by permission of the *Los Angeles Times*.

5

Anticipating the Sequence in Vice Control

Many types of behavior that are not harmful in moderation become *vices* if they are done so much that they impair health, work, or other important concerns. For example, everyone eats, and most adults drink some alcoholic beverages, but compulsive overeating and heavy drinking are vices. Gambling is a vice for those who regularly bet more than they can afford to lose, especially if they wager by hunch alone, hence usually lose. Having sex is a vice if done with disregard for its consequences and morality. Throughout history, many people have taken mood-changing drugs, but drug use becomes a vice when people depend on it to an extent that threatens their ability to fulfill their obligations to others and to maintain their own health.

The focus in this chapter is on government efforts to control the vices related to alcoholic beverages, prostitution, gambling, and illegal drugs. Efforts to control these vices tend to go through a typical sequence. A major step in the sequence is prohibition, but it is frequently ineffective and wasteful as the primary control method because it increases linkages between the vice and predatory crimes. Historically, the control measures that have most often succeeded are preventive education, treatment for those who engage in the vice, and sometimes licensing of vices while limiting their visibility and their accessibility to minors or to extreme addicts. They are most likely to dampen indulgence in vices cost-effectively and reduce the incidence of associated crime.

Victimizing and
"Victimless" Crimes

If people harm only themselves by their vice, as when overeating creates dangerous obesity, government reactions usually are limited to public health education and treatment. A vice is most often declared criminal when others are injured because of it, as when a violent or reckless act that hurts someone is ascribed to the perpetrator's drunkenness or when a craving for drugs is blamed for a thief's stealing.

Crimes—that is, acts lawfully punishable by the government—fall into two distinct categories, depending on their legal histories and the ways we count or control them. Traditional crimes may be categorized as "victimizing," but vice crimes are often viewed as "victimless."

In the acts that we most consistently have viewed as crimes, such as theft or assault, a criminal clearly victimizes someone else. If injury or loss is severe, and not caused by a friend or relative, it is likely to be reported to the police and become an official crime statistic. Such offenses may be called *predations* or *predatory crimes* because the perpetrators prey on others. When many people become disturbed by the prevalence of an injurious act, they are likely to get laws ordering punishment of the injurers. Laws against predations are cumulative; they are seldom repealed. Furthermore, the government tends to designate certain victimizing acts as crimes whenever new inventions create new ways to injure others. For example, after invention of the automobile, dangerous driving came to be viewed as a social problem, and laws were passed to make speeding and reckless driving criminal. More recently, insider trading on the stock market, polluting the air, and spreading computer "viruses" became crimes; victims mobilized support for laws to punish the offenders.

Contrastingly, a vice such as drinking, using drugs, gambling, or buying or selling sex is usually a voluntary activity on the part of all involved in it. Neither the sellers nor the consumers of goods or services for a vice view themselves as victimizing anyone else, and they object to police efforts to suppress their conduct. Laws to have the government punish a vice are sought by nonparticipants who oppose it on moral grounds or are distressed by its physical or economic costs to others. Laws against vices do not accumulate in the course of history, as do those against predations, because reactions to vices go through a series of changes that in time usually modify or even repeal these laws.

The Sequence of Vice-Control Efforts

The long-run trend for most anti-vice laws has been to reduce or abolish the penalties for engaging in the relevant vice, but such change is often temporarily halted or reversed. Despite discontinuity and variations, a sequence of seven overlapping phases in government reactions to vices may be discerned. These are summarized in Exhibit 5.1 for the four vices that seem to have most often concerned lawmakers: drunkenness, prostitution, gambling, and drug abuse. The duration of each phase varies by vice and by the state or country legislating against the vice. Each phase begins before those preceding have fully ended, and there is often regression to an earlier stage before movement to a later one. For some vices, all phases have not yet occurred; only time will tell if all phases are inevitable.

Tolerance

All peoples, in all times, have engaged in vices of some sort, to some degree. Communities have tended to tolerate these vices or to deal on a personal, private level with the problems they create. The government does not get involved, except perhaps when predatory crimes, severe public health problems, or unemployability develop that may be related to a vice.

Today, the belief that alcohol and drug abuse, prostitution, and gambling are harmful is widespread in Europe and America. But for centuries before World War I, their suppression by government was either nonexistent or very limited. Use of addictive drugs, such as opiates and cocaine, was not nationally punishable in the United States until 1916. The 18th Amendment to the U.S. Constitution, which prohibited alcoholic beverages, went into effect in 1920 and was repealed in 1932. Gambling and prostitution have been punished as crimes mainly by state or local laws, which vary greatly.

Prohibition's Beginnings

Political movements for punishment of a vice are first led by what sociologist Howard Becker (1964) called *moral entrepreneurs*, persons who devote themselves almost full-time to this objective. The rhetoric of these zealots portrays the vice both as extremely damaging and as irresistible,

	Vice			
Phase	Reckless Consumption of Alcoholic Beverages	Prostitution	Gambling	Illegal Drug Use
1. Initial Tolerance	Alcohol use is fully accepted	Prostitution is very open	Wagering is widespread	Psychoactive substances are uncontrolled
2. Prohibition Beginnings	Moral entrepreneurs organize anti-vice campaigns, often appealing to prejudices against some religious or ethnic groups alleged to be in favor of the vice.			
3. Enforcement Dominance	Vice-prohibition enforcement agencies take over anti-vice campaigns, seeking more funds, severer penalties, and greater investigative power.			
4. Organized Corruption	Demand persists for service to vices. Organized crime grows to supply it, and uses its large profits to corrupt governments and businesses.			
5. Predations From Vices	Drunks commit petty thefts and forgery.	Pimps control prostitutes, some violently.	Bettors' bad checks become a problem.	Addicts steal, burglarize, and rob widely.
6. Anti-Vice Innovation	Disease view of drunks is promoted.	Antidisease measures are emphasized.	Gamblers Anonymous promoted.	Methadone and other types of treatment become more prevalent.
7. Curbs Mainly on Visibility	Bars are limited and minors are banned from them, but they remain widespread.	Paid sex is allowed if it is discrete and not called prostitution.	Licensed gambling expands and openly advertises.	Some types of drugs are decriminalized or legalized in a few places and at certain times, if hidden.

Exhibit 5.1. Sequence of Control Efforts for Four Vices

especially to youths. Horrible effects are easy to find among addicts to alcohol, gambling, or drugs and among prostitutes. They provide examples that prohibitionists dramatize and imply are customary with the vice. In fact, however, most people who indulge in these vices avoid extreme consequences.

Current vice-control efforts are analogous to the punishment of deviant religious practices that has at times appeared in most of the world, and in some parts still today. Despite extreme penalties, such as crucifixion and burning at the stake, punishment alone generally has been as unsuccessful in suppressing religious heretics as more civilized penalties have been in deterring the adherents of vice. Coincidentally, moral entrepreneurs often seek vice prohibitions by appealing to prejudices against religious, racial, or national groups.

The Temperance Movement that produced the 18th Amendment to the U.S. Constitution, prohibiting manufacture or sale of alcoholic beverages, is a good example of the effectiveness of moral entrepreneurs. The movement was mobilized by Methodist middle- and upper-class descendants of early settlers from Britain. They were prejudiced against the new poor immigrants of Catholic faith from Ireland and Southern and Eastern Europe, who drank more openly than the Protestant elites (Gusfield, 1963).

Similarly, whites blamed African Americans for the spread of marijuana, and blamed Chinese immigrants for the spread of opiates, although both of these drugs had avid distributors and promoters among whites.

Policy Domination
by Enforcement Agencies

Once vice laws are enacted, specialized police agencies must enforce them. But it is always difficult to catch and convict people for vices, because unlike predatory crimes, they do not produce victims who report the lawbreaking to the police. Also, most vices can be readily concealed.

When lawmakers are unfamiliar with a vice, their information on its danger and on prospects of suppressing it come mostly from moral entrepreneurs. But enforcers of a vice prohibition, although they may have a more sophisticated understanding of the vice, acquire a vested interest in the cause when it becomes the source of their budget, prestige, and power. They refer to the vice as a crime. To cope with a vice's persistence, enforcers usually appeal to legislators and the media, which are largely accessible to enforcers, for more funds for their agencies, fewer restraints on their investigations, and severer penalties.

Laws to suppress vices also prohibit less readily hidden, related behavior. It is often easier to catch and convict for acts associated with vices than for the vices themselves. Thus, possessing illegal drugs is more often prosecuted than their use; being in the presence of unlawful gambling is more often prosecuted than betting; soliciting for paid sex or accepting money for it is more often the basis for prostitution arrests than actually having sex for a fee.

Still, only a tiny fraction of illegal vice is punished. Massive police raids on brothels, casinos, bookie joints, or drug sale areas almost always produce many more arrests than convictions. Thus much police effort consists only of harassing alleged prostitutes, drug peddlers, or others to make them leave locations where complaints are received about their aggressive solicitation; the focus is on reducing the vice's visibility.

Throughout U.S. history, police scandals have disproportionately involved officers of vice squads. Whenever a criminal vice is widespread (e.g., marijuana use or prostitution), many of the investigating officers also have indulged in it, or had friends or family who did. They were then unlikely to have much moral outrage at the vice. Many officers have been convicted of helping themselves to some of the considerable cash, and even drugs or guns, they discover in their raids.

Police combating drug traffic often make exploratory searches, and then if they find anything illegal, invent prior reasons that would justify the search. But in 1961, the U.S. Supreme Court in *Mapp v. Ohio* made it illegal for courts to accept evidence seized without a warrant or a prior probable cause for arrest. The result was about a 75% increase in "dropsy" cases, in which the police claim that arrest for drug possession was justified because they saw the defendant drop something that appeared to be narcotics (Barlow, 1968)—as though most people with drugs have "butter fingers."

Corrupt police and other local officials, more common formerly than today, have a quasi-licensing function for establishments serving popular but illegal vices. For an investment in a house of prostitution or an illegal gambling center to be profitable, the place has to attract customers, has to be widely known. Vice operators have therefore often reached agreements on regular payoffs to politicians and police before they opened their businesses. When moral entrepreneurs complain intensely about such practices, corrupted police may switch to "tipping off" the operators before a raid so that there is little lawbreaking evident when police arrive. Or they may raid without a warrant, fully aware that charges will be dismissed later because of the illegal search.

Convictions for serious vice crimes are achieved mainly by dropping charges against arrestees who inform on others, or by having detectives pretend to engage in the illegal activity in order to catch offenders.

Because vices are compulsively pursued and easily hidden, arrests reduce a vice's visibility much more than its prevalence. Thus law enforcement claims of success in suppressing a vice usually have only short-term credibility. Before long, there are reports of the vice's return. For example, spending billions to stop the import, manufacture, or sale of illegal drugs has been like throwing money into a bottomless pit. Only briefly has the supply of the prohibited substances been curtailed. Prices on the illicit market sometimes rise briefly after "crackdowns," perhaps making some buyers take the drugs less often and reducing the number of new users, but for compulsive addicts it is another story. Those who steal or sell sex to buy drugs must hustle more when prices rise, but soon more drugs arrive and prices drop.

Heroin and cocaine bring more then 100 times as much in the United States as in the countries where their raw materials are grown and processed. As long as the price users will pay is so many times the cost of getting the substance, many persons are eager to make money in this commerce. Closing down any supply channel soon expands business through others. Nabbing the head of a large vice-serving organization only creates new opportunities for others to rise to the top.

The United States has paid many millions of dollars for eradication of drug crops in Colombia, Peru, Turkey, and other countries. It has paid millions to the farmers there to subsidize the production of alternative crops, and additional millions for destruction of drug-processing plants, such as cocaine refineries. But, a sophisticated economic analysis concludes, "When account is taken of the structure of prices in the cocaine industry and the ability of farmers and refiners to make behavioral adaptions, none of these programs has much prospect for affecting the flow of cocaine to the U.S." (Reuter, 1992).

The failure of these suppression efforts demonstrates the vitality of free enterprise capitalism, even when it is illegal.

Corruption by Organized Crime

Laws criminalizing previously legitimate enterprises either give law-breakers new economic opportunities or change respectable business persons into criminals. When a vice is popular despite laws against it, large criminal organizations develop to serve it. Law-abiding persons, by definition, cannot enter this trade.

Prohibition of the manufacture or sale of alcoholic beverages during the 1920s and early 1930s essentially handed over a huge segment of our economy—the manufacture, import, and wholesale or retail sale of beer, wine, and liquor—to those willing to violate the law. Because drinking was customary among large segments of our population, with much wine and "moonshine" already home-made, especially in rural areas, many local vendors were available to sell these beverages. In addition, much was smuggled in from Canada, Latin America, and elsewhere. Often local officials, already dominated by corrupt political machines, overlooked the operation of speakeasies in exchange for payoffs.

In 1920, when Prohibition was enacted, the newest large immigrant group in U.S. cities came from Southern Italy. Italians, already accustomed to wine as a food, had relatively little drunkenness. But with the passage of prohibition, they made or imported much Italian wine and quickly expanded to supply non-Italian markets. In addition, the Italians, like other new working-class immigrant groups, then lived predominantly in the slum areas of large cities, where law enforcement was least vigorous and political corruption greatest. These features helped them compete well in bootlegging and other vice-services.

Italians also had advantages in conducting illegal activities based on the criminal organizations they had developed in Sicily and the Naples area to resist absentee landlords. Such groups operated with codes of secrecy, using violence and extortion. The Italian organizations are often called "the Mafia," and it is alleged that all such organizations are united in one national or world hierarchy, but such claims are disputed and probably erroneous.

Nonetheless, during the Prohibition era, some Italian groups rapidly came to dominate illegal distribution of alcoholic beverages in several of our largest cities. With the capital and power this activity gave them, they often also took control of illegal gambling and brothels, and extorted from legitimate businesses payments for "protection." When Prohibition was repealed, federations or "families" of these Italian groups each controlled a different region. They sometimes feuded violently for illegal business turf, but they also developed legal businesses, such as clubs and resorts.

As Italians moved out of the slums and advanced in legitimate occupations or businesses, especially after World War II, most were replaced in organized crime by African American, Latino, or other ethnic groups newer to the slums (Ianni, 1972, 1974; Skolnick, 1978).

The Increase in Vice-Propelled Predation

When a prohibited vice is costly, devotees without enough legitimate income to pay for it often engage in crimes for money. Drinking and gambling have long been associated with arrests for petty theft or forgery—mostly victimizing friends or family, however, and therefore unprosecuted.

The most serious problem of drug addiction for most of us is property crime by addicts. The typical "street addict" pays $20 to $50 daily for drugs, and sometimes much more. The more a drug costs and the lower the legal income of its users, the more crimes they commit to pay for it and for their other living expenses. Cocaine and heroin addiction are blamed for more than a third of all robbery, burglary and murder, and for most prostitution. Of 611 interviewed Miami juvenile delinquents, whose ages ranged from 12 to 17 and averaged 15, more than 90% had used some form of cocaine three or more times per week in the 3 months prior to the interviews; 82% had used marijuana; most had also drunk alcohol and used additional types of drugs. To pay for this vice, almost all were involved in drug dealing (e.g., as sellers or lookouts) and in theft; two-thirds committed robbery and most of the females were prostitutes (Inciardi, Horowitz, & Pottieger, 1993).

Studies show that when heroin addicts increase their dosages of narcotics, or when other criminals begin drug use, the amount of money they get by crime and their offense rate increase exponentially. When drug use by addicts peaks, they shift from less violent thefts and burglaries to violent robberies (Anglin & Speckart, 1988; Horney, Osgood, & Marshall, 1995).

Frenzied, Innovative, and Unstable Vice-Control Efforts

When prohibition laws fail to stop vices and vice-induced predations, moral entrepreneurs and sympathetic officials frantically seek to increase enforcement efforts and penalties. Increasing the severity of authorized penalties has always been a legislator's easiest reaction to complaints about crime rates. But such laws are often passed with little or no thought about the feasibility or cost of enforcing them.

When drug use surged in the 1960s, and again around 1990, state and federal punishments escalated rapidly in response to vigorous lobbying by top antidrug officials. Sentences permitted for drug sales increased to include life imprisonment and even death. Although no one was executed for selling drugs, some youths with little drug or other criminal experience received years in prison for possessing small amounts of an illegal substance. In parts of Texas, judges were said to inflict longer terms for transfer of a few marijuana cigarettes than they usually imposed for homicides, although many judges drank whiskey, a drug more disabling than marijuana.

In 1986, when President Reagan announced a new "war on drugs," federal antidrug laws were enacted that mandate 5 years in prison with no parole for selling one fifth of an ounce of crack cocaine, and 10 years for 2 ounces or more. These apply even if the seller has no prior criminal record. Similar penalties occur for small amounts of other illegal drugs. Many federal prisoners are so-called mules, usually poor peasants from Latin America with little or no prior crime, some of them women, even pregnant ones. For a few hundred dollars from smugglers, they bring drugs into the United States, often sealed in plastic bags that they swallow. Many states have copied the federal statutes or enacted severer ones.

The result of the drug "war" has been a massive increase in prisoners, at a cost of $50,000 or more for each new cell and $15,000 or more per inmate for annual operations. Since 1990, federal prisons have held more inmates for drug crimes than for property offenses (McWilliams, 1994).

When law enforcement clearly fails to curtail a vice, movements develop for approaches other than arrest and punishment. Judges offer addicts, alcoholics, or gamblers a reduction or abolition of penalties on condition that they participate in treatment programs. In 1967, New York State was estimated to have half the nation's 500,000 heroin addicts. It established a Narcotics Addiction Control Commission, which in 5 years spent a billion dollars. The commission subsidized almost every type of addiction therapy, much of it imposed involuntarily in incarceration where addicted felons could elect to receive about 3 years of treatment as an alternative to a longer prison term. But heroin use in New York increased, and in 1973 the state reversed its policy by enacting what was called "the nation's toughest drug law." It mandated long prison terms for possession or sale of any illegal drug, expanded police and courts to prosecute these cases, and made it easier to grant lower penalties to addicts for informing on others. Yet after 3 years it was concluded that "heroin use was as widespread in mid-1976 as it had been when the 1973 [law] revision took place," and that any deterrence by the law was only temporary (Joint Committee, 1977). In 1979 the law was again changed, reducing penalties for small amounts of drugs and allowing flexibility in sentencing, changes that already prevailed in most courts through plea bargaining that ignored the law.

During the 1970s, 11 states, with Oregon and Alaska in the forefront, responded to the failure of severe penalties to reduce marijuana use by formally cutting the authorized punishment to a small fine, or eliminating it altogether, if the amount involved was small or was grown for home use. Surveys showed that these changes did not raise marijuana's popularity. But in the 1980s, federal enforcement leaders persuaded state and federal legislators to react to the spread of cocaine by enacting severer laws against all drugs. The federal Omnibus Drug Control Bill of 1988 discouraged state variations in penalties and created in the White House an Office of National Drug Control Policy, whose director the press called the "drug czar." Federal sentencing guidelines allowed large sentence reductions only for cooperation in providing evidence to convict others.

All these expensive actions had no enduring effects on the price or availability of illegal drugs. Drug use by high school seniors declined during the 1980s, but rose somewhat in the 1990s, surveys showed. (But, as Chapter 4 indicates, most criminally active juvenile lawbreakers drop out of high school before their senior year and are therefore less likely to be counted in such surveys.) The clearest drug use changes have been only in fads and fashions; some substances or ways of taking drugs gained popularity, notably crack cocaine in the mid-1980s, while use of some other drugs declined. If a vice is both popular and easily hidden, the number of police who can be assigned to combat it are always too few to reduce its pursuit.

Attempts to Limit Visibility and Damage

When outlawed vices are widespread despite increased arrests, convictions, and imprisonments and despite millions spent on treatment programs, the vices are often gradually made legal. This relaxation of vice control efforts occurred widely in the United States after years of futile use of the criminal law to try to stop alcohol drinking and gambling. Criminal penalties persist for some forms of these vices—if they are public, if children are exposed to them, or if anyone is endangered or injured because of them—but they no longer are nearly as completely prohibited as they once were, either nationally or locally. Instead, there is more emphasis on education and treatment to reduce them. At some point, society begins to question whether severe penalties for engaging in vice are profitable.

During the 1980s and 1990s, such conservative savants as economist Milton Friedman, former Secretary of State Charles Schultz, and commentator William Buckley pointed out the futility of our antidrug policies. They called for more reliance on education and treatment to reduce this vice. At the same time, Alcoholics Anonymous and Gamblers Anonymous became more popular.

Reckless Consumption of Alcoholic Beverages

The vice that perhaps best illustrates the sequence of vice control just described is alcohol abuse. Between the end of Prohibition and the 1960s, most arrests in the United States for the vice of alcohol abuse were for public intoxication. Police rounded up persons too drunk to walk without staggering, and jailed them if no one came to take them home. In skid row neighborhoods, they collected van loads of drunks who were either released when sober or given a few days in jail. This approach was a revolving door for many alcoholics, as they would soon be rearrested.

Trends in Alcohol Abuse and Its Control

Today alcoholism, which can be defined as a self-injuring lack of control over cravings for alcoholic beverages, is regarded as a sickness rather than a sin, in sharp contrast to assessments by Prohibition advocates. Public drunkenness is no longer a crime. Drunks are now either left alone or transported by the police or others to a detoxification center.

Of course, many are still arrested for crimes ascribed to drunkenness, most often for that catchall offense, "disorderly conduct." Drunkenness is also blamed for about half the auto deaths, and also for many fights, homicides, rapes, child molestations, fire deaths, and drownings. Because drunkenness can have such grim consequences, sellers of alcoholic beverages remain highly regulated through federal, state, and local restrictions on their business locations, hours, and advertising; their employment of anyone with a criminal record; and their sales to juveniles or to persons already intoxicated.

Furthermore, although alcoholism is called a disease, the law still holds drinkers responsible for knowing when they have consumed too much for tasks such as driving and therefore could endanger others. People are jailed and fined for "driving while under the influence" (abbreviated "DUI" here, but often "DWI" for "driving while intoxicated" or "while impaired"). About 2% of these arrests are ascribed to drugs other than alcohol. Since 1970, DUI arrests have risen more than five times as rapidly as the number of licensed drivers. Arrest rates are highest among 21-year-olds, peaking at one arrest annually for every 39 licensed drivers of that age (Cohen, 1992). The United States has the world's lowest auto-caused death rate per mile but the most auto-driven miles per person and by far the most vehicles. Thus it has the largest total number of highway deaths.

Nevertheless, drinking alcoholic beverages remains popular in many segments of the U.S. population. Household surveys in 1994 found that 54% of all persons in the United States over 12 years old had drunk alcoholic beverages in the past month, including 22% of 12-to 17-year-olds, 63% of 18- to 35-year-olds, and 54% of persons over 35. Rates for women were about 80% of those for men (U.S. Department of Health and Human Services [USHHS], 1995a, p. 85). Rates of "heavy drinking," defined as five or more drinks on one occasion 5 or more days of the past month, were 10% for males and 2.5% for females; the totals peaked at 13% for 18- to 25-year-olds (U.S. Department of Health and Human Services [USHHS], 1995b, pp. 22-24). Surveys of high school seniors and of college students alone generally report higher rates of alcohol use than do national household surveys.

Alcoholics Anonymous (AA), a voluntary organization of alcoholics dedicated to helping one another control an illness they feel powerless to deal with alone, has grown rapidly. Although some studies claim similar success for other treatments, and many alcoholics become abstinent on their own, the longest and most rigorous follow-up survey (Vaillant, 1983) found AA to be the most effective treatment. Nevertheless, many chronic drinkers still ignore their intoxication, refuse to recognize the danger of drunk driving, and cannot adequately inhibit their lust or anger while under alcohol's influence.

Profitable Treatments and Penalties

Judges and other officials often order participation in AA or other therapy as part of a penalty, but these efforts usually fail if coerced.

Evidently an alcoholic must voluntarily choose to reform for the effort to have a lasting effect, but support from ex-alcoholics often helps. A search for AA help is prompted by "hitting bottom" or reaching "the last straw" in misfortune from alcoholism. "Bottom" varies for different persons; a minor disgrace turns some around, but others change only after utter degradation and physical debility, or never.

Lobbying by MADD—Mothers Against Drunk Driving—has produced mandatory jail terms for DUI and breath tests for drivers suspected by the police of drunkenness. Yet Laurence Ross's (1992) research on DUI laws, for more than 20 years in many jurisdictions, shows that it is publicity about penalty risk, not the penalty itself, that reduces DUI. Publicity on any new laws or crackdowns temporarily reduce drunk-driving arrests, but the effects soon decline and offense rates rise again. Surveys show that half of American adults admit driving after they "had too much to drink," and 37% admit doing it in the past year (Gilbert, 1988).

The probability of being stopped and punished is apparently too low to deter them. Ross (1992) and associates found that despite laws mandating jail terms for all DUIs in Arizona, only 1% of convicted DUIs in the Phoenix area were jailed. When laws mandated jail after a second conviction, only 45% of DUI arrestees in New Mexico and 70% in Indiana were at least briefly confined. Not only did judges often ignore these laws, but sheriffs frequently did not impose the sentences when courts ordered them. A 1981 California law prescribing murder charges for killings by drunken drivers had by 1991 been applied in only 30 of 1,100 such cases.

Ross (1992) calls DUI a "folk crime," implying that most efforts to diminish it will be futile. As he points out, DUI is inevitable because drinking is so strongly associated in our culture with maximum enjoyment in dining, social mixing, and much recreation, yet driving some miles is so often necessary for these activities.

John Braithwaite (1989, p. 166) says that laws against drunk driving have had little effect because we do not greatly shame such drivers. Polls linked a drop in Oklahoma drunk driving to an increase in people being blamed and shamed for it (Grasmick, Bursik, & Arneklen, 1993). The most effective solution to drunkenness problems may therefore be to alter our culture, to make drinking customs less dangerous. Already there is a shift in preferences from hard drinks—whiskey, vodka, and gin—to wine or beer, and even to alcohol-free wine or beer.

Australian data show that drivers are most deterred from drinking if cars are selected randomly for breathtesting, especially if such stopping is frequent and much publicized (Homel, 1988, 1990). Apparently, persons unwilling to admit being too drunk to drive do not get behind the wheel if they are likely to be tested and found drunk no matter how well they drive. In the United States, random tests that lead to drunk driving charges are often dismissed under our Constitution's Fourth Amendment, which demands that police search only when they have probable cause to believe the suspect is guilty. Yet roadblocks may legally stop all cars.

Incapacitation of drunk drivers now is achieved not by jailing, but by mandating installation of an antidrunkenness interlock on the driver's car. To start a vehicle with this device, the driver must breathe into an ignition attachment that will prevent its turning on if there is alcohol on the breath. These devices have proved more effective than license suspension in reducing further drunk driving (Morse & Elliott, 1992). A 1993 California law requires that a person convicted of drunk driving twice in 7 years be forbidden to drive without an interlock.

Apparently the most profitable penalties for drunk driving are heavy fines, which seem to deter most drinking drivers appreciably more than any other punishments. However, jailing those who cannot pay the fines turns potential profits into losses for the government. Fines of a specified number of days' earnings, the "day fines" described in Chapter 2, are more equitable, and are probably more readily collected from poor persons than are identical fines for everyone.

Favorable effects in reducing DUI are also reported for house arrest with electronic monitoring, rather than jailing (Lilly et al., 1992). Electronic monitoring is less costly to the state and to the offender's dependents than confinement, especially in the several jurisdictions that make the convicted person pay the cost of this monitoring.

Clearly, controlling the damage to society from excessive alcohol use requires pragmatic research on what works most profitably for different types of persons.

Prostitution

Prostitution, called "the oldest profession," is the sale of sex. It depends on the traditional double standard regarding sex. Men were expected to "sow their wild oats" before marriage and even when wed, but women were to have sex only in marriage. Mathematically, such a double standard could only exist if a small percentage of women had sex with many men. This double standard created a second one: Women were "good" or "pure" if without "carnal knowledge" outside of marriage, and otherwise "bad" or "fallen."

These double standards have by no means disappeared but they are now much less rigid than formerly. A January 1991 news release by the federal Centers for Disease Control reported that 70% of 18-year-old women in the United States had had sexual intercourse. The more that premarital and extra-marital sex are available at no charge, and the greater the fear of AIDS, the smaller is prostitution's market. But prostitution probably has been reduced most by growth in other job opportunities for women.

In the United States all prostitution has long been illegal, except in one state. In 1971, Nevada made licensed prostitution a matter of county option. It prevails only in rural counties near the tourist centers—Las Vegas, Reno, and Tahoe.

Arguments for licensing brothels are that prostitution has never been effectively suppressed, and that licensing permits authorities to assure that house prostitutes are not infected and not employed unwillingly or other-wise mistreated. In the Netherlands, Germany, Austria, and elsewhere, licensed brothels are banned from the main streets but are conspicuously lit with red lights at night, and they often have suggestively clad women on display in their windows. The women must be regularly tested for venereal diseases, especially for AIDS.

Elsewhere, throughout the world, unlicensed prostitutes seek custom-ers at bars, often in a paid arrangement with bartenders. Others solicit on the street, at airports, and in hotels, especially during conventions. Sex for a fee is reportedly available at some massage parlors, as well as by "escort services" and dating agencies. At some clinics for marital problems and impotence, "sexual surrogates" train men in sexual arousal and inter-course by acting out techniques with them, practices that may sometimes be illegal but are rarely prosecuted.

Many people view a woman's giving sexual favors for money rather than for love as exploitative by the male and demeaning to her. Others assert that what a woman does with her body is no one else's business. Pioneering a social movement to promote this view was the San Francisco group COYOTE, for "Call Off Your Old Tired Ethics."

Why do women become prostitutes? Much of the impetus is economic. Historian Barbara Hobson (1987) shows that for centuries, poor women have had the limited choice of marriage, a menial job, or prostitution. Many prostitutes have been unable to find other employment or at least none that is nearly as remunerative as prostitution. In addition, Caplan

(1984) ascribes teenage prostitution in the United States to the sad fact that some runaways from hate-filled homes find that panderers and pimps are their only friends.

Many prostitutes are from Third World countries, and are recruited by international cartels engaged in pimping and pandering. According to Kathleen Barry's vivid volumes (e.g., Barry, 1995), international groups move prostitutes from one city or country to another. Several Third World nations, she claims, routinely provide brothels for their armed forces.

Julie Pearl (1987) estimated that in the 16 largest American cities, total government costs for arrest, conviction, and punishment of a prostitute average about $2,000, ranging from a low of $942 in Chicago to a high of $7,038 in Philadelphia. Given these costs and the "victimless" nature of prostitution, police are likely to make arrests only where conspicuous soliciting by prostitutes generates complaints, especially from businesses.

Sweden has maximum decriminalization of prostitution, because it does not punish taking money for sex. A few other nations come close to Sweden's example, as in Denmark, where sex for money is prohibited only if it is a woman's sole income; she must have or seek an additional source of legal income. By law in Britain and other nations, and usually by police practice in the United States and elsewhere, conspicuously soliciting customers for prostitution is treated as a crime, but giving sex for payment is not.

The trend in most of the United States today is to decriminalize all types of sexual activities, even when compulsively pursued as vices, if adults participate in them voluntarily and in private. AIDS and other sex-linked diseases are prevented mainly by education, testing, and distribution of condoms.

Gambling

Wagering has always been popular, but is often deplored as a vice be-cause of its cost to heavy losers and to their dependents. It also violates cus-tomary views that income should come only from work and investment.

Nevertheless, most nations have long had much gambling. In the United States, Nevada in 1931 became the first state to license most types of commercially organized gambling. In several other states, betting on horse races was legal, but only at the track. New Hampshire created a state lottery in 1964, and one state after another approved various kinds of gambling in subsequent years. By 1994, all but two states, Utah and

Hawaii, had legalized some combination of lotteries, casinos, gambling card-parlors, bingo games, and off-track betting centers for horse races and other athletic events (*Los Angeles Times*, Oct. 2, 1994). Some types of gambling are prohibited in many U.S. localities, but such bans are always widely violated, as many people want to bet.

Influential arguments for legalization of gambling have been that prohibition persistently fails and that legalization ends control of gambling by organized criminals and their corruption of government officials. In recent years, however, the most influential argument seems to have been that governments can gain income if they provide a gambling service, such as a lottery, or if they impose license fees and taxes on gambling services offered by others. Lotteries yield an average of 3.3% of state income, generally allotted to education (Clotfelder & Cook, 1989).

Predictably, gambling no longer is invisible. State lotteries, as well as licensed privately operated casinos, advertise lavishly to give people the delusion that they have appreciable prospects of "making it rich" by wagering.

It is most assuredly a delusion. The odds in state lotteries are commonly set so that only about half the money from tickets is paid back in winnings. Therefore, ticket buyers should expect to lose, on the average, 50 cents for every dollar they spend. Slot machines return about 98% of the money they receive. However, many players operate several slot machines at once and as fast as they can, so they often experience being ahead, but in reality they tend to keep betting until they run out of money. Although only a negligible fraction of the frequent patrons of commercial gambling or state lotteries are ahead overall, selective memory makes them recall their wins or near wins and forget their losses.

Lotteries are a form of regressive taxation, because they especially appeal to poor people. Gambling is also said to be the fastest growing teenage vice in the 1990s, and some states have begun to require school education against it. Yet many politicians also promote state lotteries because they are popular, and because they can fund the expansion of other types of popular government services without requiring an unpopular increase in taxes.

Gambling Mentality and Criminality

The psychology of compulsive gambling explains its prevalence, as well as the persistent risk taking of predatory criminals. It has been shown repeatedly, both with humans and with animals, that behavior tends to become habitual if it is always followed by reward and soon ceases if the reward stops. But the behavior continues most doggedly if rewards follow only intermittently and unpredictably—a pattern all too familiar to compulsive gamblers.

Psychologist B. F. Skinner (1953) proved this principle dramatically in a classic experiment he called "superstition in the pigeon." When bits of food are dropped one at a time at purely random intervals into a cage of hungry pigeons, soon all will be repeating odd movements: some will bow their heads, some will scrape their feet, others will shake their tails, and so forth. They repeat whatever they were doing when they found food, which makes it more likely that they will be doing the same thing again the next time they find food, although they are given food on an erratic schedule. Skinner observed:

> The efficacy of such schedules in generating high rates [of behavior repetition] is well known to proprietors of gambling establishments. Slot machines, roulette wheels, dice cages, horse races, and so on pay off on a schedule of variable-rate reinforcement. . . . The pathological gambler exemplifies the result. Like the pigeon . . . he is the victim of an unpredictable . . . reinforcement. The long-term net gain or loss is almost irrelevant in accounting for the effectiveness of this schedule. (p. 104)

Predatory criminals, especially if not professional, tend to have this sort of superstitious gambling mentality, ascribing their fortunes or failures at crime mainly to luck. After a run of success they develop superstitions about the procedures that made them lucky, then ritualistically repeat them. Many criminals thus acquire a modus operandi that makes it easier for detectives to trace offenses to them. Also, they spend freely and are very generous when a crime has reaped significant funds, because they feel lucky, but their heavy spending pattern soon forces them to gamble with crime again.

Some reduction of compulsive gambling and of much predatory crime might result from more education in our schools on the laws of probability and of variable reward. These principles make it inevitable that in the long run, almost all who persist in most forms of gambling—including theft, burglary, and robbery—will lose. Even if thieves have a high success rate, such as not being caught 90% of the time, they tend to repeat their offense at a rate certain to result in arrest before long (Glaser, 1978, chap. 5). But both compulsive gamblers and criminals resist recognizing and admitting their prospects of failure.

Profitable Preventives for Gambling

Compulsive gamblers, chronic alcoholics, and drug addicts often take money or goods from their families and commit other property offenses to continue their addiction. Society thus has a stake in reducing this vice. Yet gambling arrests are few, and those that occur tend to be for the misdemeanor charge "being in the presence of public gambling," typically dice games on sidewalks.

Other types of measures seem more profitable. When Britain legalized casinos in 1968, it forbade their advertising, even on matchbooks or in the telephone book. In the United States, columnist Neal Pierce proposed in 1989 that lottery tickets carry conspicuous warnings against compulsive gambling, much as cigarette packages warn users of cancer risks. Sweden discourages heavy betting at race tracks by forbidding announcement of odds until the race is over. We have no visible social movement for such reforms, but we should.

Treatment is another profitable option. Gamblers Anonymous is an organization modeled on Alcoholics Anonymous, with a similar success record. A small-scale survey of its U.S. members found them typically to be male, married, aged 40 to 50, employed, and high school graduates (Gowen & Speyerer, 1995). Like AA, Gamblers Anonymous includes more middle-class than very poor addicted persons. Also like AA, it cannot attract potential members until they "hit bottom," a level that they perceive very diversely.

Illegal Drug Use

Narcotics are the bane of our criminal justice system, and control efforts have been much more extensive than for any vice except possibly alcohol use during Prohibition. Attempts to diminish the use of drugs by punishment have been tremendously costly, but usually seem to have no effect on the prevalence of drug abusers and their predations. As psychopharmacologist Ronald Siegel (1989) shows in his book *Intoxication*, many humans everywhere, throughout history, as well as most other animals, after trying mood-changing substances, get intense cravings for more. When aware of the quick and even euphoric relief from some types of discomfort that certain drugs at times provide, many will spend large sums or take great risks to get them whenever the discomforts recur.

The dilemma of combating the vice of drug use is that the effects of legal and illegal mood-changing substances overlap. The impact of all such "psychoactive substances" depends a great deal on the amount and speed of consumption. The law prohibits marijuana, cocaine, and the opiates but allows our intake of items that can be equally disabling, including whiskey, wine, and beer, as well as tranquilizers, sedatives, analgesics, stimulants, and antidepressants sold in drug stores, some without prescription. Legal psychoactive substances are regularly prescribed to control rebellious or disorderly persons, at almost all ages, both in and out of penal and mental health institutions. Many adults are tranquilized or sedated almost always, although their physicians know that the drugs they prescribe for them are addictive (Hughes & Brewin, 1979). We may have more "zombies" from legal than from illegal drugs.

During the Civil War, hypodermic needles and morphine distributed to wounded soldiers caused many to become addicted. From then until the 1940s, most drug addiction in the United States came from medically prescribed morphine for major pain or from excessive use of laudanum, codeine, or other opiates sold without prescription in "tonics" or as "cures" for diverse ailments or discomforts.

The Harrison Act of 1914 established federal restriction of opiate distribution to medical channels, in accordance with an international agreement reached in The Hague 2 years earlier. Congress added cocaine to the law's control, although it was not covered by this treaty and is a stimulant, whereas opiates are relaxants. Federal marijuana controls were not created until 1937. Marijuana is generally regarded as a "soft" drug, not nearly as dangerous as the opiates and cocaine, but it is sometimes called a "gateway drug" because of the claim that its use leads to trying "hard" substances. Since World War II, new federal drug prohibitions have repeatedly been enacted, most covering more substances or imposing severer penalties than their predecessors.

In Britain, in contrast, opiate addiction was long seen as primarily a medical problem. British national health offices maintained a roster of addicts reported by physicians, who were allowed to prescribe opiates to prevent withdrawal illness from sudden abstinence. Reducing drug dependence was encouraged, but rates of achieving it were low. The United States initially had a similar program, but after 1920 a separate Narcotics Division established in the Treasury's Prohibition enforcement unit harassed and prosecuted physicians who prescribed drugs for addicts (Musto, 1987).

Heroin, a morphine derivative, has a quicker and more powerful impact than other opiates. Physicians therefore preferred it for emergency pain relief and relief of severe coughing. But because heroin's quick effects are appealing to addicts, the Narcotics Division in 1924 forbade its medical use in the United States. It is still prescribed in European nations. Canada initially followed the United States in banning heroin, but in 1985 permitted its prescription by physicians.

In a 1994 survey of households in the United States, more than a third of persons over 11 years old reported use of illegal drugs at some time in their lives. Those who reported using illegal drugs in the preceding month were 10% of children aged 12 to 17; 13% of youths 18 to 25; 8% of persons 26 to 34; and only 3% of those over 34 (USHHS, 1995b, p. 60). Such surveys doubtless undercount the prevalence of drug use, partly because users are afraid to respond truthfully and partly because active offenders and the homeless are unlikely to be included in survey samples (Mieczkowski, 1996). Of male arrestees in 12 major cities in 1994, the percentages found by urine tests to have recently consumed illegal drugs ranged from 23% in Portland, Oregon, to 64% in Washington, D.C. Their most used drug was marijuana, particularly for students, with cocaine next, followed by opiates (National Institute of Justice, 1995a).

Most illegal users in the United States are neither heavily addicted nor involved in much other crime. For example, many physicians, nurses, and pharmacists become addicted by taking opiates for pain. There are numerous examples, in the United States and other countries, of persons able to get opiates through medical channels who maintained addiction for 30 to 50 years of their long and well-respected lives. Some people use drugs intermittently for recreation with others, but are seldom arrested. In typical adolescent social worlds, using drugs, especially marijuana, is often routine in "partying," or in social breaks to relieve boredom (Glassner & Loughlin, 1987). Feasible police and court actions are unlikely to catch a large percentage of this group of users.

Trends in Drug Crimes

Before World War II, opiates were used mostly by women or elderly persons of both sexes who became addicted through medical treatment for various pains. However, our medical morphine supply was preempted by the Armed Forces during World War II. When "civilian" users could not get opiates legally, plane and ship crew members traveling internationally found it profitable to smuggle heroin into the United States to sell at high prices.

After the war, drug distribution became an organized crime specialty, not only for heroin but also for marijuana and cocaine. Criminal groups, based mostly in the slums, sold to dispersed addicts and encouraged drug use by youths seeking psychedelic experiences (Ball, 1965; Finestone, 1957; Musto, 1987). In the growing "hippie" subculture, a search for euphoria or relaxation with drugs spread among youths of many locations and incomes. In the 1950s and thereafter, adult criminal addicts were mostly from the small fraction of drug-abusing juveniles who did not stop using as they matured.

Greatly impeding efforts to ban drug use is the fact that all widely used illegal drugs are or can be grown or manufactured in many places. In addition, for every substance in short supply, substitute drugs exist or are quickly developed. Amphetamines, especially methedrine ("speed"), are commonly used instead of cocaine, as they are cheaper and are made in secret chemical laboratories scattered throughout the United States. Arrest of any individual involved in drug production usually impairs the drug supply only briefly, because the trade consists of many independent entrepreneurs in diverse roles, in all types of illegal drug distribution, and most getting their highest income from it. Others hurry to replace anyone removed from the industry by arrest.

In the mid-1980s, "crack" cocaine, which is cooked with baking soda and water to form smokable crystals, quickly replaced heroin as the "hard drug" most often leading to arrests. It soon sold for only $5 to $10 for a dose that is intensely stimulating for about half an hour, after which more is so craved that high risks are taken to obtain it. Crack is used in such volume that those who steal, rob, or are prostitutes to support their use of it skew the statistics on the frequency of these crimes. Its addicts include youths, many in gangs that prepare and sell crack for high incomes, and long-term addicts who replaced much of their former heroin use with the new forms of cocaine (Johnson, Golub, & Fagan, 1995). Because about 95% of arrestees for crack cocaine have been nonwhites, acute racial bias in control efforts is alleged.

Regular drug users develop a subculture that includes drug-taking rituals, and they exchange information and opinion on substances and their sources. Most youths on probation for selling drugs, a Washington, D.C., study found, are users who augment their legitimate earnings by part-time drug dealing. They average about $30 per hour in this illegal work, which is well over twice what their jobs pay (MacCoun & Reuter,

1992). But unemployed "street addicts" are especially predatory in seeking funds for drugs. In slums, notably in New York City, a vacated building often deteriorates quickly because addicts soon strip it of salable plumbing and light fixtures, and then make it their hangout or "shooting gallery."

Most avid users and sellers of drugs have had so much income from lawbreaking that their crime patterns cannot be easily ended. Even if they stop drug use, whenever they fall short of funds many are readily tempted to engage in the types of crimes—such as shoplifting, burglary, prostitution, or drug selling—that they previously pursued with high success. A 24-year follow-up of heroin addicts released from incarceration between 1962 and 1964 found that many died each year. They typically alternated drug-free periods of legal work with periods of drugs and crime, but most eventually became fully abstinent (Hser, Anglin, & Powers, 1993).

Treatment of Drug Addiction

Three major types of treatment for illegal drug users have developed in the United States: outpatient methadone maintenance, a type of legalization of opiates; therapeutic residences; and outpatient drug-free therapy. Since the escalation of penalties for drug use, much treatment of convicted drug addicts has been mandated, in conjunction with incarceration, parole, or probation. However, some voluntary treatment is undertaken.

Methadone

Methadone is a synthetic opiate that in our country is given to heroin addicts orally rather than by injection. The dosage they receive is sufficiently high to cause withdrawal illness if they stop taking it and to prevent much additional sensation if they take heroin, yet it is not too high to prevent their working. In Britain and elsewhere, methadone is often injected.

In the United States, methadone is usually given only to advanced addicts who have failed with other types of treatments, and many wait long for admission to these programs. Some are sent by the courts or referred by social service agencies. Their age averages nearly 40, most are nonwhite, and about a third are women. They generally take methadone for 3 or more years (Hubbard et al., 1989). Those maintained on methadone must come daily to drink a solution of it in front of staff, to prevent their selling it to the many addicts not in these programs who want to buy methadone to relieve withdrawal symptoms. Those given methadone legally must leave a urine sample to be tested for other drugs. Many who are new to a methadone program check its effectiveness by trying heroin, or they may continue to use other drugs simply to be sociable with their friends.

Antidrug activists, especially those with a vested interest in other types of treatment, often object to methadone maintenance because it keeps its subjects addicted. But methadone program administrators encourage their patients to reduce their dosage voluntarily over a long term and eventually to abstain. In most large-scale follow-up studies of opiate addiction treatments, no other method rates as highly as methadone in keeping addicts voluntarily participating in the program, free of crime, and employed.

It should be stressed, however, that long-term heroin addicts typically have much experience in crime and little in legitimate employment. When on methadone, they often continue using alcohol and other drugs. Thus they may have a hard time reforming completely. They have even lower success rates if coerced into methadone programs—for example, as a condition of parole or probation—than when they enter voluntarily (Anglin, Brecht, & Maddahian, 1989).

Addicts in such programs who are employed and have a conventional social life, often including marriage, dislike coming to the center daily for the methadone. Permission to take home several days' supply is controversial, but a British study found that it increases patients' persistence in attending school, work, and counseling, as well as in testing negatively for other drugs (Ghodse, 1989). One dose of LAAM, a derivative of methadone, prevents withdrawal effects for several days. A British physician concludes, from much experience, that because addicts on LAAM need go less often for treatment, they identify more with a drug-free lifestyle (Ghodse, 1989).

The limitation of all maintenance treatment is that most opiate addicts take a drug for the feelings it gives them, and for this they prefer heroin to methadone, and methadone to LAAM.

Therapeutic Communities

Addicts who have lived on crime, never married, and heavily used alcohol plus many other kinds of drugs may benefit from a stay in a therapeutic community. The residents of such communities are very diverse; the average age is about 27 (Hubbard et al., 1989). These organizations impose a regimen of menial work for newcomers, and they devote several hours daily to group talk sessions and rituals in which staff, mainly ex-addicts, berate patients. The staff and sometimes the residents do much public speaking to get community support and employment. Treatment communities introduce their longest-term residents, most of whom have become staff, to display their treatment successes.

A majority of addicts do not join therapeutic communities. Others continue some drug use while in them, and over three-fourths leave or are expelled in less than a year. Treatment communities often deliberately impose a waiting period for entrance in order to screen out those not heavily committed to seeking their treatment, who soon cease efforts to enter.

Many of these residential centers have long been government funded. They treat residents as requiring aid in maturation, receive welfare funds and food stamps for them, and are often assigned clients on parole or probation. Their ex-addicts and other employees frequently bully and nag newer members for even petty deviance. Skoll (1992) finds that they tend to instill expectations of nonrecovery, despite claims to be therapeutic. Yet some, notably Delancey Street in San Francisco and Phoenix Houses in New York City (both with some branches elsewhere), have long been quite autonomous and have many successes with formerly advanced addicts.

For addicts in New York state prisons, therapeutic community programs called "Stay'n Out," modeled on Phoenix Houses and run by ex-addict state employees from these communities, have since the 1970s had significant success rates. Those in Stay'n Out had lower rearrest rates than similar inmates who were waiting to enter it or were in other types of treatment programs in the prison. The longer inmates were in this program, the better was their postrelease record (Lipton, 1996).

Drug-Free Outpatient Clinics

Those sent to outpatient clinics are usually unadvanced drug abusers, average age 25, about 80% whites. Most enter as a condition of probation or under parental pressure because they use marijuana or other non-opiate drugs. Their main treatment is group counseling, although some clinics offer individual counseling and diverse referrals to meet each client's needs.

Rates of drug use reported by patients after 3 to 5 years in the clinics is about half what they report when admitted. How much of this progress is due to the program and how much to normal maturation cannot be estimated. These outpatient clinics seek mainly to reform marijuana users, but their attendance tends to be high only if required for continued employment or as a condition of probation; their reduction in drug use was less than that reported for users of other types of drugs (Hubbard et al., 1989; Lipton, 1996).

Drug-free outpatient clinics and therapeutic communities share some features: Both are highly variable in effectiveness and cost; both keep those who shared a drug-use subculture interacting with each other, instead of assimilating into nondrug social worlds. Unfortunately, psychotherapeutic programs in residences and clinics are often evaluated only by whether they use officially prescribed methods, rather than by long-run follow-up studies of how much these methods change clients, as compared to change of similar clients in other programs or no program.

Current Drug-Control Developments

Simplistic "cures" for drug addiction, ranging from chemical "drug antagonists" to acupuncture, have shown little impact for most cases. Nevertheless, more complex treatment programs using ex-addicts do seem to work. The Clinton administration advocated court-linked local treatment programs, modeled on one in Miami that is reported to reduce drug use more cost-effectively than do jails (Finn & Newlyn, 1993). These programs, now in many other cities, offer diverse types of treatment and also assist in housing and job procurement.

The effort to treat addictions can be very cost-effective. A RAND study found that treatment programs to control cocaine addiction are seven times as cost-effective as law-enforcement efforts to punish cocaine use (Rydell & Everingham, 1994). For example, the Los Angeles Drug Court treatment program

> is based on the 12-step program pioneered by Alcoholics Anonymous. In addition to the daily meetings and frequent urine tests, participants . . . pay a $200 fee. . . .
>
> "It completely changed my life," said Amelia Garnica, 37, who said she had been using drugs since she was 14. Garnica entered the program in May 1995 after she was caught using heroin near MacArthur Park, where she was living as a transient.
>
> Garnica described herself as one of 12 alcohol and drug addicts in a family of 13. "I didn't know no other way to live," she said. (Hong, 1996)[1]

Treatment programs for heroin and other opiates have also been effective in keeping addicts away from crime. In Britain's initial system, which lasted more than 40 years, addicts got heroin prescriptions from their physicians, had them filled, and bought needles at a local pharmacy at nominal cost, thus satisfying their cravings without having to steal or to destroy their health with contaminated drugs or needles. Prior to 1960, only about 300 in Great Britain's 50 million population were registered addicts; most had jobs and good reputations.

From the 1960s on, the number of British addicts grew, as "hippie" subcultures promoted drug use for intoxication, heightened appreciation of rock music, and allegedly greater enjoyment of sex. British physicians were hounded by youths wanting registration as addicts, and many of those registered pressed for larger dosages, possibly to sell. In 1967, when registered addicts totaled 1,800, the British government limited authority to prescribe heroin for addicts in the London area to a few clinics that made strong efforts to shift their patients to methadone or to smaller heroin dosages. Many addicts then became more reliant on black-market heroin and adopted the street-addict lifestyle. By 1988, registered opiate addicts in Britain totaled 19,179 (Ghodse, 1989, p. 44), but some experts guessed that there were twice as many regular users. The numbers had increased dramatically, but in comparison it was estimated that the United States, with about four times Britain's population, then had 500,000 chronic opiate users.

AIDS, a disease discovered during the 1980s, spread rapidly among intravenous drug users, who frequently share needles. The British and Dutch began to give new needles to drug addicts at no charge, in exchange for used needles. Although many feared that this practice would encourage intravenous heroin use, evidence that it did not and that it curbed the spread of AIDS prompted needle exchanges in several American cities.

Because of concern with curbing AIDS, physicians began to replace police in much leadership of drug control efforts. British physicians now prescribe cocaine as well as heroin for persons addicted to them, with either sometimes provided in cigarettes rather than by injection. The Swiss now lead in replacing police and courts with a medical approach, followed by the Netherlands, Spain, other European countries, and Australia (Nadelmann, 1995; Reuter, Falco, & MacCoun, 1993).

All nations continue to incarcerate large-scale illegal drug dealers, but the Dutch stopped punishing possession of drugs for personal use. They provide liberal treatment for addicts desiring it, and have much antidrug education. They send regularly scheduled buses to places where addicts congregate, to provide methadone to be consumed at the bus and to exchange new needles for used, possibly AIDS-contaminated ones. The Dutch in the 1970s legalized the sale of marijuana at specified youth centers and cafes, but banned its advertising or other sales promotion. Polls showed that legalization was followed by a decline in marijuana use.

Profitable Penalties for Illegal Drug Use

Research has shown that breaking drug habits is a good way to reduce crime, but treatment requires persistence. Drug-abusing probationers of many types who are unemployed or have unstable employment histories were found to have lower rates of revoked probation if, in addition to getting frequent randomly scheduled drug tests, they are placed on house arrest with electronic monitoring. Interviews with those monitored for the first 90 days after their release show that this sentence alters their work and play habits and schedules; keeps them at home more instead of out carousing; and increases their rates of employment, money saving, and contact with their families (Glaser & Watts, 1992). Monitored home confinement also reduced recidivism rates when combined with mandatory treatment as conditions of probation (Jolin & Stipak, 1992). For those with a disorderly life but little experience in crime, monitoring plus drug and alcohol testing at randomly scheduled times, and possibly treatment, are less expensive than being locked up in jail. Incarceration is much more likely to reduce job prospects of such users and to foster their predatory lawbreaking on release.

For employed petty drug offenders, fines or community service or both are almost always the most profitable penalties. Such punishments not only reduce recidivism rates more than does jailing, but they also can give governments more added income than costs (Glaser & Gordon, 1990b; Gordon & Glaser, 1991). It is a gross waste of human potential and of taxpayers' money to impose long prison terms on such drug users. Yet mandatory penalties, especially in federal courts, now often give job-holders 5- or 10-year prison sentences.

In contrast, addicts who have long engaged in predatory crimes or in drug trafficking must be incapacitated for long terms to prevent them from continuing felony careers that endanger others. They should be treated for their addiction while incarcerated, and their releases should be conditional, with close supervision and drug tests.

A dozen states reduced marijuana penalties during the 1970s, before the federal "drug czar" in the 1980s pressured them to conform to a national standard. As in European countries that decriminalized small-scale possession of this drug, penalty reduction was not followed by an increase in the number of users. Indeed, some hard-drug users changed to marijuana when it was decriminalized, and drug overdose cases in hospital emergency rooms declined (Model, 1993). This experience suggests the desirability of allowing state policies to deviate from federal guidelines. Rand Corporation researchers Haaga and Reuter (1990) observe that "because no community has solved its drug problem, each could adopt different strategies and see what works after the fact; the wider the variety, the more information to be gained from the experiment" (p. 73).

No one who has lost a child to drugs or who sympathizes with persons who have is likely to welcome proposals for legalization. Many also justify opposition to lesser penalties by pointing to "crack babies," infants weighing but a few pounds at birth as a result of their mother's crack cocaine use. These babies are kept alive through intensive hospital care, with intravenous feeding in artificial respirators, at huge cost. They are destined to be forever physically and mentally retarded.

But no one who studies the facts can deny that government efforts at drug prohibition have largely failed and that some decriminalization efforts have reduced drug abuse. Furthermore, many—perhaps most—heroin addicts eventually outgrow heavy drug use and crime without therapy programs, as shown in Patrick Biernacki's (1986) study of 101 such ex-addicts. Dan Waldorf and associates (Waldorf, Reinarman, & Murphy, 1991) demonstrated that cocaine users also often grow out of the habit. The same is true for marijuana and other drugs as well. More life-history data on illegal drug use are needed to help us make drug policies more profitable for society. As the directors of the Rand Drug Policy Research Center concluded in their June 1995 newsletter,

> Drugs are not a temporary problem that can be vanquished by a sudden and swift attack. Rather, we face a deep-rooted and persistent problem, like disease and poverty, that must be dealt with on an ongoing basis with long-term strategies. . . . We will never eradicate illicit drug usage. But we can get smarter . . . and . . . reduce drug use . . . consequences for the generation of children now coming of age. ("Three Strikes," 1995, p. 1)

Conclusion

Government attempts to control vices are beneficially evolving to reflect the following profitable perspectives:

• Vices are generally learned socially, mostly from trusted friends, and are usually pursued with one or more associates rather than alone. Therefore, a high priority, when trying to reduce vices, is to attract their adherents to alternative activities with other people.

• Vices seem to relieve some sort of stress in addicts, whether of loneliness, boredom, physical discomfort, or a sense of failure. Therefore, promotion of healthier methods to alleviate stress is desirable, particularly physical fitness activities, other legitimate types of recreation or hobbies, and satisfying jobs.

• Pursuit of vices gives people a sense of being experts, or connoisseurs, in exotic, exciting, and prestigious experiences for which they are admired by associates, who share with them a disdain of the "squares" who are unaware of such pleasures. These attractions are sometimes maintained but made less damaging by curbing the most injurious forms of a vice while making other forms more available. Promoting use of wines and beers instead of whiskey, for instance, seems to have reduced the consumption of hard liquor. Prohibitionists often demand total abstinence, but this approach is rejected by most of our population, who are moderate in their vices. Also, people change over time, and many gradually pursue their vices less avidly, as they acquire alternative interests.

• Because vices provide intermittent rather than continuous gratifications, and sometimes are fleetingly euphoric, the memory of pleasures from vices creates a psychological craving that is extremely persistent or recurrent. Some alternative activities suggested above, such as physical fitness pursuits and other forms of recreation, also produce intermittent highs that may compete with vices in their appeal.

Laws that ban a vice undoubtedly deter many from trying it. Yet vices are too easily concealed to be greatly limited by prohibitions, and efforts to ban them promote organized and predatory crime. They also overload and corrupt criminal justice agencies. But many prohibition laws are retained even when unenforceable, to symbolize official opposition to a vice. Politicians who question such laws are often unfairly branded as soft on the vice. Nevertheless, much can be learned from the past vice-control failures described in this chapter.

For all vice control we should consider the counsel of Bakalar and Grinspoon (1984), who urged that instead of so much reliance on prohibition, we "place more confidence in the judgment of the average person and the recuperative powers of society than we have been willing to show" (p. 145). Also, in these and other efforts at more profitable crime control, we should be more willing to experiment. However, rigorous assessment of scientific experiments and pilot projects should be used to test innovative ideas before they are adopted as federal policies.

Note

1. Reprinted by permission of the *Los Angeles Times*.

6

Curbing Crimes of Rage

Crimes of rage—assault, manslaughter, and murder committed in an intense emotional state—disturb the public more than any other types of offenses. We have a morbid fascination with news stories about the disgruntled employee who fatally attacks a manager, or neighbors or family members who commit violence. We are wary of those volatile persons who, out of drunkenness or a generalized resentment of society, react to provocations with disproportionate violence. Perhaps we worry that we could somehow lose control of our own normal emotions—anger and fear—and let them become the passions of rage and panic. These passions are mighty engines for violent crimes.

This chapter focuses on the lawbreakings that mainly express rage. Excluded from our concerns here are relatively dispassionate assaults or killings for money, such as those of professional robbers and hit men, which are discussed in Chapter 9. The anger that precedes rage has many causes, both biological and social. The key to controlling crimes of rage, therefore, is ameliorating the anger and reducing the means for implementing violent emotions. The chapter ends with a look at domestic violence, which creates special crime-control problems because of our society's ambivalence regarding the nature of family relationships.

Assault, Manslaughter, and Homicide

Assault is a violent attack on another person, whether or not it causes injury. A shot fired or an object thrown at someone may, largely by chance, kill or injure the target, or it may miss its target altogether and hurt no one. Nevertheless, all are assaults.

The penalty, however, depends partly on the result, and especially on the motives ascribed to the attack. Assault is excused if committed in self-defense or to stop a serious crime. It is a criminal act if done with what the courts regard as excessive force, such as a killing to stop the theft of a candy bar. If no one is hit, a violent attack is usually not punishable, but it could be if it is inferred that blows, thrown objects, or bullets were intended to hurt, or even to kill.

Statistics on assault are unreliable. In the law, "simple" or "petty" assault can include even a slight shove, but it is imprecisely distinguished from the usually more brutal attacks called "aggravated" or "felonious" assault. These severe assaults are the ones that are most often referred to the police. Yet most assaults of both types are not reported to the police, especially if they take place within the family. They may also go unreported to interviewers for the National Crime Survey. After defining each common type of victimizing crime to samples of the population, the NCS interviewers ask if anyone in the home has suffered it in the past half year. Police also differ in how completely they record the assaults that are reported to them.

Our best data on violence rates are on killings, for they are almost always counted by the police. They also appear in public health statistics on the causes of death, compiled from physicians' and coroners' death certificates.

Murder committed with premeditation and malicious intent is called *homicide*, but many states differentiate between first and second degree murder by the extent of malice and premeditation. *Manslaughter* is unintentional killing. It is usually punished more severely if it results from an assault with intent to hurt, rather than from negligence (as in inattentive driving).

Although reported assault rates have risen over the past three decades, they are, as already mentioned, inexact measures. Assault rates are often only inferred from murder rates. Murder rates known to the police, and the much less complete data on assault, were once shown to be correlated almost identically with age, gender, race, and other variables (Pittman & Handy, 1964). Therefore, it has long been thought that one could extrapolate the correlates of assault from those of the more fully known variations in murder rates. This notion may now be changing, however, as Tonry (1995a) infers:

Given the greater availability of ever-more-lethal firearms, the proportion of assaults proving fatal (that is, the ratio of homicides to assaults) should be increasing. To the contrary, it has steadily fallen. This suggests that much of the apparent increase in assault rates reflects higher reporting and recording rather than a higher incidence of assault. (pp. 20-22)

The changes in assault reporting procedures may differ geographically.

The chances of someone in the United States being a murder victim are more accurately known. The annual rate of homicide doubled in three decades, from about 1 in 20,000 persons in 1960 to about 1 in 10,000 in 1990 (Holmes & Holmes, 1994, p. 6), although the odds have declined slightly since 1990. But most people are still very unlikely to be murdered. The United States has always had much higher homicide rates than other similarly developed nations, such as those of Western Europe, but much lower rates than some less developed ones, such as Mexico, Brazil, Colombia, the Philippines, Rwanda, and Sudan.

At least 40% of murders in the United States probably are victim-precipitated, in that the victim struck the first blow in the interaction that culminated in his or her death. Reported victim precipitation varied from 22% to 38% in different studies, but in 21% to 44% of the cases reported in those studies there was no indication of who struck the first blow. If we infer that victim precipitation occurred in about the same proportion of the lethal altercations in which the precipitator could not be determined as of the reported ones, then clearly more than 40% of the killings were begun by the person killed in the fight (Curtis, 1974; Wolfgang, 1958; Voss & Hepburn, 1968). Regardless of the precise percentage of victim-precipitated murders, in a substantial number of murders it is often only chance that determines who is the killer and who is killed.

Self-reported crime data from successive yearly interviews in the National Youth Survey's sample show that an early record of alcohol or marijuana use and of several serious offenses are the best predictors of involvement in violent crimes. They also show that each successive serious offense makes further violent crime more probable, but that nonspecialization persists. Therefore, the "probability of arrest for a non-serious offense is certainly as high as for a serious offense at any point in the [criminal] career" (Elliott, 1994, p. 18). In Denmark, also, the probability of arrest for a violent crime was found to increase with each arrest for any type of serious offense (Brennan, Mednick, & John, 1989).

Causes of Potentially Violent Passions

In all societies, violence is committed mostly by males. About seven times as many men as women are arrested for homicide in the United States, and the ratio is similar for assault. This difference is often explained biologically. In almost all mammals the males do most of the fighting, possibly because pregnancy and nursing handicap females in physical combat. Differences between the sexes in average upper-body strength and in hormones are also cited as explanations. Yet the fact that most cultures view violence as a virtue for males and as improper for females is probably more influential.

Biological Factors

Nevertheless, biological factors do play a role in creating the passions that lead to violent crime. Humans, male and female, share with other animals the types of physiological reactions that accompany intense emotions. This similarity across species is shown when a sudden noise occurs. All humans, dogs, cats, birds, and other beasts that hear, say, a big bang experience arousal of their *autonomic nervous systems*. Their muscles tense, senses sharpen, and hearts speed as their bodies automatically mobilize for fight or flight.

Some have claimed that all human emotions are reducible to four broad types—fear, anger, depression, and happiness—each linked to a distinct pattern of autonomic system reaction (Kemper, 1987). Goleman (1995, pp. 289-290) cites a longer list of types of feelings, drawn from many languages and from diverse cultures: anger, sadness, fear, enjoyment, love, surprise, disgust, and shame. One could add guilt, pride, hate, and ecstasy as other common designations of distinct feelings. It is because emotions mix; are culturally interpreted; and vary in intensity, setting, and associated conduct that they get such a variety of labels.

In addition to having an autonomic nervous system, humans and other animals have a *central nervous system*. However, this system is much more highly developed in humans than in other species. It gives us the ability to interpret our circumstances in words and to direct our conduct on the basis of these interpretations. The result is deliberate and ostensibly rational guidance of behavior. To an appreciable extent, then, the central nervous system can inhibit the expression of emotions in conduct. We learn from family, friends, schools, religious institutions, and other sources, and may also develop individually, ideas on when certain expressions of emotion are improper, and when they are permissible or even desirable. But the proper functioning of the central nervous system is crucial to such inhibition.

Diverse brain abnormalities, endocrinal imbalances, and low levels of blood sugar or of the neurotransmitter serotonin, as well as other body conditions, affect ease of emotional arousal and ability to inhibit it. Persons who are persistently violent are the most likely to have hereditary central nervous system sluggishness or to have had perinatal complications (Kandel & Mednick, 1991; Moffitt, 1993). Artificially induced brain abnormalities also play a role. Stimulants, such as cocaine or amphetamines, make emotions more easily aroused. Alcohol, opiates, and other depressant drugs, as well as fatigue, reduce the central nervous system's ability to inhibit emotions.

Social Feedback and Audience Effects

A distinctive feature of emotions is that their expression by one person tends to arouse or intensify similar feelings in others. This process, which has been called "circular reaction" (Blumer, 1939) and "excitation transfer" (Zillman, 1979), is called *social feedback* here. Until this feedback process is interrupted by distracting new external or internal stimuli, passionate interaction tends to intensify the feelings of those participating, as well as the feelings of those observing or hearing it. The external stimuli that distract them can be any other sights or sounds that get their attention; internal stimuli include other thoughts (e.g., remembering an appointment) and other feelings (e.g., pain, fatigue, or nausea).

Social feedback typically begins when anger makes a person's voice rise. This tone evokes anger in anyone yelled at, and soon both are shouting at each other, unless the anger of one has aroused fear in the other. Supreme Court Justice Oliver Wendell Holmes referred to social feedback of fear when he said that free speech does not include the right to cry "Fire!" in a crowded theater. Such shouts of fear, by arousing similar emotions in the audience, can elevate fear to panic and start such rushing to the exits that people are trampled or trample others to death.

Some popular singers—for example, the Beatles, Elvis Presley, or Frank Sinatra in their primes—can also precipitate social feedback, moving adoring audiences to screaming and sighing and intensifying ecstasy until some swoon from it. A more common form of social feedback occurs among mourners at a funeral. The crying of one or two heightens the sadness of others, who soon are also weeping.

Individuals may even experience social feedback in communicating to themselves, when in private contemplations they "work themselves up into a stew" of rage, love, anxiety, or gloom. This process can be interrupted or even reversed by new stimuli from external events, or by the usually unvoiced communication to ourselves that we call "thinking" or "reflection." Our thinking can be a shared process in "discussion" or "talking it out," if it is done more in collaboration than in conflict with others.

An analysis of 159 verbal interaction sequences that ended in assault or homicide noted another cause of potentially violent passions: *audience effects.* "Violence is evoked most readily if one or more others are present when unfavorable remarks are exchanged" (Felson & Steadman, 1983). Someone who is humiliated in public, thereby losing face in front of others, is especially likely to reach a state of uncontrollable rage, because of the audience's perceived or anticipated social feedback of negative emotional reactions. Probably none of the murders these researchers studied would have occurred if habits of cooler response had prevailed in at least one disputant, or if either participants or audiences had departed at the first sign of anger. Instead, social feedback intensified anger to rage and a deadly weapon was used or a fatal blow struck. Nonlethal assaults develop similarly, but end when someone is hurt, flees, or the quarrel is otherwise interrupted.

Inequality

Sophisticated statistical analyses of data from different countries show that homicide rates and indices of economic inequality are correlated in all nations, but are most correlated in democracies (Avison & Loring, 1986; Krahn, Hartnagel, & Gartrell, 1986; Messner, 1989). Perhaps democracy promotes more outrage at inequalities because it also promotes norms of equality.

The fact that inequality in income and wealth increased in the United States from 1970 to 1990 may largely account for the growth in violent crime rates during that period. But as Chapter 1 indicated, the slight decline of these rates in the 1990s may also reflect a drop in the percentage of teenagers in the total U.S. population, because teenagers have the highest crime rates.

National homicide rates also generally rise with diversity in ethnic and language groups within a country, which may promote bias and misunderstandings, as well as inequality.

Within our largest cities, rates of violent crimes reported to the police (homicides, rapes, robberies, and assaults) are correlated with area rates of poverty and economic inequality (Blau & Blau, 1982; Messner, 1982; Williams, 1984). Data on 26 neighborhoods within Manhattan showed that their homicide rates were closely associated with their proportions of people in extreme poverty, and their percentages of the divorced or separated (Messner & Tardiff, 1986).

Homicide today is the leading cause of death of African American males aged 15 to 24; their rates are at least seven times those of white males in this age group. This discrepancy may partly result from white flight to suburbs between 1970 and 1990, which was closely correlated with increases in robbery rates in the cities they left (Liska & Bellair, 1995). Yet for both races, urban homicide rates are so closely linked with rates of female-headed households, male unemployment, and residence in the slums, that the differences between these two racial groups on such variables suffice to explain fully their contrast in homicide rates (Sampson, 1987).

Subcultural Violence

A Southern subculture of violence is frequently alleged in the United States, because police-reported homicide and assault rates have long been highest in the former Confederate states. Compared with other regions, Southern property crime rates are not so exceptional. One explanation for the high rates of violence is that these states have the highest rates of extreme poverty; for all 50 states, homicide rates are closely related to the percentage of the population that is very poor. This correlation applies especially to *primary homicides*, the murders between friends or relatives that are more likely to express rage, rather than to the less passionate killings of strangers, as occur in the course of robbery (Dawson & Langan, 1994; Loftin & Hill, 1974; Parker & Smith, 1979).

There are also indicators of higher tolerance for deadly violence between intimates in the South than prevails elsewhere. Anthropologist Henry Lundsgaarde's (1977) *Murder in Space City* showed that when Houston police ascribed a killing to a spouse's provocation, such as adultery, or simply to an argument in which both parties were drunk, they were unlikely to charge the accused with murder and often did not prosecute for any crime. Until 1974, the Texas Penal Code excused killing one's spouse or the spouse's lover if they were caught in the act of adultery.

Southern states also have the nation's highest rates of gun ownership and hunting, which puts the means for killing more readily at hand. Surveys have found that both Southern-reared persons and gun owners everywhere are more approving than others of violence in defense of abused women or children or of burglary victims. They are not much different in reacting to verbal affronts (Dixon & Lizotte, 1987).

The South imposes the death penalty on convicted murderers much more than other regions do but still executes less than 1% of them. Its killers sentenced to prison get shorter terms than are given for murder in states that rarely or never use capital punishment (Glaser, 1979).

One can infer that in the South especially, and in the rest of the nation to a lesser extent, an angry assault in response to physical abuse of one's person or family is a "folk crime." It is forgiven even if it has deadly results, because most people can see themselves reacting in a similar rage to such provocations. But if a killing seems unprovoked, the South is more willing to execute.

Differences in violence rates between the South and other regions have declined in recent decades, mostly because these rates rose in the rest of the country (Kowalski & Petee, 1991). Increases in violence in the North and West followed large migrations there from areas of higher violence, such as the South and Latin America.

Mass Media

One controversial issue is whether spectators become aggressive from seeing violence in films, television, newspaper accounts, and sports (especially boxing, wrestling, hockey, and football). Many psychologists once held that watching violence has a "cathartic effect," helping spectators get rid of violent impulses vicariously instead of by aggressive acts. More rigorous research, however, shows that watching violence prompts similar conduct by persons already so inclined if they see people like themselves reacting violently in circumstances familiar to them. Although the most violent films are animated cartoons and fairy tales, they evoke little audience violence because they are unrealistic. On the other hand, theater owners have learned at great cost that realistic films about teenage gang fights prompt conflict and "tearing up the place" by the already-delinquent audiences that such films attract.

In August 1996, newspapers reported a study by the Markle Foundation in New York that found a potential link between mass media and nonviolence. High school students who as preschoolers had watched educational television most, such as *Sesame Street* and *Mr. Rogers' Neighborhood*, had the highest grade-point averages in high school English, science, and mathematics courses. Because high academic grades are correlated with nondelinquency, perhaps delinquency results from the type of TV show watched rather than from the total amount of watching.

Home Experiences

A study of more than 400 children that investigated their propensity for violence when they were about 8 years old and then reexamined them a decade later found that the most violent children not only spent more time watching TV but also had weaker identifications with their mothers. Teenage boys' violence was especially related to violence in the home. Experiencing parental warmth and enthusiasm, which the researchers called "nurturance," as well as being in middle-class homes and doing well in school, were closely associated with nonviolence at 8 and at 18, for both sexes (Lefkowitz, Eron, Welder, & Huesemann, 1977).

A 30-year follow-up of boys classified as aggressive when they were 5 to 9 years old found that those least supervised as young children were the most aggressive as adolescents and as adults. They also came from homes with the most conflict between parents, the most corporal punishment from fathers, and the least affection and family leadership from mothers (McCord, 1983). Indeed, family counseling research has repeatedly shown that conflict in families tends to be predicted by conflicts in the homes where the family members were reared.

"Saving Face"

Anger escalates to rage most readily among intimates, because their lives are much involved; they are more indifferent to the conduct of strangers, because their lives are less likely to be affected by these persons. Primary homicides have thus long been the most common type of murder and the most passionate. Although killings by strangers, such as the professional murders discussed in Chapter 9, seem to be growing in frequency, only in mystery stories do most murders result from careful planning.

Primary violence tends to evolve from an escalation of emotions in what Erving Goffman (1967) called "character contests"—people trying to impress each other with their personal qualities. Such contests prevail in the teasing and "kidding" conversations of everyday life. Participants in them strive to show superiority and to avoid the embarrassment of displaying inferiority. As Peter Blau (1964, pp. 43-47) pointed out, we keep trying to impress others but not to be impressed by them. Thus many character contests are "zero-sum" games, as one person's "loss of face" is the other's gain.

Such contests are common in social gatherings as diverse as a street-corner group of delinquents, where each tries to appear tougher or cooler than the others, and a cocktail party of intellectuals who compete in display of erudition, artistic taste, or wit. Violence may result from such character contests as a last resort for people who have run out of ways to display their self-importance by verbal or other nonviolent responses. As Braithwaite (1992) notes, "Much crime, particularly violent crime, is motivated by the humiliation of the offender and the offender's perceived right to humiliate the victim" (p. 81). Also relevant in about half the apparently rage-driven felonies is inebriation. If the perpetrator—and often the victim—has been drinking, social feedback more readily escalates the emotions of all participants (Roth, 1994b).

David Luckenbill (1977), in analyzing exchanges that culminated in murder, always found that "opponents sought to establish or maintain 'face' at the other's expense" (p. 176). Pride came before their falls. All the fatal contests he studied evolved after one person did what another viewed as a threat to face, and neither of them backed down before violence became deadly. The initial perceived threat could be a disrespectful remark, a refusal to obey an order, or an alleged false statement. When both are drinking, the precipitating event can be a very trivial annoyance that would ordinarily be ignored.

Profitable Policies for Violence Prevention

The social costs of passionate crimes are immense. When such crimes occur among intimates, a family may lose a member to either imprisonment or fatality. The lives of all survivors of violent crime may be radically altered by the physical and psychological distress; they may feel obligated to move from the neighborhood or come to distrust their friends or become unable to perform their jobs. People who lose control of their emotions and are convicted of crimes of passion face the stigma of criminalization.

The economic costs are substantial as well. The expense of caring for severely wounded victims of passionate crime affects society as a whole, as does the expense of arresting, sentencing, and incarcerating perpetrators. Of course, none of this expense erases the social costs of such crime.

Thus the most profitable approach for controlling crimes of rage is to prevent them in the first place. Among the efforts to prevent violence are training in other ways of resolving differences, gun control, and severe penalties for murder.

Education

People need training at home and school to know ways of calmly negotiating disagreements, or they will run out of alternatives too readily. Violence is avoided by peaceful discussions without nasty remarks.

A major provocation to fighting among males is a challenge to manliness. This sort of fighting is often not so much from anger as from fear of being humiliated by backing away from a fight. This is the sexist "face" that males too often literally die to save. Toys and games, sports, and mass media have long promoted the image of the hero who has the ability and desire to fight physically or to use guns. Such an image is intended primarily for males (although the gender difference is diminishing). Less violence in boys' and men's play; less favorable attention to macho demeanor; and fewer stereotyped, separate roles for each gender in employment, housework, and recreation would probably reduce the need to prove manliness.

High violence rates and low educational level are closely correlated. It follows that violence is diminished by all the methods of reducing childhood-transition criminality that were urged in Chapter 4, such as parenting classes, Head Start, "lighted schoolhouses," welfare reform, and help in the transition from school to work. School classrooms themselves play a major role in training students to discuss their differences and control their anger, Also, democratically run clubs and democratic meetings for children, beginning at the earliest age, provide some of the best training in nonviolent resolution of differences.

New York City elementary schools have developed what they call "The Resolving Conflict Creatively Program" (RCCP). It includes elementary and secondary school curricula, teacher training, a student mediator program, and parent training. The elementary schools have 51 "workshops" for students covering 16 topical units, such as "communication," "acknowledging feelings," "resolving conflict creatively," "appreciating diversity," and "bias awareness." The secondary school curriculum reviews the elementary school's topics, then emphasizes concepts and skills of conflict resolution and intergroup relationships.

RCCP training for teachers encompasses 20 hours of after-school sessions with much role playing, plus 6 to 10 subsequent classroom visits by instructors.

An RCCP mediator program is begun in schools that have had an RCCP program for a year or more, with teachers who have used the program regularly. Students apply to become mediators and are selected by teachers, sometimes after secret ballots on student preferences. Student mediators are supervised by one teacher who gives them 2 days of initial training, holds bi-weekly sessions to review their experiences, and is available as a consultant. RCCP mediators work in pairs, wearing a "Mediator" T-shirt. They patrol the lunchrooms in elementary schools, and if they see a fight, instead of intervening physically they ask the students if they wish to mediate, which most do. In secondary schools they mainly mediate quarrels referred to them. In any case, the mediation is done in the privacy of a separate room, usually during the lunch hour, and the mediators are given much autonomy but are to seek consensus on what the disputants agree on and what remains to be settled.

The RCCP Parent Involvement Program provides 60 hours of training for two or three parents per school, to lead workshops for other parents on intergroup relations, family communication, and conflict resolution.

Evaluations of RCCP thus far stress student tests, which show that most master the curricula topics. Teacher and student testimonials also attest to changed attitudes and behavior. Possibly RCCP, and "Beacon" after-school programs (discussed in Chapter 4) account for much of the recent decline in New York City violence rates. More rigorous assessments of its impact are under way (DeJong, 1995).

Less extensive programs analogous to RCCP are now widespread. In some Los Angeles public schools, for example, classes in temper control, for sixth to ninth graders who have had problems from flying into a rage, are reported to be effective in reducing their school and home difficulties. In many cities, police officers are involved in the student violence reduction programs as part of the growing emphasis on community policing, which is discussed in Chapter 10.

Gun Control

Although gun ownership in Europe was historically a monopoly of the military and the aristocracy, Europeans who settled North America during the 1600s and 1700s made sure that almost all their adult males, and many boys, had at least one gun. These were used mostly for hunting, because wild game was the principal source of meat, with the hides and furs used for clothing or export. Guns were also used to control Indians, slaves, and outlaws. In addition, the European custom of dueling spread to the upper classes of the South and evolved into gun fights in the West.

Because guns are now used in the United States for 70% of murders, and in many robberies and rapes, some people infer that these crimes could be drastically reduced by allowing almost no one except the police and the armed forces to have guns. An opposite belief is that many more citizens should have guns for self-protection. These are the two extreme views in the debate on gun control. The reality is that weak controls prevail, which vary among the states.

Arguments for Gun Control

Those who want more gun control point out that in no other large, technologically developed nation is there as much handgun and assault gun ownership per capita as in the United States, and in no other developed country are murder and robbery rates as high. Also, because assaults and robberies in other nations less often employ guns, a smaller percentage are fatal. Guns have finally surpassed motor vehicles as the leading cause of traumatic deaths in the United States, according to a February 3, 1995, newspaper report from a violence research center at the University of California at Davis.

Canada has little regulation of rifles and shotguns, used for hunting in its vast terrain, but it rigidly controls handguns, which are more often used for crime; it has less than half the U.S. murder rate. Western European nations greatly restrict ownership of any type of gun; the per capita murder rate in England is about one-seventh and in France one-fifth that of the United States'. Rates of killings by means other than guns are also lower in these countries than in the United States (Chappell & Strang, 1992).

All kinds of lethal shooting increase with the prevalence of firearms. Of the more than 30,000 deaths from guns annually in the United States, about half are suicides, 40% homicides, and 10% accidents (Wright & Rossi, 1986). Rates of suicide by gun are correlated with rates of homicide and of accident by gun, but all diminish with stricter gun control laws (Lester, 1987). A loaded handgun is acutely dangerous to children who may find it and play with it; to adults who handle it carelessly; and to angry or despondent persons, especially when drunk. Too often they impulsively kill others or themselves because the weapon is readily available.

The rise in juvenile use of firearms is also cause for concern. Murders committed with guns by juveniles increased by 79% during the 1980s, robberies by juveniles with guns also rose, and those aged 15 to 19 had the highest rates of death by bullet. Surveys of students of inner-city neighborhoods found that 45% had been threatened or shot at with guns while going to and from school (Blumstein, 1995; Mock, 1994; Zawitz, 1995). Higher figures are often reported in newspapers for schools in high-crime neighborhoods. Gun prevalence probably explains why 82% of U.S. murder victims aged 15 to 19 were killed by firearms, compared to 70% of all murder victims (Roth, 1994a).

Arguments Against Gun Control

The Second Amendment to our Constitution reads: "A well-regulated Militia, being necessary to the security of a free State, the right of the people to keep and bear Arms shall not be infringed." Although gun advocates usually quote only the words after the last comma, federal courts focus on the words about a militia. The judges declare that this 1787 Amendment was motivated mainly by fear that the federal government would interfere, as the British had, with the separate militias formed from self-armed citizens in each of the 13 colonies (Newton & Zimring, 1969, appendix J). Today, the role of the colonial militias is filled by the National Guard units of each state. In addition, in many states voluntary groups unofficially call themselves "militias." They engage in military training and war games with guns.

Gun advocates marshal historical evidence to oppose the federal court interpretation of the Second Amendment (Halbrook, 1984). They insist that the right to bear arms is essential to our liberties. But they ignore liberty's survival in Canada, Australia, and Western Europe without widespread distribution of handguns.

Gun advocates also argue that residents or employees can be present in homes and stores more continuously than police, and arming citizens therefore prevents crimes at these places. Kleck and Gertz (1995) estimate that close to 2.5 million defensive uses of guns occur annually in the United States, perhaps preventing millions of crimes.

Traditionally, state laws have provided that persons who meet specified criteria, such as age and lack of a criminal record or mental ailment, may be licensed to carry a concealed handgun—if they convince officials that they need it. In 1985 the National Rifle Association, the principal organization of private gun owners, began to lobby for laws allowing anyone who meets the criteria to be issued such a license on request, without showing any need for it. These are often called "shall" laws because they change the crucial wording from "may be licensed" to "shall be licensed." Since 1985, at least 15 states have changed their laws to the "shall" form.

The effects of these changes have been assessed for Miami, Jacksonville, and Tampa in Florida; the Portland area in Oregon; and Jackson, Mississippi. In the four areas other than Portland, the monthly rate of homicide by gun rose after "shall" laws increased the availability of handguns. Rates of non-gun homicide did not rise. Portland had much lower rates of homicide than the Southern areas both before and after this change, but taking the five areas together, homicide rates increased 26% with the "shall" legislation (McDowall, Loftin, & Wiersema, 1995).

Polls show that, of all respondents, gun owners fear crime least. Therefore, fear reduction might be a strong argument for opposing gun controls. Fear is stressful and prompts much spending for security devices like locks and bars. It also makes people stay home at night when they could enjoy going out. However, polls also show that most people who fear crime do not want guns (Hemenway, Solnick, & Azrael, 1995).

Most attempts to disarm cities by buying handguns for $50 or some other flat sum each, or by providing free tickets to popular events in exchange for guns, yield few weapons, the bulk of them inferior. Buying back the estimated 225 million privately owned firearms in the United States at $50 would cost well over a billion dollars, but most devotees would not sell their last guns for anything but an enormous sum. Handguns are also durable and easily hidden.

Incidentally, more than half the handguns that police identify as involved in crimes were stolen. They are usually taken in home burglaries, mostly by teenagers who carry out all portable valuables that they find.

The stringent controls long established in Western Europe and Japan authorize civilian ownership of few handguns and hardly any assault rifles, require prior approval for their sale or transfer, and confiscate those unauthorized. Three conditions make such controls unlikely in the United States in the near future and of limited crime-control value even if attempted.

First, the strength of opposition to gun control is enormous. The National Rifle Association mobilizes millions of letter writers and thousands of demonstrators on short notice to harass legislators considering gun control laws. It is funded not only by its avid members, but by manufacturers, importers, and dealers in guns, who also have their own lobbyists, and by state organizations.

Some extreme right-wing groups—called "survivalists" and linked to militia groups—are wary of dictatorships developing in the United States or of the United Nations taking control of this country. They propagate a fear that authorities will use gun registration records to seize all private weapons, then suppress liberties. This fear was especially intense when Communists controlled the Soviet Union. These extremists viewed as Communist conspirators almost anyone with more liberal political views than theirs. Some of their members were charged with terrorism and other crimes, notably the 1995 Oklahoma City federal courthouse bombing.

Legislators, responding to polls and to their own beliefs, enacted new gun control measures in the 1990s. Because state laws are diverse both in wording and in enforcement, John Hinckley on one afternoon could buy in Louisville, Kentucky, the two handguns with which he tried to assassinate President Reagan. Most handguns seized by the police in New York City were traced to dealers in states with weaker controls, such as South Carolina. Some federal laws for more uniform controls have been enacted, notably against sale of assault guns, but lobbyists' efforts have left serious loopholes in them.

Second, to control the sheer volume and dispersion of private guns in the United States is a formidable problem. Half of our 260 million people are in homes with guns. It has been estimated that households with firearms average three guns each, and that half have handguns. Because most gun owners oppose controls, it would be impossible to register all legally acquired handguns and to confiscate those deemed illegal. Attempts to do so would create much resistance, sometimes lethal.

Surveys of male high school students find that nearly a third have owned a gun and more than a fifth still do, most often a handgun. About an eighth report always carrying their gun, and most say that they do so for protection (Sheley, McGee, & Wright, 1992; Wright, Sheley, & Smith, 1992). Increasingly, however, parents are held criminally responsible for their juvenile offspring's illegal gun possession or gun crime, and any student bringing a gun to school is expelled.

Third, it is unlikely that gun controls would promptly disarm criminals. Surveys of prison inmates who used guns find that most did not buy them from legitimate dealers; the bulk were either stolen or acquired by purchase or trade from others operating outside the law. It is estimated that half of all gun transactions involve used guns (Cook, 1991, p. 39). They are often traded openly at swap meets and garage sales, even in states with relatively strict controls, such as California. When handguns are scarce, and at other times, criminals saw off the barrels of rifles or shotguns to make them more concealable. They can then be used at short range with deadlier effects than most handguns.

Many states have laws requiring prison terms for using a gun in a crime. Their impact is less than was expected, however, for defense lawyers readily get prosecutors to drop the gun charge in exchange for guilty pleas on other charges (Loftin, Heumann, & McDowall, 1983).

Some Feasible U.S. Gun Controls

About two thirds of our adult population support gun control (Kleck, 1991, pp. 379-380), and half the gun owners and most nonowners agree that certain people should not be allowed to acquire firearms (Hemenway et al., 1995). However, less than a third endorse banning all ownership of guns by private citizens (Kleck, 1991, pp. 379-380). Thus there are realistic prospects that limited gun controls can be established in the United States. They would gradually reduce criminals' ready access to handguns, as well as diminish accidental shootings and suicides. Such changes can come from achieving as many as possible of the following nine goals:

• *Nationally uniform licensing and monitoring of gun sales, to ban sales to ex-felons, mentally disturbed persons, and juveniles:* The U.S. Treasury Department's Bureau of Alcohol, Tobacco and Firearms already enforces such rules for what the National Firearms Control Act imperfectly defines as "assault weapons," but the ban could gradually be extended to all handguns. Eventually, registration could be required for all transfers of guns by gift or sale. Licensed dealers, for a fee yielding a reasonable profit, would check the would-be recipient's record. All guns now must have serial numbers, and the serial numbers of new guns are usually recorded by manufacturers and most dealers in conjunction with registering product warranties. If a serial number were recorded for every gun transfer, and any gun with its serial number removed or altered were subject to confiscation and destruction, the distribution of guns could gradually be controlled more thoroughly. Profitable penalties for violators of such laws would be a large fine for a single weapon (preferably a day fine, so the amount would be dependent on income), plus jail or prison terms for large-scale or repeated sales.

• *Nationally available instant check on the criminal records and mental health history of anyone wishing to buy a gun:* Virginia already has such a program, it works well, and it is expected that the rest of the country will follow. A prospective gun purchaser shows the licensed dealer two types of personal identification, one with a current photograph, and fills out a form; the dealer then makes a toll-free call to a state computer center that checks the person's record. The dealer sends the form in with a report on the gun purchase. Only about half those who challenge their nonqualification for buying a gun are eventually allowed to purchase one.

• *Government payments for voluntary registration of all guns now owned, with owners' criminal and mental health records then checked; confiscation of guns from those whose criminal or mental health histories prevent their qualification for ownership; and confiscation of unregistered guns after some future date:* Registration of newly purchased guns can be mandated and be financed by license fees, but incentives such as government payments would be needed to motivate much registration of previously owned guns. All these proposals would be resisted by many or evaded if enacted, but they would gradually diminish ready access to guns by emotionally upset or criminal persons.

• *Limits on the types of guns offered for sale:* To further disarm U.S. civilians who are not clearly law-abiding, mature, and mentally stable, limitations should be enacted on the manufacture and import of handguns; on the calibre, ammunition storage capacity, and automatic firing potential of all guns sold to the civilian population; and on ammunition sale and distribution.

• *Training, testing, and licensing for the handling and secure storage of registered guns and ammunition:* Such procedures are currently followed by the armed forces. Extending them to the civilian population would reduce accidental shootings and weapons theft.

• *Bans against possession of many usable guns by one owner:* Owners now usually have several guns, and some collect dozens, scores, or hundreds. Often the guns are antiques, but as long as they can be fired, they are dangerous. Even if the owner would do no wrong, the guns may be stolen for use in crime.

• *Government purchasing offices in high-violence areas to buy guns for a reasonable price with no questions asked:* These guns would be destroyed except for some that might be useful to the police or the armed forces. Records would be kept on guns bought, and researchers would assess the impact of the program.

• *Bans against public sale of armor-piercing handgun bullets, and of guns made so predominantly of plastic as to be passable through metal detectors at airports and elsewhere:* Handgun bullets usually have soft metal heads that will not penetrate body armor well. Police are especially anxious to have a ban on more penetrating bullets, as many at times wear body armor. Although plastic guns of the type described are not yet known to be available, they can conceivably be made. An effort should be made to prevent their manufacture or import.

• *Special training and deployment of police patrols to identify and seize illegally carried guns:* For 29 weeks in 1992-1993, a federally funded, controlled experiment in Kansas City, Missouri, in an 80- by 10-block area with high crime rates, added two patrol cars from 7 p.m. to 1 a.m. Each car had two officers specially trained to spot guns in cars or under clothing of suspects when stopping vehicles to check any type of law violation. They averaged one car check every 40 minutes, many more in some periods than in others, and appreciably increased seizures of illegal gun. Gun crimes in this area decreased significantly during this period, although they did not in adjacent areas and in a control area (Sherman, Shaw, & Rogan, 1995). Similar programs have begun in other cities.

All these proposed restrictions would be resisted by advocates of gun ownership and their organizations. Realistically, therefore, these proposals can be enacted only piecemeal. And even if they were all enacted right away, bombing and other types of killing are still likely to be committed by the most avid, most violence-prone individuals. Thus none of the proposals would have an immediate, great impact on crime rates.

It should also be noted that gun violence rates are determined not so much by the number and distribution of guns or by laws restricting gun ownership as by cultural values, customs, and confidence in police and other government agencies that affect gun use. Survey data indicate that gun ownership for household protection varies inversely with confidence in the police and the courts (Young, McDowall, & Loftin, 1987). If community policing, discussed in Chapter 9, brings more youths and adults into collaboration with law enforcers, a major fringe benefit is likely to be less public fear of crime and less desire for gun ownership.

Switzerland provides an interesting model. It is among the most technologically advanced, affluent, and democratic countries. Its universal military service for males places guns in most households for defense against invasion, yet it has relatively low crime rates. Its government is very decentralized, with numerous local decisions made at town meetings (Clinard, 1978). Switzerland's record supports this book's repeated contention, also made by Cullen (1994) and others, that the most effective crime preventives are informal social controls through community interaction across age, gender, and other social barriers.

Enacting the preceding gun control policies in this country would help to instill informal social controls like Switzerland's. Gradually, only ownership of registered guns would be respectable, as in Western Europe. If these proposals could slowly change our culture's attitude toward lethal violence, we might finally achieve lower killing rates.

Capital Punishment

The death penalty has long been abolished in most technologically advanced nations; in the remainder, including the United States, its use is limited, as Exhibit 6.1 shows. For more than 20 years in the United States, executions have been authorized only for murder and treason.

About 40 states currently mandate capital punishment for certain crimes, but few actually impose it. Until 1995, 14 states and the District of Columbia banned the death penalty, but in that year it was restored in New York, missed restoration by only a few legislator votes in Massachusetts, and was reconsidered in several other states. Because of court challenges, the status of the death penalty remains uncertain even where voters favor it. Executions are unlikely to occur for at least 10 years in states like New York that have restored the death penalty. Yet national polls show that a majority favor it in our country, and they demand it as the punishment for the most heinous crimes.

EXECUTIONS IN THE UNITED STATES, 1930-94

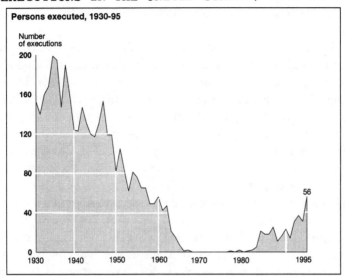

Exhibit 6.1.   Executions in the United States, 1930-1994
SOURCE: Stephan and Snell (1996, p. 2).

The strongest moral argument for the death penalty is that it is the only punishment that fully avenges a murder. It is also assumed to be a deterrent to others. Walter Berns's (1979) book *For Capital Punishment* asserts:

> The criminal law must be made awful, by which I mean awe-inspiring, or commanding "profound respect or reverential fear" . . . and in our day the only punishment that can do this is capital punishment. (p. 173)

Berns also focuses on the need for retribution by death for killers of revered figures, such as John F. Kennedy and Martin Luther King, Jr.

Moral arguments against the death penalty stress that because life is sacred, the government should never be a cold-blooded executioner. But when a heinous murder arouses public anger, demands for revenge have more appeal than remarks on the sanctity of the killer's life. Some opponents of the death penalty also contend that the publicity and drama of executions by the government promote rather than deter potential murderers. In 1990, for example, Oklahoma carried out the death penalty for the first time in 25 years, and in the following year its rates of argument-related killings of strangers (murders not associated with robberies, rapes, or other felonies, or between intimates) rose significantly (Cochran, Chamlin, & Seth, 1994).

Capital punishment also has an incapacitation function, commonly asserted as "Only a killer who is dead will not kill again." One should note, however, that in 80% of solved murders, the killing is done by a family member or associate, rather than by a stranger (Dawson & Langan, 1994). Relatively few of these "primary" murderers are convicted of new felonies after release from prison; the best predictor of postrelease recidivism is the releasee's total prior felony record. Released convicts who have been lifelong, versatile predators are far more likely to commit a new murder. The "career criminals," discussed in Chapter 9, begin persistent lawbreaking before their teen years, are unspecialized in their crimes, are frequently assaultive, drink heavily, and use drugs. They are highly recidivistic. The probability that their next crime will be a killing is greater than the probability that the typical primary murderer will commit a second killing. Primary murderers are usually older when first confined, are much older at release, and have demonstrated little prior criminality.

Many sophisticated statistical analyses refute the few claiming that capital punishment deters the public from committing murder (Klein, Forst, & Filator, 1978). In the states and countries that have adopted, abolished, or restored the death penalty, there has been no pattern of increase or decrease in murders following these changes; the only pattern is lower murder rates where murderers get long prison terms rather than the death penalty (Archer, Gartner, & Beittel, 1983; Forst, 1977; Glaser, 1979). It has been shown that homicide is reduced as much by certainty of any kind of severe penalty as by the prospect of capital punishment (Kleck, 1979).

Capital punishment advocates contend that if it were used more, its deterrent effect would become evident. But when it had greater use it did not reduce murder rates, and its use is unlikely to be much higher, for many factors inhibit officials from making the irreversible decision to impose death. Four Southern states—Florida, Georgia, Louisiana, and Texas—have conducted most of the executions in the United States since 1977. Yet less than 1% of killers are executed even in these states. In 1994 there were only 31 executions in the United States, even though at the end of that year 2,890 persons were imprisoned under sentence of death, including more than 300 each in Texas, California, and Florida (Stephan & Snell, 1996). The number of executions (see Exhibit 6.2) has always been far less than the number of death sentences imposed.

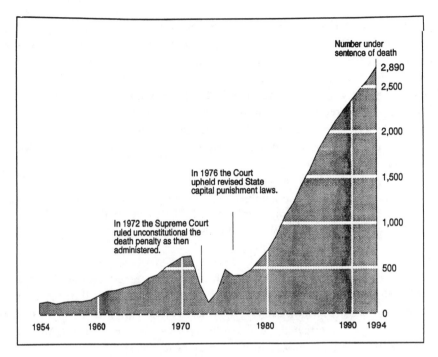

Exhibit 6.2.   Persons Under Sentence of Death in the United States, 1954-
1994
SOURCE: Stephan and Snell (1996, p. 11).

The ability even to arrest and prosecute murderers is spotty. Most
primary murders are solved by the police. Often the murderer turns
himself or herself in, and frequently witnesses saw the crime or heard the
quarrel that preceded it. But the police solve only a minority of killings
committed in robberies with victims who are strangers to the offender.
And less than 1% of assassinations of organized crime figures result in
successful prosecution. These killings are done by professional "hit men"
who murder for pay (discussed in Chapter 9). They kill in states with or
without the death penalty, confident of not being caught.

Many claim that the death penalty has never been applied fairly.
Wherever it is used, the differences between the murderers executed and
those spared are so inconsistent that its use seems haphazard (Zimring &
Hawkins, 1986, p. 89). In South Carolina's 16 judicial districts, the percentage of murders legally eligible for capital punishment in which the prosecutor requested the death penalty ranged from 17 to 87 (Paternoster, 1991,
p. 181). It has been shown in several states that those executed are not the

most heinous killers, but are disproportionately African Americans who killed whites; they are practically never whites who killed blacks (Gross & Mauro, 1989; Tonry, 1995a, pp. 42-43). In 1977, the Supreme Court ruled that capital punishment for rape is illegal because in the South, the only area where it was then much used, it was applied almost exclusively against blacks convicted for rape of whites, and not against whites who raped blacks (*Coker v. Georgia*, 431 U.S. 992; see also Bedau, 1982, pp. 58-61). Statutes authorizing capital punishment, Gross and Mauro (1989) point out, give courts

> the power to threaten to kill thousands, but to do it only to dozens. . . . One lesson is clear from experience: this is a power that we cannot exercise fairly and without discrimination. (p. 224)

Yale's Law Professor Charles L. Black, Jr., used the phrase "The Inevitability of Caprice and Mistake" as the subtitle for the first (1974) and the second (1981) editions of his book *Capital Punishment*. He contended that no statute has reliably distinguished, or can, the types of homicide for which it requires the death penalty from those that it exempts.

A further argument is that there are always questions about the basic causes of a murder. Was it the killer's heredity, or the way he or she was reared in childhood? Because no killers can choose either of these, are they fully responsible for their deadly acts? We excuse a murder if we ascribe it to mental illness or idiocy, but we often cannot identify these conditions with certainty. In Britain and in New York State, sharp declines in acquittals on grounds of insanity occurred when the death penalty ceased to be mandatory for first degree murder. (The defense of insanity is discussed in Chapter 7.) In a classic experiment, people were given descriptions of murder trials and asked to decide if the accused was guilty in each. A randomly selected half, who were told that death was the mandatory penalty for murder, acquitted the accused significantly more often than did those told that the penalty was life in prison (Hester & Smith, 1973). These findings imply that punishment is more certain, hence may have more deterrent value, if death is not a possible penalty.

Those who support capital punishment point out the presumed economy of killing a convicted murderer rather than paying for room, board, and guarding in prison until natural death. However, our efforts to avoid unwarranted executions result in so much extra time of trial and appellate courts in these cases, and of defense and prosecution lawyers, that the cost of a capital punishment case is several times the cost of a life term in prison. A New York study showed that it costs $660,000 to imprison a man for 40 years, but $1.8 million to execute him (Uelman, 1983). California's estimated capital case costs are $6,500 a day to operate a court room, including salaries of all personnel, for an average of 50 days, or $325,000; prosecution, including attorneys, investigators, and other staff and consultants, $400,000 to $500,000; defense, paid by the government unless the defendant is very affluent, $300,000 to $500,000, including investigators and advisers; 5 to 10 or more years are spent appealing death penalties to higher courts, at what can be an additional million or more in costs ($3 or $4 million if it goes to the U.S. Supreme Court), plus well over $20,000 per year for secure presentence confinement (Lindner, 1993).

Finally, one irrefutable argument against capital punishment is that when courts are mistaken about someone's guilt, the error cannot be corrected. Hundreds have been proved innocent after courts convicted them of crimes, including some sentenced to death or even executed (Huff, Rattner, & Sagarin, 1986; Prejean, 1994, pp. 218-221). No one knows what percentage of those convicted are completely innocent, but many claim it is at least several percent. Erroneous convictions are spurred by political pressure on police and prosecutors to solve notorious offenses and by their reliance on criminal informers, from whom they seek incriminating testimony in exchange for a reduction in charges or sentence or other inducements. Thomas Jefferson is quoted on the masthead of the *Quaker Service Bulletin* as having asserted: "I shall ask for the abolition of the punishment of death until I have the infallibility of human judgment demonstrated to me."

The possibility that the public may change its views on the death penalty was suggested by the inconsistent responses in a Field poll in California, published March 1, 1990. Although 80% of its telephoned sample favored the death penalty for murderers, 67% then said that rather than a sentence of death they would endorse a sentence of "life in prison without parole, with the requirement that convicts work in prison and give their pay to the victim's survivors."

However, polls that do not suggest alternative penalties find that most Americans would support the death penalty even if it proved no more deterrent than life imprisonment (Zimring & Hawkins, 1986, p. 16). Many people are comforted by a capital punishment law, even if not protected by it. "A life for a life" seems just. Faith that the death penalty reduces crime was compared in a 1989 cartoon by Marlette with ancient beliefs that a human sacrifice appeases the gods. Politicians regularly exploit such popular delusions, and pretend to be tougher on crime than their opponents because they were earlier or more vehemently for the death penalty. Feelings are often more influential than facts.

Domestic Violence

One of the most perplexing crimes of rage is *domestic violence*, assaults and even killings that take place between family members. A home should be a haven from the stresses and threats of the outside world; one's family should be a source of support and nurturance. Yet 40% of the violence suffered by adults at home comes from spouses, and another 19% from ex-spouses (Langan & Innes, 1986). As for the children, a quarter of a Kaiser Foundation national sample of 1,000 15- to 17-year-olds said that they had been beaten at home severely enough to have skin scarred or bruised, noses bloodied, or bones broken (*Los Angeles Times*, Dec. 7, 1995, pp. E1, E7).

Domestic violence is said to be the leading cause of injury to women. The April 20, 1993 *Los Angeles Times*, reporting on a national poll, asserted that, "More than 1 of 3 Americans say they have witnessed a man beating his wife or girl friend" (1 in 3 polled say they've seen women being beaten, *Los Angeles Times*, April 30, 1993, Part A).[1] Of course, some women do batter their husbands or boyfriends, and the rate may be rising. In Los Angeles, between 1987 and 1995, women rose from 7% to 14% of arrestees for do- mestic violence (J. Johnson, 1996). But American women rarely kill. When they do, their victim is most often a spouse or other male intimate. How- ever, only an eighth of murdered men are killed by their female partners, whereas more than half of murdered women are killed by their male partners (Frieze & Browne, 1989, p. 204).

Wife beating was legal in most of the world until recently, because a wife was considered her husband's property, as though she were his slave. A batterer typically claims a right to control his wife; his violence is part of a pattern of verbal insults, nagging, other nonviolent efforts to maintain dominance, and a sometimes successful effort to convince her of his right to authority (Barnett & LaViolette, 1993; Tifft, 1993). Because wife beating reflects the tradition of male dominance in our society, it has long been widely accepted by both the criminal justice system and the public at large. Police, neighbors, and social scientists viewed it as noncriminal unless life-endangering and were mostly unaware of its prevalence in American society. Only recently has wife beating been exposed to the kind of debate and policy making that may substantially reduce its occurrence.

Deterrence Versus Therapy
for Spouse Batterers

A landmark national study of intact families in the United States estimated that annually in 2 out of 3 families, one spouse threw something at the other; in 1 of 6, a spouse struck the other; in 3 of 200, one "beat up" the other; in 1 of 200, one of them used a knife or a gun (Strauss, Gelles, & Steinmetz, 1980).

Battering is correlated with poverty. In recent National Crime Surveys, women with family incomes under $10,000 reported 11 incidents of violence per 1,000 persons, as contrasted with a rate of only 2 per 1,000 for those with family incomes over $30,000. Within each income group, about the same average rates were reported by black, white, and Hispanic women, and by those in central cities, suburbs, and rural areas (Bureau of Justice Statistics, 1994). However, more blacks and Hispanics were poor.

The higher rates of reported violence in poor families seem to be partly due to more honesty about it there than in the middle class. If parents and children are questioned separately about spousal violence, they more often disagree in middle-class families than in lower-class families (Okun, 1986).

Frustration seems to be a common cause of spousal battery. Unemployed men have been shown to be twice as likely as full-time employed men to use severe violence on their wives. Unemployed men were also three times as likely to be beaten by their wives (Strauss et al., 1980). Similarly, battering is more likely to be used by high school or college dropouts than by graduates. One study found that men who are underachievers in relation to their level of education are more likely than others to use violence against their mates (Frieze & Browne, 1989). Battering is also reported to become more frequent when the wife is pregnant (*Los Angeles Times*, Dec. 3, 1995).

Like most interpersonal violence in our society, that between spouses is especially associated with drunkenness. Frieze and Browne (1989) summarize:

> Abusive men with severe alcohol or drug problems are apt to abuse their partners both when drunk and when sober, are violent more frequently, and inflict more serious injuries on their partners than do abusive men

who do not have a history of alcohol or drug problems. They are also
more apt to attack their partners sexually and are more likely to be violent
outside the home. (p. 192)

Although spouses of both genders are violent with each other, especially when both are drunk, the male is most often the initiator and is much
more likely to inflict serious injury. The subculture of violence held up as
a model to certain groups of American males may be a main source of this
battering. Some evidence for the influence of early socialization comes
from findings that domestic assaults typically occur more often in the
family from which the batterers come than in the homes of their abused
spouses (Pagelow, 1981, pp. 168-171).

The Battered Wife Syndrome

Wives do not usually call police when their husbands beat them, or if
they call, they soon decline to press charges. So prevalent is this pattern
that it has been dubbed the battered wife syndrome. The battered
woman's ineffectiveness in demanding better treatment seems to be due
to her fear of retaliation, her economic dependence on her husband
(especially when there are small children), her prior love for him, and,
usually, his later show of contrition. Economic dependence is apparently
a major factor. One of the best predictors that a battered wife will leave
her spouse is her own ample earnings.

Most marital quarrels are followed by forgiveness. Typically after
violence that occurs when both spouses have been drinking, guilt and
remorse come with sobriety, often to both. Lenore Walker (1984) noted a
three-phase cycle in spousal violence: (a) tension building; (b) the acute
battering incident; (c) loving contrition. Such cycles keep recurring, Jean
Giles-Sims (1983) pointed out, because contrition after a battering gratifies
both parties and reinforces the assailant's prior behavior. But repeated
contrition induces in the victim what Walker calls "learned helplessness,"
which is pleasing to the assailant but is destructive of the victim's ability
to seek, or even see, feasible alternatives to the abusive situation.

Many claim that if such cycles are not interrupted by drastic changes
in the relationship, the violence increases in frequency and severity. The
"last straw" that precipitates a prompt departure by the battered spouse
is usually an increased severity in beating, especially use of a weapon
(Okun, 1986).

Penalties and Remedies for Spouse Battery

In the past few decades, the women's movement has brought more attention to wife battering, which has led to research on the prevalence, distribution, and causes of this problem. Women's groups have also demanded enforcement of assault laws against batterers. But enforcement was at first quite lax. Extensive observation of police-citizen encounters by ride-along social scientists in 1977 in three metropolitan areas found that police chose not to arrest despite grounds to do so in 83% of marital violence cases (Sherman, 1992a). Male officers denied that their leniency came from sympathy with the batterers, pointing out that prosecutors are reluctant to file charges because the victims soon become unwilling to testify against their spouses.

Meanwhile, efforts by the women's movement resulted in a growing number of shelters for battered women in metropolitan areas, plus crisis hot lines to call for help, counseling, legal aid, and other assistance. One review observes:

> Shelters have received very high ratings for general helpfulness and for . . . decreasing violence. These ratings are based on "consumer survey" studies rather than on measurements of violence before and after shelter residency. (Saunders & Azar, 1992, p. 204)

Interestingly, the rates of women killing men have dropped most in the states that have increased help for battered women (Browne & Williams, 1989).

Courts often mandate that the assailant in a wife-battering case get counseling (sometimes with his wife), post a money bond to be forfeited if battering recurs, and live away from home temporarily. This sort of penalty is especially difficult to enforce on poor spouses. Also, rigorous evaluations fail to confirm the effectiveness of court-mandated treatments (Hamberger & Hastings, 1993).

The Domestic Abuse Intervention Program (DAIP) of Duluth, Minnesota, has been an influential effort to implement court-mandated treatment. It requires that police bring in spouse batterers, by arrest if necessary, and protect the victim by enforcing any court sanctions. It also provides safe housing, if needed. In addition, it imposes on one or both spouses a court-mandated 12-week group counseling program in anger management and related cognitive themes, plus a 12-week program of education on abusive behavior and thought. DAIP collects information from all agencies involved in order to monitor these programs. An evaluation indicates considerable dropout, however, much of it occurring when one or both spouses leave the area, and finds no clear evidence of predominant reform of the remaining couples. Yet this Duluth effort is reported to have been copied in at least 20 cities, including Milwaukee and Baltimore (Hamberger & Hastings, 1993, p. 215; Tifft, 1993, pp. 126-130, 184-185).

Another program that was once much copied was one in New York City. It trained police to counsel people in family quarrels instead of arresting them. The main claim for the program's success was that counseled victims called police about further assaults more often than did uncounseled victims, which was viewed as evidence that victims were satisfied with their counseling (Bard, 1970).

This policy was dramatically reversed after 1985, however, when a controlled experiment in Minneapolis was much publicized. In this research, police responding to calls about home quarrels were directed, in a random sequence, to use only one of three approaches: advise and mediate; order the alleged aggressor to leave the home for 8 hours; arrest. The lowest rate of renewed violence in the next 6 months followed arrest, although almost half the arrestees were released the same day and only 14% were held for more than a week. The experiment was done in very poor neighborhoods, and more of the couples were unmarried than current or ex-spouses (Sherman, 1992a; Sherman & Berk, 1984).

In the National Crime Survey, the women who reported domestic battering and who called the police had less repetition of violence than those who did not call the police (Langan & Innes, 1986). Women injured in subsequent attacks cited the Minneapolis experiment in suing police for prior failure to arrest the men who battered them (Sherman & Cohn, 1989; Steinman, 1988).

The National Institute of Justice funded five replications of the Minneapolis experiment, in different cities, and usually in better neighborhoods with fewer unmarried couples. But the results challenged the prior study's conclusions: No matter what the police did in Omaha, Milwaukee, Indianapolis, Miami, or Charlotte, North Carolina, the researchers found no significant differences in battering recurrence rates (Buzawa & Buzawa, 1996, pp. 112-120). In fact, some cities reported more recurrence of battering by arrestees than by nonarrestees.

These are the conclusions supported by research findings thus far in all cities:

◆ Arrest consistently reduces spousal beatings by employed suspects more than it does beatings by unemployed suspects (Berk, Cambell, Klap, & Western, 1992; Sherman, 1992a, p. 32, 1992b, chap. 1). Those who work have a stake in their jobs that makes arrest a deterrent for them.

◆ The weaker a suspect's social bonds, the more likely it is that arrest will increase subsequent violence (Sherman, 1992a, 1992b).

◆ "Sanctions are likelier to deter wife beaters with less severe histories than those with more severe histories" for this offense (Fagan, 1993).

◆ In about half of domestic violence calls to the police, the accused is gone by the time the police arrive. In these cases, notifying the household that the local prosecutor will issue a warrant for the arrest of the accused apparently reduces further beatings even more than arresting the accused when present. This was a surprising finding of the Omaha replication (Sherman, 1992b, p. 16).

In short, formal penalties, such as arrest, work only for those with a stake in conformity to the law, which may be derived from being employed, never before being arrested, or being formally married (rather than informally cohabiting) (Sherman, Smith, Schmidt, & Rogan, 1992).

Policies for responding to wife beating remain diverse, confusing, and contradictory. Despite "the debate regarding research findings . . . 40 states have mandatory arrest statutes of some kind which are not likely to be overturned anytime soon" (Mignon & Holmes, 1995, p. 440); yet in about two thirds of the conflicts between intimates for which police are called, arrests are not made (p. 433). Counties vary in their willingness to allow a battered wife to drop charges after prosecution begins, but an Indianapolis experiment suggests that the probability of renewed battering following a warrant arrest declines where the wife is permitted to drop charges (Ford & Regoli, 1993).

In the long run, the optimum policies to reduce spouse-battering rates include more and better education and counseling for marriage. The major factors in this crime's eventual decline are likely to be women's progress in achieving the same occupational statuses and compensation levels as men, plus a more equitable division of child care and housekeeping tasks, so that spouses have more equal and collaborative roles.

Remedies for Child Battering and Neglect

Even more than wife beating, violence of parents or guardians against children has long been viewed as outside the law's domain. Children are regarded as possessions of their real or surrogate parents. Indeed, the killing of children, especially in infancy, was until recently accepted in many countries as a parent's prerogative. Of course, children are usually the members of a household least able to resist assault, and they are most often aggravating in their conduct. About 90% of American parents sometimes spank their children. But the violence that concerns us here is too severe for justification as discipline.

Interest in child battering surged after much publicity was given a 1962 article in the *Journal of the American Medical Association* titled "The Battered Child Syndrome," by physician Harry Kempe and associates (Kempe, Silverman, Steele, Droegemueller, & Silver, 1962). The syndrome includes broken bones imperfectly healed because the children were not taken to physicians, black-and-blue areas, and bruises. Many nurses, teachers, and physicians reported that they frequently saw these symptoms in children but that the parents ascribed them to accidents. If the child disagreed, the parent's word was accepted by other adults.

Child battering is a crime with far-reaching consequences. Children, in dealing with younger siblings and later with their own children and spouses, copy parental patterns of habitual threats or acts of violence (Strauss & Gelles, 1990). Unless they learn other patterns elsewhere, this is the only type of reaction they regard as proper.

As with wife beating, researchers find child battering most often in the poorest and least educated families, but it is far from absent in the middle and upper classes. Many adults have unrealistic expectations of small children and can readily be roused to a fury by normal childishness. Adult anger at a child's sloppy eating, breaking of things, lack of toilet training, or crying often gets out of control. Many adults slap and shake infants and toddlers to make them stop crying, but usually such young children respond only by crying harder; if violence then becomes more vigorous, serious injuries or death may result. Most homicide of children under age 4 is by family members. Extreme reactions are most common in young and inexperienced parents or stepparents, especially under stress, and in baby-sitters who have not been parents.

Often linked with child battering is the crime of child neglect, which includes any inexcusable failure to give a child food, shelter, or care. Neglect may express either indifference or anger at being a parent. Contributing to the delinquency of a minor by engaging in crime with a child, encouraging absence from school, or abandoning a child are other legally punished parenting offenses. They have higher rates with stepparents than with biological parents but occur with both, and only a small fraction are prosecuted.

Violence toward or neglect of children used to be prevented mostly by having enough relatives and neighbors around to share in child care. Grandparents, aunts, uncles, older siblings, and others all helped parents when needed. This sharing persists where traditions support it, as in most Asian and Latin American countries where extended families are close, but it has diminished in the United States as families have scattered and broken up. A more feasible optimum alternative to care by the extended family is for several families to cooperate in caring for each other's children. However, commercial child care is the usual alternative, with quite variable cost and quality.

Instruction on child care for actual and prospective parents is a preventive for child battery and neglect that seems to be growing in popularity. Missouri in 1984 was the first state to mandate such instruction in all its school districts. By 1990, 53,000 prospective parents had been taught in its Parents as Teachers (PAT) program, for which enrollment could begin as early as the third trimester of pregnancy and continue for 3 years after birth. The PAT program includes both classroom instruction and individual home visits. The volunteer instructors were 1,400 selected parents who had completed a 34-hour training course (Walters, 1990). Many states, notably Hawaii, have federally assisted "Healthy Start" programs that send trained visitors to stressed mothers to improve family functioning, enhance child health, and prevent abuse (Earle, 1995).

After the Kempe group's 1962 article on the battered child syndrome, state and local governments increasingly required that teachers, nurses, and physicians report symptoms of child battering to the police. To reform child batterers, courts frequently had parents attend presumably therapeutic sessions with similar parents, often in organizations such as Parents United or Parents Anonymous. The latter group, founded in 1970, now has over 1,200 local branches. Most participants are mothers, but the severest battering is ascribed to fathers and stepfathers, who rarely attend. Mothers usually attend Parents Anonymous under court orders mandating attendance if they are to gain or retain custody of their children. Graduate students who attended Parents Anonymous as researchers have described the participants as lonely women, self-righteously denying that they mistreated their children, and blaming the judge for requiring their attendance at these meetings. While there, they were more preoccupied with gossip and small talk about their social lives than with parenting problems. Competent instruction and testing on effective parenting seems preferable to such nondirective group therapy for incompetent parents.

Another possible treatment is behavior modification. Psychologists have developed programmed texts and classes to instruct parents on how to make rewards and penalties contingent on their children's behavior. They ask parents to keep records on their children's pleasing and displeasing conduct, their reactions to it, and the sequence of verbal and gestural exchanges between them and the children that culminate in violence. Discussion of these records with psychologists, or simply recording these details, increases parents' insight into their child care problems and thus helps defuse the escalation of anger that may create a crisis.

Conclusion

Social feedback frequently escalates the anger of persons who are engaged in "character contests," especially in the presence of an audience. Violence is a last resort of those unable "to save face" by words in such contests, especially when drunk. Anger then expressed in lethal acts is therefore often over trivial issues.

Rates of homicide in an area increase with indices of economic inequality, ethnic diversity, and percentage of teenagers. Although depictions of violence in the mass media are often blamed for high violence rates in our society, research indicates that the media prompt violence only in those already inclined to it. The most influential models of violence for young people are assaultive parents.

Some feel that more stringent gun control would greatly reduce homicides. But eliminating or greatly limiting private ownership of guns in the United States would be difficult and is likely to remove more guns from the hands of law-abiding citizens than of criminals. Yet the number of guns can slowly be reduced, which probably would cut homicide, suicide, and robbery rates, as well as fatal accidents.

Capital punishment, another alleged remedy for violence, is geographically associated with higher rather than lower homicide rates, and its abolition or restoration has not generally altered these rates. Those who are sentenced to death constitute a haphazardly selected, very small (less than 1%) subgroup of convicted murderers. When the penalty for homicide is so indefinite, it has little deterrent value. The years of waiting for final decisions in capital cases further reduces their possible deterrent effect. Furthermore, court proceedings in these cases create legal costs for the government several times the cost of life imprisonment. Death is clearly an unprofitable penalty.

Domestic violence is a crime of rage that has been difficult to control. Police traditionally avoided intervening if called for wife beating. When they experimented with arresting the assailants, the results were contradictory. The need remains for more adequate research on which interventions work best for what types of spouse beaters. But the best bet for reducing this crime seems to be changes in our culture that produce more equality for men and women.

Children are the most battered persons in our society. Police intervention in child beating has surged since medical revelation in the 1960s of how frequently it causes serious injuries. Education in parenting may be the best preventive. It can be provided routinely in schools for everyone and as a condition of probation for offenders.

In fact, the best preventive for all crimes of rage is more training and modeling of ways to handle one's anger. Many persons, at all ages, can improve their ability to settle differences amicably, especially by participating in organizations with democratic rather than authoritative decision making. Penalties that provide such training and experience in orderly interaction before release from confinement or discharge from probation, are likely to be more profitable than those striving to maintain dictatorial control on all details of an offender's conduct at all times.

Note

1. *L. A.Times*, Apr. 20, 1993. Reprinted by permission.

7

Suppressing Sex Crimes

The crimes discussed in this chapter are committed by persons who criminally seek sex with someone who does not want it or who cannot make sound judgments about it. These include rape, sexual molestation of children, and indecent exposure. Although those who commit sex crimes are expressing the passion of sexual lust, sexual arousal may or may not actually occur.

In sex crimes, especially in rape cases, lust is often mixed with rage. Lenore Walker (1984) found that 59% of battered women reported being forced to have sex with their assaulter after being beaten. Child batterers also often sexually abuse their victims.

The most sensationalized sex crimes involving adults tend to be cases of rapists who also murder their victims. In recent years, as well, the issue of acquaintance rape has been a topic of discussion on college campuses and talk shows. But the sex crime that most inflames the public these days involves the sexual molestation of children. A number of laws have been passed, at both the state and federal levels, that aim to prevent and punish the sexual exploitation of children. This chapter examines the causes of such crimes and some methods for preventing and penalizing specific types of sex offenders, who are thought to differ in some important respects. But it also examines some penalties and treatment methods advocated for all types of sex offenders, in the hopes of repairing inappropriate sexual attitudes and controlling inappropriate behavior.

The chapter ends with an investigation of insanity, idiocy, and incompetency defenses for passionate crimes, including crimes of rage, panic, fear, and lust. Sex crimes, in particular, seem to raise questions about the sanity of offenders. The public may have some understanding of how anger becomes rage, but most people have a hard time understanding how sexual desire can be transmuted into attacks involving both bizarre sexual practices and extreme expressions of rage. The dilemma is how to punish someone who has committed a heinous crime without comprehension.

Forcible Rape

Rape was long defined by law as a man's use of force or the threat of force to have sexual intercourse with a woman not his wife, against her will. This is the classic definition of *forcible rape*. The law also included having sex with a woman when she was unconscious or too mentally deficient, deranged, or young to be lawfully capable of consent. (Unlawful sexual intercourse with someone who is too young is classified as *statutory rape* as opposed to forcible rape.) In this legal tradition, rape is viewed as a form of theft that takes away much of a woman's "value" to other men.

Note that the traditional definition of rape excludes wives as victims. A marriage license was thus not only a hitting license (as Chapter 6 explains), but also, a license for sex—whenever the husband wanted it. Webster's dictionary does not exclude spouses when defining rape, and wives knew when their husbands raped them, but the law did not. Beginning in the 1970s, women's groups tried to change laws on *spousal rape*, and by 1992 they had succeeded completely or in part in all the states but North Carolina and Oklahoma (Allison & Wrightsman, 1993, p. 89; Russell, 1994, appendix III). Although about one seventh of samples of ever-married women over 18 tell interviewers that their husbands have raped them, spousal rape is rarely reported to the police and even more rarely prosecuted (Russell, 1994, chap. 5).

Rape in general was long one of the most underreported crimes in police statistics because women who reported it could expect to be leered at by male officers, repeatedly questioned by police and prosecutors, badgered on the witness stand by defense attorneys as though they were the accused, and embarrassed by snide or skeptical remarks from others, even from members of their own families. Especially in the four out of five cases when the rape is by an acquaintance rather than a stranger and when it occurs on dates (so-called acquaintance rape or date rape), the victim is treated as though "she asked for it."

This situation has changed somewhat because of promotion by the women's movement of counseling and other assistance to rape victims.

Many women have been educated to report rape promptly to the police, without first washing away the evidence. Hospitals are given "rape kits" containing glass slides for collecting semen, and envelopes or other containers to collect hair, skin from under fingernails, and other evidence useful in prosecuting rapists. Designated nurses are specially trained to use these kits, and large hospitals try always to have one such nurse on hand (Martin, DiNitto, Maxwell, & Norton, 1985). Unfortunately, these programs have often been eliminated because of their cost and infrequent use.

Rape victims are said to be at first dazed and disorganized and then to suffer tremors, nausea, insomnia or nightmares, irritability, loss of appetite, and inability to concentrate. These effects last for weeks or months, or they may quickly stop but recur much later. Often rape victims are traumatized enough to leave jobs, homes, or schools. They have major disruptions in relationships with men, including breakups of engagements or marriages; mothers become excessively irritable with their children (Allison & Wrightsman, 1993, chap. 8). Over a fourth of female suicide attempters are said to be rape victims (Katz & Mazur, 1979).

During the past few decades, crime reports have shown the incidence of rape to be increasing. Most police announcements of rape rate increases have been spurious, however. The only change has been a rise in the percentage of rape incidents in which the police were notified. The National Crime Survey's findings from 1970 to 1992 show a 22% drop in rape rates, from 1.8 to 1.4 annually per 100,000 females age 12 or over. But among women who reported that they were raped, the percentage who said that they notified the police of the offense increased by two thirds, from about 30% to more than 50% (Bureau of Justice Statistics, 1991, table 6; 1994, tables 3, 101).

Although adult women seem to be learning how to cope assertively with rape, girls and young women still tend to suffer in silence. The National Youth Survey, which annually contacted a representative sample of 1,700 youngsters 17 to 19 years old, found that about 8% of the girls reported being sexually assaulted in the preceding year. Of these, only 1 in 20 said she notified the police, and less than 1 in 4 informed her parents. About 70% told their friends, and almost all said that only the friends were concerned and supportive; parents and others frequently were described as more condemning than sympathetic (Ageton, 1983).

Despite their advances in combating forcible rape, most women report fear of rape, whether or not from personal experience. Their estimates of the probability of being raped are much higher than actual risks (Gordon & Riger, 1989).

Cultural Causes of Rape

Forcible rape is an artifact of traditional views on the relationship between the sexes. As mentioned earlier, as long as wives are viewed as the property of their husbands, or women are viewed as subservient to men, husbands consider it their right to demand sex with their wives. In addition, in a male-dominated society, men rationalize rape by the second of two double standards described in Chapter 5 regarding prostitution: They judge women as bad or good according to whether the women seem promiscuous. This mentality still leads many men to feel they have a right to "go all the way" whenever "going part way" is easier than they expected. "Meaning stretchers" are young men who misinterpret gestures of friendship or affection from their dates or other women, especially with those who were easier "pick ups" than they had expected.

In addition, of course, attitudes and propensities toward violence are inculcated at an early age. One study followed up 908 persons who as children had suffered neglect or physical or sexual abuse, and a control group of 667 similar children not known to have been mistreated (Widom, 1995). The abused were found to be about four times as likely as the control group to be arrested later for a sex crime, and the neglected were about twice as likely as the control group to get such an arrest. Sexually abused girls who were later arrested for sex crimes tended to be accused of prostitution. Boys abused physically or sexually, or neglected, were later more likely than the control group to be arrested for rape or for other illegal sex acts. The early mistreatment of these children, perhaps within a culture of violence in their neighborhoods, may have fostered both their early victimization by others and their own violence.

Much acquaintance or date rape also evolves from "rating and dating" subcultures, which begin in middle school, are perhaps emphasized most by high school students, but are still widespread thereafter among unmarried adults. In such subcultures, prestige with peers and self-esteem depend greatly on popularity and on attractiveness to popular members of the opposite sex. This attitude is evident in male conversations that exaggerate success in "scoring" with women. Such braggarts, plus popular pornography, motivate other males to seek sexual conquests as a sign of their manliness. Some who fail at seduction try increasingly drastic

ways to "score," culminating in rape. Or when several young men together pick up one or more young women, a rivalry may develop as to
who will be the most successful seducer. The result is the frequently
reported rapes at fraternity parties (Sanday, 1990) or by gangs.

When I worked in an Illinois youth prison, the convicted rapists with
little or no prior criminal records that I met were youths who had experienced neither realistic sex education nor friendships with girls or with
more experienced males. When they heard other boys' sex talk in high
school and read pornography, they misconceived how women are sexually aroused and moved too rapidly and too roughly for sexual intimacy
with women they hardly knew. When rebuffed they became more desper-
ate, stalked women, and after unsuccessful attempts without a weapon,
used a weapon as a threat to gain submission. Their parents, of course,
were shocked when their sons were arrested. In one case, when the son
was released on bail, his father took him to a prostitute to introduce him
to unforced sex.

Unrealistic attitudes about sex are often intertwined with cultural
acceptance of violence in relationships with the opposite sex. In a Los
Angeles high school survey, 43% of the boys and 46% of the girls reported
being subjected to violence by dates one or more times (O'Keefe, in press;
O'Keefe & Treister, in press). In this sample, 84% were juniors or seniors,
and half classified themselves as from families of low social-economic
status, with 53% Latino, 13% African American, 20% white, 7% Asian
American, and 7% "other." The most common aggressive acts, experienced by about a third of each gender, were "pushing, grabbing, or
shoving." Also frequent were throwing objects at or slapping the date.
Nearly 10% reported use or threat of a knife or gun against them by their
date. One sixth of the girls and a tenth of the boys asserted that their date
forced sexual acts on them. Interviews indicated cultural norms that a girl
should respond physically to boys who "get fresh."

Prevention of Forcible Rape

The AIDS epidemic, by increasing fear of infection during sexual intercourse, may reduce male pursuit of sex outside of marriage. Yet rape will
be fully prevented only when all men learn that female desire and arousal,
as well as male sexual satisfaction, depend on mutual affection and
respect. This insight is incompatible with the delusions on female sexual
psychology conveyed by pornography, which should be countered by

realistic sex education and discussion in homes, schools, churches, and elsewhere.

Women looking for an effective way to stop men from forcing sex on them have a dilemma: Should they appeal to the potential rapist's better nature, or should they fight? Statistics indicate that reasoning may stop a young and inept "seducer," but it is unlikely to stop an aggressive man. Screaming and struggling will either make the attacker flee (especially if others might hear) or will impede sexual penetration, but it may also evoke greater violence. Fighting the attacker is most risky in the one fourth of rapes in which the male has a deadly weapon (Allison & Wrightsman, 1993, chap. 12).

Suzanne Ageton's (1983) advice for preventing rape, from studying teenage victims, is that women should

- Check their own behavior for any unintended sexual messages to a man
- Be alert to unwanted sexual cues from men
- Clearly communicate their sexual limits
- React immediately and negatively to unwanted sexual pressure

For safety, women should depart promptly from any man who uses or threatens physical violence and then avoid him.

Profitable Penalties for Rape

In prosecuted rapes, most rapists are strangers to the victim. But in confidential surveys, 80% of women who report rape identify the men as someone they knew. The closer the prior relationship, the less likely the woman is to report the rape to the police, and if reported, the less probable its prosecution.

The fear that they will be humiliated in court has long prevented women from proceeding with rape prosecutions. Since the 1970s, however, the women's movement has helped to change laws and rulings that once put the burden of proof on the rape victim. It is now much less necessary for prosecutors of rape to prove that the victim resisted vigorously, and the defense can no longer refer to the woman's prior sex life to discredit rape charges. Drastic legal reform came first to Michigan, in 1974. Police and prosecutors said that Michigan's changes made rape cases more "winnable." Reports of forcible rape in that state increased 30% from 1972 to 1977, arrests rose 62%, and convictions for the most brutal types of rapes grew 90%. Less drastic laws in California did not much affect arrest and conviction rates, but penalties became severer (Allison & Wrightsman, 1993, chaps. 9, 10; Polk, 1985).

With rapists, as with other lawbreakers, prior criminality best predicts the methods that will most effectively reform them. Recidivism rates are lowest for those who have strong bonds with conventional persons, no prior criminal record, and stable school or work histories. They are likely to get much benefit from counseling that gives them practice in communicating with women, even with rape victims, as has been provided at a few prisons and mental hospitals (Brecher, 1978).

Rapists' recidivism rates not only for rape, but also for other crimes, increase with the number and variety of their prior juvenile and adult offenses. In a Dutch study of persistence in serious crime, rapists and robbers with prior criminal records were the two categories of released prisoners who had the highest recidivism rates (Block & van der Werff, 1990).

Rapes range in rapidity from a sudden attack by an unseen assailant to a gradually more persistent physical domination by a date who is at first gentle and endearing. Many sudden rapists are versatile predators who, while prowling to commit a burglary or other crime, encounter a woman alone. In this and other offenses, they arrogantly seize anything they desire that they think they can get away with. The most criminalized offenders, as Chapter 9 concludes, are profitably curbed only by long confinement.

Statutory Rape

Male sex with a female below the "age of consent," which is 16 or 18 in most states but younger in some, is a crime even if the two engage in sex by mutual consent or if she seduces him. Criminologists and often the law call such a crime *statutory rape*, but it has different names in various state laws; in California, it is one form of "unlawful sexual intercourse."

In some states, statutory rape is simply one form of the crime of rape and may receive the same penalties. In practice, however, statutory rape is punished less severely than forcible rape or not prosecuted at all, especially if male and female are about the same age.

The federal Centers for Disease Control in January 1991 announced that in 1988, 52% of women ages 15 to 19 said in confidential polling that they had engaged in premarital sex, including 70% of 18-year-olds. This finding suggests that most young women today have been statutorily raped. A

1989 National Opinion Research Center poll showed that decline in sexual activity from fear of AIDS was widespread but occurred least among teenagers—again indicating that sex before the age of consent is common.

Aware of such statistics on early sex, legislators in several states tried to lower their state's age of consent to 14 or 15, with variable success. Such changes in law prevent much statutory rape simply by redefining it. The rationale seems to be that sexual activity, at any age for which sex by mutual consent is popular (and certainly that seems to be the case for older teenagers), is probably not readily curtailed by the threat of criminal punishment, because sexual activity is unlikely to be viewed by these participants as victimizing. However, the seduction of girls in their early teens, especially by more mature males, is exploitative. Lowering the age of consent to one where sex is infrequent and usually condemned and making the penalty severer when there is a large age difference between participants may make such acts more shameful.

More profitable than changing the criminal law on youngsters engaging in sex is educating them about their risks, especially the risks of pregnancy and of AIDS and other sexually transmitted diseases. Many persons oppose sex education in the schools, believing that it implies adult approval of sex at a young age. Yet high school sex instruction, plus clinics giving contraceptive advice or assistance, do reduce unwanted pregnancies and sexually transmitted diseases.

Sexual Molestation of Children

Adults of all ages customarily show affection to children by a pat on the head, a caress, a hug, a pinch on the cheek. A few go beyond these innocent gestures to stroke and feel children's genitals, get children to feel their genitals, or engage in sex acts with children. Men commit most of this misconduct, some molesting young girls and others young boys; 97% of arrestees for child molestation are males (Greenfield, 1996). An adult's craving for child sex partners is called *pedophilia*, and male sex acts with young boys are called *pederasty*.

Pedophiles range in age from teens to the elderly. Convicted pedophiles over 50 are conspicuous in prisons because most men there for other crimes are younger. Pedophiles, in contrast to rapists, usually do not have prior records of other types of lawbreaking. However, two thirds of state prisoners convicted of rape or sexual assault had victims under 18, and half of the victims were under 12, so that these prisoners, too, are child molesters.

Surveys find that 20% to 30% of adult women recall being sexually molested when they were young girls, generally by men they knew from home or the neighborhood. Many men also report being sexually molested in childhood, often homosexually. Three fourths of child-molestation victims are females, however (Greenfield, 1996).

For both sexes, the most frequent childhood sexual molestation is from schoolmates, as part of the teasing or bullying common among children. The *Los Angeles Times* on June 2, 1993, reported national survey findings that 4 in 5 American teenagers had suffered sexual harassment in school, and 1 in 10 "had been forced to commit a sexual act, beyond kissing, during school hours" (*Los Angeles Times*, June 2, 1993).[1] A fourth of the girls and a 10th of the boys reported sexual harassment by school employees.

Psychotherapists who try to get their adult patients to articulate "repressed memories" of being abused during their childhood, especially by their parents or other close relatives, have generated much controversy recently. Some prosecutions and suits based on the recovery of repressed memories have succeeded, but in many cases the courts have ruled that the memories came from the therapists' suggestions, sometimes to patients whom they had first hypnotized. Because children tend to say what they think adults wish to hear, some commentators assert that "sexual accuse" is a more frequent problem than sexual abuse. Others, however, claim that less than 10% of the charges are fictitious (Saunders & Azar, 1992). At this time, we have neither exact knowledge of the dimensions of this problem nor satisfactory solutions to it.

Causes of Child Molestation

Generally, clinicians have the impression that most adult child molesters themselves suffered molestation as children, which was seldom reported to the police and, indeed, was usually unknown to anyone but the participants. But no well-validated research has produced a definitive answer about the motivations of child molesters.

However, some psychiatrists to whom many of these cases have been referred, notably Adele Mayer (1985), offer persuasive theories. Mayer identifies three types of child molester:

- *Regressed pedophiles:* They act out with children their adolescent sex fantasies when frustrated as adults. Although seldom arrested for this crime until older, many regressed pedophiles reveal to psychiatrists that they started fondling children sexually when they were teenagers. Most then stop because of society's taboos, and gain interest in adult females, but revert to child molesting in later years, particularly when drunk. Typically, arrestees either insist they were only fondling the child with no sexual intent, or they blame it on drunkenness.

• *Fixated pedophiles:* They persist, from an early age on, in seeking sex only from children. Although some marry, they continue their pedophilia intermittently. Many seek homosexual acts with teenage boys, whom they pay. For decades, youths from poor neighborhoods found quick money for a heterosexual date from such a homosexual source, a pattern that Reiss (1961) called "the social integration of queers and peers." In large cities, so-called chicken hawks are pimps for this market; for a fee they recruit runaway boys, or "chickens," to send to adult male customers. Frequently, fixated pedophiles are assaulted and robbed by the youths they approach.

• *Mysopedics:* They are the rarest but most dangerous type of pedophile. They are sadistic, often homicidal. Revelations that they have raped, tortured, killed, dismembered, and in a few cases, even eaten portions of children, as well as adults, shock the world. Notorious examples are Chicago's suburban contractor John Wayne Gacy, who buried scores of bodies of his male victims under the cement of his basement, and Milwaukee's cannibalistic Jeffrey Dahmer. Although mysopedics are often regarded as insane, courts define many as sane and sentence them to prison or to death, rather than committing them to a mental hospital.

Prevention of Child Molestation

Many pedophiles have great interest in pornographic movies and publications with pictures of children involved in sex acts. Internationally distributed copies of "kiddie porn" magazines—with such English titles as *Lollitots, How to Pick Up Little Girls,* and *Where the Young Ones Are*—are reported to be sold in the tens of thousands. Suppression of such publications would help prevent child molestation, but suppression is, of course, much limited by concern for freedom of the press under the First Amendment to the U.S. Constitution and by difficulty in formulating legally adequate definitions for obscenity or pornography. Thus suppression of child pornography is only partially achieved by local zoning ordinances, state laws, and U.S. postal regulations.

"Target hardening" is another possible preventative. It includes teaching children to avoid strangers and keeping them under the surveillance of responsible adults. However, the predominance of employed parents and the high rate of divorce in the United States today produce a growing number of latchkey children who have no adults at home when they finish their day at school. Many pedophiles befriend these children at video-game places, parks, and other locales where children congregate when school is out. "Lighted schoolhouse" programs or other well-supervised neighborhood youth centers, and sometimes collaborative or government-subsidized child care, all discussed in Chapter 4, could alleviate the problem.

Profitable Penalties for Child Molestation

First-offense child molesters, like other first-timers, have relatively low recidivism rates (Romero & Williams, 1985). Those who do recidivate, however, tend to repeat the same type of crime, for they seem to be Mayer's (1985) fixated type. Most insist that they were always falsely accused, but when charges are made each time by different people and in scattered places, it seems unlikely that the accused were innocent.

Criminal prosecution of child molesters is handicapped by the uncertain quality of many child victims as witnesses. Much research is now directed to assessing and improving children's recall, and to reducing their susceptibility to suggestions on what to report (Zaragoza, Graham, Hall, Hirschan, & Ben Porath, 1995).

There is also concern that the repeated interrogation of child victims by family, police, prosecutors, and defense lawyers may not only be suggestive, but also psychologically damaging. Sweden and Israel pioneered in having social workers, in locations outside the courts, get the testimony of child witnesses to crimes. They ask the children questions that attorneys submit to the judge, who may edit those that are leading or otherwise objectionable. Audio- or videotapes of interrogation sessions are then played in the court. Efforts to duplicate such practices in the United States have been impeded because the Sixth Amendment to our Constitution guarantees accused persons the right to be confronted by the witnesses against them. Yet prosecution and defense sometimes agree to accept depositions that children give out of court.

Psychotherapists usually insist that a child molester's reformation is impossible until he admits guilt. Many never do. Usually the sexually abused child is returned to the family home, sometimes even when the abuser lives there, although the abuser may be on probation and required to receive therapy. Diverse treatment approaches have not been well tested, but some claim success (Saunders & Azar, 1992).

Because of the fear of pedophilia, loitering around a schoolyard is now a misdemeanor in most jurisdictions. Parental fears often exceed the reality, however, which has created malicious accusations against innocent adults. Employees or volunteers at day care centers, scout troops, and schools—often highly respected persons—have been removed permanently from their positions after being charged with child molestation. They are then terribly stigmatized not only if convicted, but even if fully exonerated. Such mistakes also create the continuing danger of giving children excessive fear of strangers, making parents even more hysterical, and producing further false accusations.

Indecent Exposure

Many women have been startled by a man's suddenly exposing his genitals to them. This sex crime, commonly called "flashing," is ascribed almost exclusively to males. About 20% of women college students say that they have encountered flashing; because this crime's victims include females of all ages, it is probable that most will eventually have such an experience. But a majority of these acts are unreported to the police.

Exposing genitalia is labeled "exhibitionism" by psychiatrists, who define it as

> the expressed impulse to expose the male genitals to an unsuspecting female as a final sexual gratification. This definition excludes exposure which preludes sexual contact, occurs in the context of public urination or intoxication, or results from severe mental disorders. (Cox, 1980, p. 4)

Exhibitionism is legally prosecuted in different states as "indecent exposure," "public indecency," or "lewdness."

Such an act victimizes a woman by invading her privacy. "Exhibitionists," Goffman (1963) observed, "spectacularly subvert the protective social control that keeps individuals interpersonally distant," so that they entrap their victims into encounters that they can "neither immediately escape . . . nor properly sustain" (p. 143). Sharon Davis (1978) found that women confronted by a flasher tend to blame themselves for his behavior.

About two thirds of all men convicted of this offense in Los Angeles County in 1984 were masturbating when they exposed themselves (Glaser & Gordon, 1990a). Women are frightened by this sight, but flashing is rarely followed by assaultive conduct. Most of these offenders seem to seek attention but are frightened if their audience moves toward them. Most disconcerting to a flasher are the few women who laugh at him.

Flashing is different from conduct in nudist cults, for nudity advocates usually isolate themselves from public view in their own camp or other facilities. If invisible to outsiders, nudists victimize no one anymore than does a person alone in a closed bathroom or bedroom, away from transparent windows; if prosecuted, however, nudists get criminal charges identical to those used against flashers who try to be seen by non-nudists.

Meyer (1992, p. 96) reports that exhibitionism usually begins during adolescence and peaks in the middle or late twenties; most arrested flashers range in age from the teens to mid-thirties, and some are older. Nearly half of the flashers in the Los Angeles study were married, a 10th were formerly married, and the rest were never married. Many exposed themselves from their home windows or from autos, and could therefore be readily traced by the police. Fines and probation with a mandate to procure psychotherapy seem to be the most profitable penalties for flashers, but the effects of these penalties on recidivism have not been assessed well.

Penalties and Treatments for All Sex Offenders

For a sex crime—particularly serial rape, homicidal rape, child molestation, or even more bizarre sexual behavior—prosecutors often request psychiatric examination and perhaps a civil court hearing initially, then drop criminal charges if the court orders mental hospitalization. Judges also refer many sex offenders for presentence evaluation by psychiatrists. In a study in an Ohio metropolis, however, Walsh (1994) found that sex offenders receiving any psychiatric diagnosis were almost certain to get a prison sentence, despite most psychiatrists recommending probation; also, similar offenders not referred to psychiatrists were given probation. Judges seemed to view any medical label as a criminal stigma.

In some states, all imprisoned sex offenders receive psychiatric examinations for possible mental hospital confinement before release on parole or discharge. Almost all releasees are diagnosed as "in remission" of any mental illness. But many states mandate therapy for all sex offenders, with programs in prisons or mental hospitals to treat those of every type, often in largely identical ways. Therapists often have male heterosexual offenders role-play themselves and their victims, and may invite actual victims or other women to discussion groups with these inmates. The visitors express women's views of these crimes, and give the inmates guidance in being at ease and behaving properly with women. Such sessions are often videotaped, then viewed and analyzed in subsequent sessions.

More research is needed on the effectiveness of this and other methods of treating sex offenders, including behavior modification, castration and brain surgery, and mandatory postrelease registration of sex offenders. At present, it is uncertain which are profitable. In addition, some of these treatments raise difficult legal, moral, and practical issues.

Learning-Theory Approaches

The treatment technique known as Relapse Prevention, based on social learning theory, views sex crimes as addictions for which the offender must be taught behavioral self-management (Laws, 1989). First, individuals must learn to recognize High Risk Situations (HRS), which are situations like those that have preceded their past offenses. For a pedophile, for instance, an HRS might consist of children alone in a shaded park; for a rapist, it might be a lone adult female. Sex offenders also learn the covert antecedents of their search for and response to an HRS, such as feelings of depression, boredom, unrest, and sexual desire. Each offender must then learn, through group and individual practice in responding to fantasies, his most effective coping responses—such as departure or alternative activities—to an HRS and its covert antecedents. Coping responses are formulated as rules for behavior in an HRS. During reviews of fantasies and of postrelease experiences, those who are treated through relapse prevention are probed about their use of such rules.

Sometimes aversive conditioning is used to treat sex offenders. A male subject wears a penile plethysmograph, which shows his development or loss of an erection, while he reports his fantasies or watches films. Giving him an electric shock, or having him break an ammonia capsule under his nose to experience a repugnant odor, makes his erection disappear. The electric shock treatment is repeated to strengthen such aversion, or the ammonia capsule is placed in a sealed jar, which the offender can re-open himself if erection recurs (Howitt, 1995, pp. 194-195; Laws, 1989, pp. 278-279).

Castration and Brain Surgery

Castration, or surgical removal or destruction of the testes, is one of the oldest ways of trying to prevent men from engaging in sex. Castrated men, called eunuchs, were used in ancient Greece and the Orient to care for or guard women. Castration does not make men incapable of erection and sexual intercourse, but it gradually reduces the frequency of such events.

The modern rationale for castrating sex offenders is that the male sex drive is caused by the hormone testosterone, created in the testes. Research on animals shows that blood testosterone levels are correlated with male sexual activity and aggression. In humans testosterone levels may rise either before or after sexual arousal, and the association of testosterone with aggression and anger is similar to that found in animal research.

Average testosterone levels are higher in young men of good physical condition than in older or debilitated men, and levels in sex offenders are similar to those in physically similar men of the same age with no sex crime record. In fact, a Minnesota study found lower average testosterone levels in men convicted of child molestation than in a group of patients in treatment for inability to achieve or maintain penile erections. Both groups were matched in age and absence of alcoholism (Gurnani & Dwyer, 1986). This finding suggests that adult men may molest children because of their impotence with adult women, but that is a very speculative interpretation.

Much castration of sex offenders is done in Europe, under court orders based on psychiatric advice. It usually does not result in immediate freedom, for European psychiatrists urge that it be followed by some months of counseling during confinement, and then by a supervised release. No rigorous comparisons have been conducted of recidivism rates for castrated and uncastrated sex offenders who are similar in all respects other than this operation, but Europeans report that only 2% to 7% of castrated offenders commit new sex crimes. These reports are based on small samples, however, with differences in the duration of the follow-up period (Greer & Stuart, 1983, p. 112; Rada, 1978, pp. 143-144).

Although statistically castration seems to be an effective treatment, critics deplore its symbolic destruction of manhood and its irreversibility, especially if the person might later be found innocent. Some object to it on abstract ethical grounds; others cite the Eighth Amendment to the U.S. Constitution, which bars "cruel and unusual punishment." Whether castration is more cruel than long incarceration can be debated. Experience in Europe indicates that the public accepts castration if imposed only on the most seriously recidivistic sex criminals.

"Chemical castration," using drugs that diminish a man's capacity for sexual arousal, is sometimes tried as an alternative to permanent surgical castration. Some have claimed that recidivism is reduced by giving male sex offenders the female sex hormone estrogen, or chemicals such as DepoProvera that reduce testosterone creation. These chemicals often have harmful side effects, however. Furthermore, one cannot guarantee that a nonconfined offender ordered to take the drug will do so, although the releasee could be required to report regularly to take it in front of a staff member at a specified office or clinic.

Another medical approach is psychosurgery for sex offenders. Lobotomies and less radical brain operations have been tried on animals, and on a few humans, to reduce sex drive or hostility. Yet the results were so inconsistent, and in some cases so spectacularly unsuccessful, that such treatment is no longer advocated (Greer & Stuart, 1983, pp. 113-115; Rada, 1978, pp. 145-147).

Mandatory Postrelease Registration

Following a series of highly publicized cases of child molestation and murder by released sex offenders, several state legislatures and the federal government reacted with new laws requiring that the public be notified of the location of such offenders. California is one of several states now requiring that released sex offenders register with their local police departments whenever they change residences. Not only rapists and child molesters must register, but also persons arrested for pimping, pandering, soliciting for homosexuality, or even seducing by a false promise of marriage. Ex-offenders complain that police use the register to harass them whenever a new sex crime occurs.

In 1995, California also established a hot line whereby parents and others can make a "900" call to the state capital (for which they are charged $10 on their phone bill), to inquire whether a person in contact with their children is a registered child molester. Inquiries cannot be made on more than two persons per call. Early reports suggest that any released sex offender identified through such calls has much trouble keeping a home and a job. Court appeals on its legality have been initiated.

On May 17, 1996, President Clinton signed federal legislation called "Megan's Law," requiring that all law-enforcement agencies inform community residents whenever sex offense prisoners are released to their community. It is named after a young New Jersey girl, Megan Kanka, slain in a pedophile attack (Bornheimer, 1996).

Civil libertarians contend that mandatory registration or notification of the community violates our legal system's presumption of innocence. They also claim that when police are pressured to solve a sex crime, and are stymied, they often halt their investigation too soon by making unfounded charges against registered sex offenders.

Insanity, Idiocy, and Incompetency Defenses

Insanity is a legal term for a person's mental condition. If a court finds that a person was insane when committing an offense, it must declare that person not guilty. Doubts about guilt also occur when a crime is perpetrated by an adult so mentally retarded, whether from birth defect or from injury or disease (such as Alzheimer's) later in life, as to have the intelligence of only a young child. Mental deficiency is called *idiocy* when, like insanity, it provides legal grounds for finding an adult perpetrator of a crime not guilty. Finally, *incompetency* describes an accused person who is incapable of participating in his or her own legal defense.

The main policy issue regarding all three states of mental incapacitation is whether they allow criminals to avoid just punishments. For example, Chapter 4 indicated that adult penalties are deemed inappropriate for very young children who commit crimes, but should this view also apply to an adult with a child's mental capacity? The mentally retarded are seldom accused of anything but petty offenses (despite the custom of misleadingly referring to sex criminals as "sex morons"), but they do on occasion commit violent acts, seemingly without awareness of their seriousness. How is society to control such behavior without violating an incapacitated person's civil rights?

Legal Definitions of Insanity

Legal rules for defining insanity are much debated, and even when such rules are accepted, there is often disagreement in applying them. These problems occur because mental states are diverse, vague, and unstable. It is notoriously hard to prove what a person's mental state was at the time of a crime when the trial is held months or years later.

Even a firm diagnosis of a well-recognized psychosis cannot pinpoint the mental state of a person who has committed a crime. Schizophrenics often misconceive who they are or what they are doing, yet are quite lucid at other times. They are also usually too withdrawn in their fantasies to commit serious crimes. Persons diagnosed with bipolar disorder, whose moods swing to a manic or to an acutely depressed state, often seem unable to control their conduct when in such extremes, but seem normal at other times. These two major forms of psychosis occur in all societies, have apparently always existed, vary greatly in severity, and foster recurrent claims that crimes ascribed to them should be dismissed as due to insanity.

The most influential definition of insanity emerged in 1843 from the trial of Daniel M'Naghten, a British woodcutter who killed the male secretary to Prime Minister Robert Peel. M'Naghten thought he was killing Peel, whom he believed was persecuting him. The court outraged the public by finding M'Naghten not guilty because his delusion "takes away from him all power of self control." The House of Lords responded to the controversy by appointing a commission of 15 judges to specify the rules warranting such a decision. The commission's answer, the *M'Naghten rule*, was eventually adopted in almost all of the English-speaking world. It declares that "every man is presumed to be sane," but

> to establish a defense on the ground of insanity, it must be clearly proved that, at the time of committing the act, the party accused was laboring under such a defect of reason, from disease of mind, as not to know the nature and quality of the act he was doing; or if he did know it, that he did not know he was doing what was wrong. (Goldstein, 1983, p. 736)

The M'Naghten rule, known as the "right and wrong test," annoyed psychiatrists. They had encountered mentally ill perpetrators of crimes who knew right from wrong, and that their crimes were wrong, but who nevertheless could not control their actions because of the mental illness.

Thus some states in this country added a *control rule*, which defines offenders as insane if they cannot control their impulses to do what they know is wrong. But psychiatrists still favored the *Durham rule*, based on a more recent case, that simply states that persons are not guilty by reason of insanity if their criminal acts were "the product of mental disease or defect." Lawyers objected, however, that this "product rule" was too broad and vague.

Since the 1980s, U.S. courts have increasingly adopted the *American Law Institute rule*, which combines M'Naghten, control, and Durham phrases:

A person is not responsible for criminal conduct if at the time of such conduct, as a result of mental disease or defect, he lacks substantial capacity either to appreciate the criminality of his conduct or to conform his conduct to the requirements of the law.

It adds, however, that

the terms "mental disease or defect" do not include an abnormality manifested only by repeated criminal or otherwise antisocial conduct. (Goldstein, 1983, p. 739)

This addition pleases prosecutors because it forces the defense to prove that the accused was mentally disturbed before and apart from, as well as during, the criminal act.

Despite shelves of publications on the merits or faults of these insanity definitions, a folk notion of what is crazy apparently governs both juries and judges. This reality was suggested by experiments in which persons eligible for jury duty were randomly selected for paid employment in simulated juries. Each jury heard tape recordings of a sex crime case, but one randomly selected third of each jury was given instructions based on the M'Naghten rule, another random third had instructions from the Durham rule, and the rest received no instructions except to decide whether the accused was not guilty because of insanity. The proportion of juries finding the defendant insane did not differ significantly with the various instructions, although discussions were longer and hung juries were a bit more frequent after Durham instructions as opposed to the other types (Simon, 1967).

Given the confusion about legal definitions, inconsistent court judgments of allegedly insane suspects should not be surprising. After killing his grandparents, Edward Kemper, a 6-foot 9-inch, 300-pound 19-year-old, was found insane and confined in a mental hospital for 5 years. He was released by a board of psychiatrists in 1969. In the year after release he killed eight women by shooting, stabbing, and strangling after attempting to rape them; he also cut off their limbs and ate parts of their bodies. Finally, he decapitated his mother and removed her larynx, discarding it in the garbage disposal. Yet in this second series of offenses, he was deemed sane.

Many trials of notorious killers have instigated vigorous battles between psychiatric experts for opposing sides seeking to explain whether the accused was insane when committing the murders. Humorist Art

Buchwald (1982) was not far from fact when he explained how his fictional defense lawyer finds psychiatric experts:

> We have lists of shrinks who believe anyone who commits a major crime is crazy, just as the government has lists of doctors who are willing to testify that anyone involved in one was sane. We don't use their lists and they don't use ours.[2]

Evolving Replacements for Insanity Laws

A major complaint against traditional sanity rules is that they require courts to find people who commit a crime either completely innocent or completely guilty. In response, several states adopted *diminished capacity laws*. These allow courts to decide that some offenders had only partial knowledge or control in their illegal acts, and therefore should be charged with a less serious crime. Thus, a murder charge could be reduced to manslaughter if the crime was committed during a state of diminished capacity.

Many such laws were repealed after 1981 in California and several other states, however, after Dan White cold-bloodedly killed San Francisco's Mayor George Moscone and Supervisor Harvey Milk. White received only an 8-year sentence for manslaughter because of "the Twinkie defense." Physicians convinced the jury that White had diminished mental capacity when he shot these men because his blood sugar level was high from overeating "junk food."

Most Americans became especially disturbed about insanity laws during the 1980s after they clearly saw on television John Hinckley shoot President Ronald Reagan and his press secretary James Brady. Despite abundant visual evidence of the shooting, Hinckley was found not guilty by reason of insanity. The court was persuaded that these shootings were due to Hinckley's delusion that killing the President would favorably impress Jody Foster, an actress whom he admired but had never met.

A flurry of changes in state insanity rules followed the Hinckley case. Idaho abolished the insanity defense soon after, although allowing an exception for defendants who absolutely did not know what they were doing. Montana had already abolished the insanity defense before the Hinckley case, but a Montana assistant attorney general was quoted in a May 14, 1982 *Los Angeles Times* report as saying: "In any case in which the defendant could raise the insanity defense before, he now puts a psychiatrist on the stand to testify about intent" ("Insanity—Valid Plea or a

Dodge?" *Los Angeles Times*, May, 1982, Part 1, pp. 1 and 16).[3] Such a development was a problem for prosecutors because the criminal law for most crimes requires proof of intent to commit the offense. Thus the Hinckley precedent made it possible for the defense to discuss the accused's mental state at the time of the crime without even addressing the sanity issue.

Another approach to the problem of letting mentally ill offenders go unpunished for crimes is to allow courts to find an accused "guilty but mentally ill." About a dozen states have followed Michigan's 1975 leadership in permitting this ruling. Someone convicted of a crime who gets this new verdict must get psychological treatment wherever administrators prefer, in prison or in a hospital. It is used mostly for sex crimes, especially child molesting (Klofas & Weisheit, 1987), which most people seem to find harder to forgive than other crimes.

Mental Incompetency

The concepts of "insanity" and "idiocy," used when excusing a crime on the basis of a perpetrator's mental condition when committing it, are often confused with "incompetency," which refers to a defendant's condition at time of trial. A basic principle of law is that no one can be convicted of a crime who is incapable of understanding the charges and proceedings, or of cooperating with a defense attorney.

Persons who are clearly psychotic or idiotic both when committing a crime and when arrested, will usually not be brought to trial, but will be referred by the prosecution for a civil hearing on mental health. If the prosecution does not request such a hearing, the defense will often try to get the criminal court to order it. If the defense persuades a court to find a defendant incompetent to stand trial, criminal proceedings must be deferred until competency is regained. That may never happen.

Some people allege that offenders found insane or incompetent "beat the rap" to avoid the prison or jail sentence that they "deserve." Yet numerous scandal investigations have shown that a competency adjudication is not necessarily a victory for the accused. Many persons who have been sent to mental hospitals as incompetent or insane were forgotten there and stayed indefinitely. Laws in many states now forbid such hospitalization for longer than the maximum period of confinement permitted for the alleged offense. At the end of this period, a civil court reviews the need for further hospitalization.

The Effectiveness of Insanity
and Incompetency Laws

The disparate penalties for crimes committed by the insane, the idiotic, and the incompetent are confusing to the public and often produce disappointing results. The question remains: How can society most effectively stop crimes committed by these people? We have an obvious stake in preventing violence, however it occurs. Attorney Denis Woychuk (1996) voices some of the reasons for using punishments, such as indefinite incarceration in a mental hospital or community registration of sex offenders, that might violate the accused's civil rights:

> Unlike the prison system, from which still-dangerous people are released every day, people in forensic hospitals who are considered dangerous because of mental disease are not supposed to go free. To hold a criminal convict beyond his sentence would violate the U.S. Constitution, but there is no term limit to incarceration for mental patients. Thus, even as a form of revenge, the . . . hospital system has features that should appeal to the public at large. It is punishment with no term limit.
>   . . . Megan's Law—the public identification and registration of child sex offenders after their release from prison . . . doesn't require a change in the mental condition of a sex offender. The man who killed eight-year-old Megan Kanka had been released from prison after duly serving his time for an offense against another child. If he had been sent to a mental hospital instead, Megan might be alive today.
>   But in New York, at least, the insanity plea would not have been available for Megan's killer. It is designed only for those individuals whose mental illness is such that they are unable to appreciate the nature of their conduct or do not know that their acts are wrong. The psychopath or sadistic pedophile who lacks empathy but knows that what he is doing is wrong does not qualify for "insanity treatment" under the M'Naghten test. (p. 213)

Hospitalization is not always the most profitable penalty, however. Follow-up studies of allegedly criminally insane persons who were held for years in mental hospitals as dangerous but were released when appellate courts found them to have been confined through illegal procedures show that few were rearrested, and most charges against these few were petty (Steadman & Cocozza, 1974; Thornberry & Jacoby, 1979). A New York State comparison of accused persons sent to mental hospitals as incompetent, and of others jailed for similar offenses (almost always minor), found incompetents confined longest. Recidivism rates for both groups were best predicted by their total number of prior confinements of any type (Steadman, 1979), not by their psychological diagnoses.

Another issue is the inconsistency with which insanity and related laws are applied. The flexibility of court decisions due to plea bargaining, and variation in local courthouse norms on bargaining, often make the outcomes of insanity, idiocy, and incompetency cases much different from what one would expect from reading the laws. A study of Wisconsin criminal cases found that courts sentence offenders who have mental disorder histories but who were not found insane more leniently than persons committing the same crimes with similar prior criminal records but no known prior mental ailment (Hochstedler, 1986). A New York State study found that many defendants first plead insanity, then negotiate a reduction of charges in exchange for dropping the insanity plea (Braff, Arvantes, & Steadman, 1983). In Louisiana, the proximity of courts to a state hospital predicted their rate of accepting insanity and incompetency pleas (Bankston, Floyd, & McSeveny, 1977); the sheriffs delivered those arrested to either a prison or a mental hospital, depending on which was nearest.

There are also international variations in court interpretations of the same rules or laws. Thus, the M'Naghten rule leads British courts to find almost a fourth of those charged with murder not guilty by reason of insanity, but U.S. courts that used this rule found insanity in only 2% or 3% of the cases (Lunde, 1976).

Achieving profitable penalties requires regular research on what courts actually do and on the consequences, rather than study only in lawbooks.

A Proposed Resolution of the Insanity Issue

In view of the haphazard decision making on insanity and incompetency, it would be well to follow the advice of Norval Morris (1982) that we abolish both the insanity defense and current use of the incompetency plea. For trying competent defendants, Morris would have courts use traditional procedures; for those deemed incompetent he would have them simulate these procedures as closely as possible to maximize fairness in deciding "who did the crime." In both types of cases, the court would then consider the offender's current mentality to order the most appropriate penalty or treatment, but would not impose longer involuntary confinement for the mentally disturbed or deficient than the maximum permitted for the competent and sane.

Coupling such practices with regular review of the decisions in such cases would be the most profitable way to protect society from crimes while protecting the mentally ill or retarded from being either erroneously accused or excessively restrained. They would not be able to avoid unpleasant consequences for their criminal acts, but we could fairly accomplish any incapacitation needed for society's protection.

Actually, the distinction between sentencing for a sanely committed crime and imposing treatment for a mentally ill perpetrator of the same act is becoming blurred. From 1960 to 1990, the common use of tranquilizers and other psychiatric drugs to treat U.S. mental patients, plus treatment policies favoring outpatient care or board-and-care homes, reduced by two-thirds the total number of days per year in mental hospitals per thousand persons. Those once hospitalized for most of their lives now have only short hospital stays.

Many of the mentally ill released from hospitals become homeless from receiving inadequate care and supervision in community treatment places, from not taking their medications, or from wandering off because they are confused or rebellious at their board-and-care places. Also, agency budget cutting allegedly leads staff to encourage some people to leave treatment facilities despite their inability to care for themselves or to get care from others. Because the costs of arresting, adjudicating, and jailing for petty crimes by the homeless mentally ill total much more than the costs of proper care for them either in hospitals or in the community, it would be profitable to improve mental health care, as well as services for the homeless (Barak, 1991; Schutt & Garrett, 1992).

Conclusion

The passion of lust can be criminally expressed in diverse ways, and the profitable penalties are equally diverse. "Flashing," for instance, seems relatively benign and is most profitably addressed through fines. Similarly, much statutory rape can be diminished simply by redefining the age of consent, and when the participants are of a similar age, education on the risks of sex may be more helpful than arrests and punishments in reducing the social costs of statutory rape.

More violent and exploitive sex crimes require more severe penalties. It seems appropriate to punish statutory rape more severely when the participants are of widely disparate ages. Forcible rape, which is often intermingled with rage, has extremely harmful effects on subsequent relationships of its victims to men and fosters much female suicide. Its prevention requires that males more realistically sense female psychology and cease viewing seduction of women as a sign of manliness. Such changes require more communication and role sharing between the sexes. The probability of recidivism by rapists, the thieves of sex, is best predicted by the earliness, intensity, and continuity of their prior offenses of all types. As with many other types of criminals, likely recidivists may be most appropriately punished by incarceration.

Adults of all ages may sexually molest children. First offenders have relatively low recidivism rates after punishment, but a "fixated" pattern, usually evident only when the perpetrator is drunk, is highly repetitive. Such pedophilia is especially difficult to treat successfully because the best source of reformation probably is sincere participation in Alcoholics Anonymous, which cannot be effectively coerced. Of course, the public demands severe penalties for sadistic or homicidal child molestation, which is conspicuous but fortunately rare.

Many nations and states mandate particular types of treatment for all sex offenders. Castration seems to reduce further offenses, especially when used as in Europe, with psychiatric treatment before and after. Both it and less drastic behavior modification treatments, as well as criminal penalties and mandatory registration of sex offenders by the police, need much more evaluation before being widely implemented.

The issues of whether a person is not guilty by reason of insanity at the time of the offense or is incompetent to be tried are raised mostly with sex offenses and other crimes of passion. The inconsistent and perhaps often unjust use of such defenses suggests that it may be wise to abolish these ways to avoid or defer a trial. Instead, courts should fairly adjudicate whether the accused perpetrated the alleged offense; if so, the most cost-effective and legitimate way of preventing its repetition should be undertaken, whether this is in a penal or mental health institution.

Notes

1. *Los Angeles Times*, June 2, 1993. Reprinted by permission.
2. *Los Angeles Times*, Art Buchwald Column, May 11, 1982.

8

Removing Crookedness
From Legitimate Occupations

Some lawbreaking occurs only because the offenders have respectable employment. There are "crooked" ways of doing things in most jobs, and in every type of business or profession. These crimes are usually small, but some of them kill or maim thousands of people, and some gain the perpetrators millions of dollars. Many people call these offenses "white-collar crimes," but that term does not describe them well.

Four broad types of crimes are considered here:

◆ Crimes of employees against their employers
◆ Crimes of employers against their employees
◆ Crimes of businesses against the public
◆ Criminal law violations by the government

These types are listed in sequence from lawbreaking by the least powerful to offenses by the elite. All four include crimes so common and separately so trivial as to be usually accepted as standard behavior, but they also include huge crimes that collectively cost their victims more than all the nation's burglaries and robberies combined.

Reducing Crimes Against Employers

Embezzlement is "fraudulent appropriation of property by a person to whom it has been entrusted" (California Penal Code). This charge is unlikely, however, unless a large amount is taken. The few people prosecuted for embezzlement are usually accused of theft or fraud. On a small scale, "fraudulent appropriation" by employees is called *pilfering*. It is very common.

Pilfering

Every large employer, such as a major corporation or a government, is cheated by many who work for it, perhaps because these organizations seem so bureaucratic, impersonal, and rich. Yet many small businesses are also cheated. Employees take things for personal use—office supplies, tools, raw materials, or finished products—that vary with the opportunities in each workplace. Employee pilfering also includes fraud by overstating hours worked or tasks completed, padding expense accounts, and giving false reasons for sick leave. Some employees rarely or never pilfer, others do it often, the rest only pilfer occasionally. Most conform to the customs in their workplace.

Many retail stores find that their losses from staff pilfering exceed those from shoplifting. Horning (1983) cites as a benchmark in American industry an average loss from employee theft of 2% of the gross national product. He further cites a newspaper report that "executive employees commit only 15 percent of the thefts," but "they were responsible for 85 percent of the total dollar losses."

Hollinger and Clark (1983) surveyed corporation employees in three major American cities. About a third of the 58% who returned their mailed questionnaires (which did not ask for names) admitted taking company property. Those who admitted stealing time, by taking extra-long lunch breaks or unwarranted sick leave, were also most likely to admit taking property. The highest offense rates were by young employees and those dissatisfied with their jobs.

Employee pilfering is reported to be frequent in other nations as well (Ditton, 1977). In Britain it is called "fiddling," and truck drivers are major actors. They deliberately overload or underdeliver, often in collusion with warehouse clerks or other employees, then peddle the goods to friends, to customers at the pubs they frequent, or to fences (Henry, 1978). Although Marxists attribute employee theft to capitalist exploitation of workers, much cheating and theft by workers was also reported in socialist countries when the government was everyone's employer. Indeed, pilfering is at least as widespread in government jobs of all nations as in businesses, and is especially common in the armed forces.

Embezzlement

Embezzlement, which generally involves thousands or even millions of dollars, can be committed only by exceptionally trusted persons with long records of presumed honesty, for only they are likely to be given control of much wealth. Typical embezzlers, therefore, are treasurers and accountants, lawyers handling large estates, salespersons handling valuable items such as jewelry, and business managers of wealthy clients. Yet computerized bookkeeping now often permits relatively obscure employees to transfer funds improperly into disguised accounts of their own. Banks lose over five times as much money by embezzlement as by robbery, but robberies are much more publicized.

In a classic study aptly called *Other People's Money*, Donald Cressey (1953/1971) found that the crimes of all 133 embezzlers he interviewed in prison began with what they regarded as an unshareable problem. It was always a large money loss or an obligation they had to keep secret because its revelation would damage their job security or alienate loved ones. Thus bank officials or lawyers, whose livelihoods depend on a reputation for good judgment, may embezzle to cover up losses from a foolish investment or gambling spree, or may spend beyond their means to avoid antagonizing someone with whom they have had an adulterous affair, who could expose them if jilted. Nettler (1984) claimed that the only problem of the embezzlers he studied was greed, but he implied unshareable problems when he said that detectives ascribe embezzlement to the "three B's—babes, booze, and bets."

The people who develop unshareable problems are often those whose craving for approval and status habitually leads them to display affluence or generosity in order to impress family, business associates, political supporters, or others. Some of them try theft from their employer when they realize that their lifestyle cannot be maintained from their earnings, but cannot be terminated without great loss of face.

In other cases, altruism leads someone to help another, but the need for help grows until it is unaffordable. The helper embezzles funds when unable to renege because the recipient has become completely dependent on this aid.

A study of women embezzlers by Dorothy Zietz (1981) confirmed Cressey's main findings regarding unshareable problems in most cases. She classified her female subjects' concern with unshareable problems into four patterns:

- ◆ "Obsessive Protectors" spent more money on their spouses or children than they could get legally.
- ◆ "Romantic Dreamers" idealized the quality of the relationships they tried to further with money.
- ◆ "Greedy Opportunists" became too addicted to luxurious lifestyles to lower their expenditures.
- ◆ "Victims of Pressure or Persuasion" were threatened by others, some-times by husbands or lovers who talked of leaving them if there were not enough money, or by other employees who became aware of some pilfering and blackmailed them.

The second stage in embezzlement, according to Cressey (1953/1971), is the conception of an illegal procedure for taking funds to solve the unshareable problem. Employees with access to much money or other company valuables know the routines and record systems installed to prevent fraud, and therefore, know how to evade them.

But the crime is not carried out, Cressey claims, until an essential third stage occurs: acceptance of a rationalization, so that the employee can regard this crime as morally justified. Not much rationalization is needed for petty pilfering, where the most common excuse probably is the often erroneous claim that "everybody does it"; more elaborate excuses are needed to preserve a favorable self-concept in larger thefts.

All three stages of embezzlement sometimes occur within a short period. However, reasoning may move either quickly or slowly.

Causes of Employee Crime

Pilfering commonly develops out of an "indulgency pattern" that develops at each workplace. Supervisors typically allow some kinds of petty theft, such as taking certain supplies for home use or leaving for a while to take care of personal matters (Gouldner, 1954). Management often believes that such disregard of pilfering will give employees a sense of obligation, but when pilfering is customary, employees assume that it is their right and resent attempts to eliminate it. Management problems are most likely to develop if standards on what employees may take are unclear or if someone tries to change them drastically and abruptly.

The rationalization that embezzlers most often report as preceding their crime is simply that it is only borrowing and that they will repay what they borrow. Many persons entrusted with other people's money, especially within households or clubs, occasionally borrow from these funds and repay before being found out. If such borrowing was easy, they readily repeat it, but unexpected developments sometimes prevent repayment.

Embezzlers often take only a small amount at a time, then suddenly become aware that the total has grown too large to repay. Usually their most ego-supportive defense at this point is that they are not adequately paid for their services and therefore deserve what they take. If the victim is a large or rich firm, part of the rationale is that it does not need the money taken, or that it is protected by insurance. In this way, embezzlers delude themselves that their offense is not really bad by prevailing moral standards.

Arrested embezzlers have a median age above 30, for to be given much trust they must have more education and work experience than childhood-transition offenders. However, most have less stable job histories and are younger than the average in their occupation. A small proportion are professional "con artists" who misrepresent their work histories and hide criminal records to get positions of trust in order to embezzle.

Prevention of Employee Crime

Obviously, employee theft can be prevented by initial screening to eliminate persons with prior criminality or costly vices; the main goal is to find competent persons with good work histories. Once hired, staff may be inspired to feel a stake in the company if they are consulted on workplace decisions, and if pay, working conditions, and prospects of advancement are good. Their offense rates are also minimized if indulgency standards are clear and reactions to violations are consistent.

A standard way to prevent employee crimes, of course, is guarding and checking. Thefts may be intercepted if workplaces are observed, lockers searched, records audited, and metal detectors installed at doors. Lie-detector tests (polygraphs) are now given to millions of employees and job applicants. But if no crimes are noted through such measures, vigilance may lag or overly predictable security routines may evoke innovations in theft and fraud. In addition, the cost of some security measures may exceed the cost of the offenses they prevent. Also, an employer's display of distrust can impair employee morale, reducing productivity. Each firm must therefore develop its own mix of security measures and indulgence to cope with risks of employee pilfering and embezzlement.

Profitable Penalties for Employee Crime

Many firms prefer to handle embezzlements without notifying the police, because publicity about their losses may hurt their business reputation. Their goals are to dismiss untrustworthy employees, deter misconduct by others, and be reimbursed for losses; they may threaten to prosecute only to foster repayment. Because those who attain positions of trust before violating them may long have met prevailing work standards well, employers can often rehire them in jobs with less access to funds. This solution is often part of a restitution agreement for installment repayments.

When embezzlers and large-scale pilferers are caught, a minimum period of confinement may be demanded by enraged victims as just desert and as deterrence to others. But complainants often soon realize that punishments are more profitable if defendants get early release on probation or parole with enforced obligations to make restitution payments, do community service, pay fines, and be restricted in their postrelease movements.

Embezzlers previously in positions of trust usually have bonds with anticriminal persons. Most have experience and skills that can lead to jobs despite their crimes. Because they lose such assets with long imprisonment, this penalty often seems unprofitable for society. Yet the public demands it for notorious offenders, and may benefit if such revenge strengthens society's values.

Reducing Crimes Against Employees:
Dangerous Working Conditions

Because a main goal in business is to maximize profits, firms try to pay the lowest wage that assures satisfactory employees, and to do any other cost-cutting that does not impair profitable sale of their products. One way to cut costs is to minimize spending for safety and sanitation.

Although hazardous working conditions do exist, they are far less visible in today's workplace than was once the case. Karl Marx and Friedrich Engels were prompted to attack capitalism largely from observing deplorable conditions in 19th-century textile mills, coal mines, and other businesses of Western Europe, especially in England. Men, women, and even young children worked long hours, under extreme stress, in dangerous and filthy places.

Today, however, in democratic countries, the imbalance of power between owners and employees has been reduced (although not eliminated). Two developments account for most of the changes: employees became unionized, and legislators sought votes by enacting child labor laws, worker's compensation acts, and other worker protections.

Criminally dangerous workplace conditions are one type of lawbreaking that can be committed only by employers. Most penalties for such offenses are initially imposed on companies by government health, safety, or other regulatory agencies, rather than by criminal courts. But as in the case of other predations, worker endangerment tends to be made criminal by cumulative laws that are rarely repealed.

Causes of Employer Crime

Historically, the most important workplace health hazards have been

+ Lead, a cause of ailments (e.g., brain damage, anemia, kidney disease, and sterility) that threaten more than 800,000 in mines, lead smelters, and battery firms, and, before being banned from paints, greatly endangered paint-factory workers and painters
+ Arsenic, a cause of lung cancer and lymph-system tumors threatening 660,000 smelter, refinery, and chemical workers
+ Benzene, a cause of leukemia and bone-marrow damage endangering at least 600,000 workers in oil refining, petrochemical plants, auto manufacture, dye-use, distilling, and painting
+ Cotton dust, the cause of "brown-lung disease," which impairs breathing and creates chronic bronchitis and emphysema and that once endangered about 600,000 textile workers
+ Asbestos, the cause of "white-lung disease" (asbestosis) in mines, shipyards, construction, and other workplaces, where it impedes breathing and often produces lung cancer
+ Coal dust, the cause of "black-lung disease," which once endangered most coal miners (updated from Simon & Eitzen, 1982, p. 111).

Many other dangerous substances whose use is regulated by the government exist in contemporary workplaces. For example, vinyl chloride is a potential source of brain or liver cancer for about 10,000 workers in plastics factories. Numerous medical technicians, uranium miners, nuclear power employees, and others risk exposure to levels of radiation that can cause bone, lung, or thyroid cancer, leukemia, sterility, and spontaneous abortion.

Prevention of Employer Crime

Employers, unions, and insurance companies collaborate in trying to avoid accidents that stop production and create sudden injuries. For instance, they all have long endorsed no-smoking rules in oil refineries, coal mines, and other places where explosions readily occur. But they diverge in willingness to spend enough to end long-run dangers from slow-acting hazards that hurt employees more than employers, such as lead, asbestos, mercury, or dust. Strong regulations, with penalties, are needed to combat such dangers.

Government efforts to regulate the use of hazardous substances and to eliminate other safety hazards do save lives. Formerly, asbestos endangered well over a million workers, but since 1970, government regulations and victims' successful lawsuits have reduced its use, although many workers remain at risk from asbestos still in buildings and furnaces. Annual deaths from coal mining within the United States have declined from a peak of 3,241 in 1907 to well under 100 in recent years. Similar reductions have occurred in Britain, France, Japan, and most other coal-mining countries (Braithwaite, 1985). According to the U.S. Public Health Service, deaths by accidents on all jobs in the United States declined from more than 16,000 in 1945 to around 12,000 in the 1980s and 1990s.

Disabling work injury totals have recently stayed fairly constant at about two million annually, despite much growth in the size of the U.S. labor force. These injuries result mainly from a decline in the number of employees needed for manufacturing and mining and an increase in the number of generally safer service and information-processing jobs. Simultaneously, freer global trade in essence "exports" our risks, for it allows developing nations to expand dangerous work for their populace, sell their products cheaply to us, and thereby get funds to purchase more technologically advanced, less riskily produced goods or services from us.

Pressures for engineering changes to reduce employee risks and to minimize costs often result in new equipment that is both less dangerous and more efficient. New methods of electroplating, plastic manufacture, and lead smelting, devised to spew less toxins into the atmosphere, are both cheaper and more productive than the methods they replaced (McCaffery, 1982).

Profitable Penalties for Uncaring Employers

Some conservative economists (e.g., Viscusi, 1983) would have the government abolish all rules and penalties for workplace safety, but publish information on risks at various jobs so that workers willing to take the risks can demand higher pay. As another alternative to government regulation, Noble (1986) calls for mobilizing workers locally to use their bargaining power to get risks controlled. But many conservatives join liberals in endorsing severe penalties for firms that knowingly create great risks without warning possible victims. And all must acknowledge that the rate of injuries and deaths from job accidents has dropped because of government regulation and, in particular, government mandates to use safer new technologies.

The government fulfills its worker-protection function mostly through various safety agencies. The U.S. Mine Safety and Health Administration, and similar state agencies, for example, were begun (and are often reorganized) after major disasters. The Occupational Safety and Health Administration (OSHA), formed in 1970, is the regulatory agency for most other worker protection in the United States. Similar agencies operate in the separate states, although some have been nearly or completely closed in budget-cutting sprees.

OSHA inspectors usually make their rounds of a company with representatives of both management and labor. The OSHA Process Safety Management Requirements, first issued in 1992, mandate largely standardized procedures for analyzing hazards, providing safety training to avoid them, setting up employee complaint channels, investigating incidents, and reporting regularly on hazards and incidents. When issued, the requirements applied to about 25,000 establishments and three million workers in all of the United States except California, Delaware, and New Jersey, which had federally approved state programs (Dennison, 1994, chap. 1). In response to management lobbying, Congress barred OSHA from penalizing "nonserious" violations unless at least 10 were found at one firm and gave OSHA only a consulting function for other violations. For most violations, fines are discretionary and average only a few hundred dollars, but repeated violations (called "willful") have brought down fines of over a million dollars. Those fined may delay enforcement pending appeal to administrative boards and subsequent appeals to the courts.

Even before Congress curbed OSHA's power to punish violators of health and safety rules, its effectiveness was being questioned. A 1989 survey by an experienced prosecutor pointed out that since OSHA's inception in 1970, deaths from workplace-created illness had increased 30% (although accidents were declining) while the average civil penalties had decreased by more than 50% (Webber, 1989). This investigator noted that OSHA has authority under state criminal laws to seek punishment for health and safety violations but imposes only civil penalties. She proposed that more use be made of criminal prosecutions to deter dangerous employers.

Conviction for most such crimes requires proof that the accused not only did, but intended to do, the criminal act. If the act is one of criminal negligence or recklessness rather than intentional, it must be proved that the defendant did not take reasonable precautions. However, when safety violations are long-standing practices of large firms, one cannot prove that any individual's intent or carelessness caused the violations. Therefore, guilt is now increasingly placed on the corporation rather than on any individual, to the chagrin of some legal traditionalists. The company is found guilty by the rules of what lawyers call *strict liability*, which means that regulatory agencies need only prove that the working conditions caused injury or ailment, rather than prove intent, negligence, or recklessness.

From extensive studies of diverse firms in many countries, John Braithwaite (1985) concluded that regulations are most effective if they differ somewhat for different establishments, because of variations from one to another. He advocates "enforced self-regulation," whereby large firms and their unions or other employee representatives collaborate in devising safety and health protection rules, with penalties. When the government approves these rules, it appoints an autonomous local board, representing all major interested parties, to monitor compliance, inform management and the government of violations, and aid in correcting them. The government spot-checks such self-regulation, and if it finds serious deficiencies, may impose penalties. This process, Braithwaite claims, produces more frequent and more thorough inspection than the government can provide, and more continuous attention to worker protection. Although critics assume that "employer self-regulation" would be business dominated (Snider, 1990), Braithwaite claims from its record in Australia that it provides the most profitable penalties for uncaring employers.

Reducing Corporate Crimes Against the Public

As individuals or corporations seek to maximize profits, they may be moved by what Adam Smith (1776/1937) in 1776 called the "invisible hand" of competition not only to increase the "wealth of nations," but also to cheat or poison the public or to use unfair means to manipulate the marketplace. Offending businesses could be sued by their victims, but until lately this sort of lawsuit was infrequent because of the difficulty and expense of individuals fighting big corporations in court. Now laws increasingly allow the government, on behalf of the public, to punish corporate predations as crimes.

Curtailing Consumer Fraud

In medieval and renaissance Europe, guilds of artisans and merchants had standards of a "just price" for sound goods, enforced by various local tribunals. With the rise of capitalist economies, however, especially in the 19th century, the principle of caveat emptor—let the buyer beware— gradually reduced controls over what was sold, how it was advertised, and what price could fairly be charged. Since then, various ways of defrauding consumers have been tested by unscrupulous companies.

Varieties of Consumer Fraud

Numerous instances of fraud can be found in the way companies sell practically every type of merchandise, service, or "investment opportunity." The prevalence of consumer fraud is shown, for example, by automobile clubs and other consumer-oriented groups that conduct such experiments as loosening a wire to impair the performance of a perfectly operating automobile, with the loose wire in plain sight when the hood is raised. The consumer groups typically find that a large proportion of the garages or service stations to which they take the automobile recommend costly repairs (Green, 1990, pp. 45-46, 215-217). "Bait and switch" techniques are also common, in which stores advertise bargains knowing in advance that they have little or none of the merchandise in stock, but then sell the customer a more profitable item (Gabor, 1994, chap. 6). Telemarketers often misrepresent what they are selling or the terms of sale. It should be noted, however, that much consumer fraud is not perpetrated by ordinary business organizations, but by professional criminals, particularly confidence men and women (discussed in Chapter 9).

As technology and our economy evolve, new ways of defrauding the public come to light. In recent years, for example, physicians, hospitals, and health maintenance organizations (HMOs) have been accused of committing frauds by performing unnecessary tests or services, billing for services not given, and overcharging for what they do perform. With payments increasingly made by the government or large insurance firms, medical or HMO personnel can easily rationalize that the payer can afford a little extra expense. The criminal law is used against only a small proportion of such offenses, although some physicians and others have been sentenced to prison in spectacular cases (Green, 1990, pp. 181-196).

The costliest frauds against the public in U.S. history occurred in the 1980s in conjunction with relaxation of government controls over savings and loan institutions (S&Ls). When federal and state rules on starting and managing these organizations were abolished or weakened as part of a deregulatory movement, many S&Ls—especially new ones—solicited deposits by promising higher interest rates than they could afford, made loans recklessly, built lavish offices, and gave high salaries and allowances to their executives.

In many cases, S&L executives engaged in activities that could be characterized as criminal rather than merely irresponsible or unethical. With the rationale that "everybody's doing it," the S&Ls shared a subculture that Calavita and Pontell (1990) called "collective embezzlement." Many S&Ls inappropriately invested depositors' funds in "junk bonds" that promised high interest rates but were actually frauds floated by criminal brokers. Also, many S&L executives engaged in illegal cover-ups to hide their operations from the government and the public. Criminal fraud and rule violations are alleged in at least 80% of the 500 S&L insolvencies.

The federal government had to deal with the crisis in this essential segment of the U.S. economy by taking over bankrupt S&Ls and paying their depositors up to the $100,000 federally insured total per account. The government recouped some of these funds by selling S&L assets, but almost always it incurred a loss. Some of these cases are still in court. It has been estimated that the government's losses will total at least $600 billion, or $3,000 per taxpayer; in comparison, the Korean War's total cost was $232 billion (Zimring & Hawkins, 1993). Because of the government's deficit budgeting, those who will end up paying most of this cost are the children of people who were taxpayers in the 1980s, when the S&L failures occurred.

The biggest single fraud related to the S&L debacle was revealed by the 1991 end of the Bank of Credit and Commerce International (BCCI). This bank began in 1972 with capital from California banks and from the oil-funded Bank of Oman, in the Persian Gulf. Its director, the Pakistani banker Agha Hasan Abedi, soon got more millions of investment funds from Britain, Japan, France, Germany, the United States, and elsewhere. BCCI established branches and subsidiaries in many countries, especially those of the Third World, promising to extend business loan opportunities everywhere. Despite BCCI's lavish campaign contributions and its other ties to Congress and to successive White House occupants of both parties, New York prosecutors found BCCI and Abedi guilty of at least $10 billion in fraud, plus money laundering and other crimes (Passas, 1995).

On a more mundane level, frauds of all sorts take place on a daily basis. A 1991 telephone survey of a national sample of U.S. adults found that about a third had been targets of fraud attempts in the prior 12 months. Fortunately, only about half the attempts were successful. The numbers of reported attempts and successes declined with the age and education of potential victims (some people "wise up"). The numbers were also unaffected by gender, minority status, or rural residence, thus contradicting common conceptions that the poor and the elderly are most often victimized (Titus, Heinzelmann, & Boyle, 1995).

Regulation of Consumer Fraud

Despite a trend toward deregulation and caveat emptor at the beginning of the 20th century, in 1934 in the wake of the stock market crash the federal government established its first real antifraud agency, the Securities and Exchange Commission (SEC). The SEC's role is to maintain the trustworthiness of stock markets and other investment agencies. It monitors issuance of stocks and bonds and diverse other operations of stock exchanges, brokers, and investment-advising services—notably large stock transactions, firm takeovers, mergers, corporation financial reporting, insider-trading, and large-scale bankruptcies. If SEC investigations reveal criminal violations of its rules, it can seek an injunction from a Federal District Court prohibiting such practices and can recommend and assist in prosecution by the Department of Justice. It can also censure, suspend, or expel members of stock exchanges, or bar individuals from further employment in securities agencies.

The SEC's effectiveness has long been in dispute, however. Some call for more and better SEC regulation to prevent costly securities crimes against the public (Seligman, 1985). But others contend that the SEC, overly zealous to convict corporations of crimes, inhibits capital formation by small businesses (Karmel, 1982), thereby hurting the U.S. economy. In reality, it seems that the SEC's regulatory function provides profitable penalties against "wayward capitalists." Susan Shapiro's (1984) study of a representative sample of closed SEC cases shows that of every 100 offenders, 93 had broken laws carrying criminal penalties. Yet criminal prosecution was begun on only 11, and of these, only 6 were indicted, 5 found guilty, and 3 sentenced to prison. On the other hand, Shapiro demonstrated, when the SEC does prosecute, the result is public benefits in fraud reduction and victim compensation that can far exceed the cost of prosecution.

The task of protecting ordinary consumers against fraud is left to other agencies. The Federal Trade Commission (FTC) was established in 1914 as an organization independent of cabinet departments, although at first its job was only to prevent business monopolies. But in 1938, Congress authorized it also to prohibit "unfair and deceptive acts or practices," hence also to have "an independent consumer protection function" that focused on deceptive advertising (Sheldon & Zweibel, 1978, p. 12). The FTC shares with the Department of Agriculture and the Food and Drug Administration (FDA), responsibility for monitoring the packaging and labeling of foods, drugs, cosmetics, pesticides, and curative devices, and for penalizing offenders. These agencies always perform imperfectly, because no amount of funding would permit them to completely check against criminal fraud in all manufacture, advertising, and purchase of all the goods and services sold to U.S. consumers.

More recently, one man, Ralph Nader, has exerted remarkable influence on government measures to protect consumers from fraud. His efforts were launched by his 1965 book *Unsafe at Any Speed*, a criticism of American automobiles, particularly the Chevrolet Corvair, one of the first American cars with a rear engine. Exposure of how General Motors' detectives tapped Nader's telephones to try to discredit him only heightened attention to his testimony to Congressional committees. This testimony spurred enactment of the National Traffic and Vehicle Safety Act of 1966, from which today's auto purchasers' protection laws evolved.

Meanwhile, Nader filed a lawsuit against General Motors for invasion of privacy. With half a million dollars from out-of-court settlement of this suit, plus income from book sales and public speaking, Nader established diverse specialized public-interest "centers" plus an umbrella organization, Public Citizen. These centers have successfully lobbied for laws against the manufacture and sale of many defective goods and services and against the use of false advertising claims. The work of the centers has been aided by numerous volunteer scientists, lawyers, and students. Their influence, and the influence of others in the "consumer movement," have tremendously expanded prosecution of consumer fraud.

Legislation spawned by this movement now requires that "price stickers" on new autos state their gasoline mileage and other attributes, and orders that autos meet a variety of safety requirements. When dangerous defects are discovered in cars or tires, the National Highway Traffic Safety Administration can now order the manufacturers to recall and repair or replace the cars at no cost to the owners. Fines can also be imposed for violations of auto-safety regulations, thus making them crimes.

Punishing Polluters Astutely

The use of chemicals by factories and mines harms the general public whenever it poisons outside air, water, or soil. This sort of pollution is a major field of crime. Pollution crimes are punishable through the Environmental Protection Agency (EPA), which was established in 1970 to consolidate functions of 10 federal agencies concerned with pollution. The EPA's pollution control efforts are augmented by efforts of the Nuclear Regulatory Commission and the Coast Guard, as well as by state environmental protection agencies.

The EPA's key enforcement device is the Environmental Impact Statement (EIS), a report on pollution risks required with each request for licensing or funding of any construction that can significantly damage the environment. Before such a project is approved, an EIS must be submitted that specifies the costs of anticipated damage to the environment and the costs of possible alternatives, as compared to the expected benefits of each (Firestone & Reed, 1983, chap. 2). Penalties may be imposed for failure to submit plans and, once they are approved, for failure to follow them. Although "slow growth" advocates want even tighter controls over potential polluters, developers complain of the expense and delay the EPA's procedures create. The EPA has also been accused of prosecuting smaller firms more readily than larger polluters, which can offer more resistance, and of putting more effort into collecting the smaller fines that it may impose on its own rather than seeking larger financial penalties through the courts (Yeager, 1993).

The safety of our water supply is a key concern of the EPA. Under the Clean Water Act of 1972, any facility other than a private household may not discharge a potential pollutant into a water source unless it first gets a permit. (Private households are controlled by local ordinances.) Other agencies punish unpiped runoffs from fertilized fields, strip mines, and logged forests.

The EPA also limits emissions from motor vehicles, the greatest source of air pollution, and from factories and power plants. Tens of thousands of vehicles that exceeded limits for noxious exhausts have been taken off the roads by the EPA, but manufacturers often successfully pressure the agency to delay anti-emission rules or their enforcement.

The most frequently prosecuted type of pollution is improper storage, transport, or disposal of hazardous waste. The interstate transportation of hazardous waste is federally controlled; punishment for improper disposal is a state and local matter. However, most local prosecutors lack access to the experts needed to prove charges of toxicity in these offenses (National Institute of Justice, 1994). Nevertheless, many local penalties, sometimes totaling in the millions of dollars, have been imposed for environmental damage due to inadequate disposal of hazardous waste; private parties have also sued successfully for damages.

Many economists contend that antipollution resources are more profitably spent by rewarding acts of prevention than by punishing pollution. Thus, most states have created tax incentives for companies that invest in air and water purification devices (Reese, 1983). But as a deterrent, some states and localities require that a polluting firm's crimes be publicized. For example, as a condition of probation, two executives of Precision Specialty Metals who pleaded "no contest" to charges of dumping cancer-causing wastes into Los Angeles sewers were fined $325,000 and ordered to do 1,000 hours of community service, as well as to advertise their offense in the *Wall Street Journal*. The Atlantic Richfield oil company agreed to establish and advertise an environmental studies scholarship fund at the University of California at Los Angeles as part of its punishment for pollution by its refinery. Antipollution laws are cumulative, and so it seems likely that profitable, innovative penalties for pollution crimes will also accumulate.

Preventing and Punishing Restraint of Trade

Restraint of trade refers to business practices that unfairly manipulate the marketplace. Its victims may be consumers or other organizations. A common way for a business to control competition is to establish a monopoly over some element of the marketplace, so the business can charge or pay what it likes without regard to the normal laws of supply and demand.

Often an industry develops not a monopoly but an oligopoly, in which a few firms have 75% to 90% or more of all sales. Oligopoly conditions also permit imperfect competition, as these firms can readily coordinate their prices to assure high profits without much risk of successful prosecution. If oligopoly members lobby successfully for protective tariffs, companies from abroad cannot compete either. The U.S. auto industry was at one time a classic example of an oligopoly, because it consisted of just a few politically powerful firms. Ultimately, however, tariffs came down enough to allow entry into the U.S. market of foreign cars that were smaller and more efficient, and the American manufacturers finally had to build similar cars to be competitive. Such a sequence also occurred in the tire industry.

The first U.S. legislation to regulate monopolies created the Interstate Commerce Commission (ICC) in 1887 to control the railroads. The railroad companies had obtained federal land grants and other subsidies for building the railways, but then charged shippers whatever they could get away with. Later the ICC gained control over interstate trucks and buses. On a broader level, in 1890 the Sherman Anti-trust Act declared criminal all "combination . . . in restraint of trade." Subsequent federal laws specifically restricted certain business mergers, purchase of stock in competing companies, exclusive contracts with one customer, interlocking directorates in competing firms, and other obstacles to free competition in interstate trade. The ICC was abolished January 1, 1996, and its remaining functions given to the Department of Transportation. However, state and federal agencies still regulate the prices and service quality of other "natural monopolies," such as electric power firms, and gas and telephone companies (the public utilities), and various government agencies still keep watch for violations of the Sherman Act.

Some contend that our standard of living would be much higher if all monopolistic practices were strictly prohibited so that many firms could develop and prosper in each field of business. Others claim that our antitrust laws are dysfunctional because they prevent mergers that would increase efficiency, that new firms soon arise to compete with successful monopolies, and therefore, that all antitrust legislation should cease (Armentaro, 1982). The trend in recent years has in fact been to accept more mergers, to prosecute less often for restraint of trade, and to negotiate lenient settlements in prosecutions (Jamieson, 1994).

The trend has been somewhat different in the global marketplace. Although multinational mergers of big companies do take place, international competition in manufacturing and distribution has also increased due to world trade expansion and reciprocal tariff reductions. Still, international oligopolies, such as the OPEC alliance of oil-producing nations, remain a serious threat. Their trade restraints can easily lead to unbearably high prices for crucial commodities. In the case of petroleum, the U.S. government has apparently decided to safeguard its access to needed supplies by overlooking the excesses of some cruel and repressive nations that have large oil supplies. Such penalties as boycotts of international oligopolies and rogue nations have apparently been adjudged too costly.

Squelching Bribery and Unlawful Campaign Funding

All societies seem to have what Gouldner (1960) called a "norm of reciprocity," the idea that anyone given anything is indebted to the giver. Repayment obligations may not be precisely calculated, and may be only informally enforced, but if people feed you, give you a gift, or do you a favor—especially if the act is not routine—you are expected to do something for them.

When a recipient cannot repay a benefit with a similar favor, an "asymmetry in exchange" develops. Peter Blau (1964) aptly pointed out that asymmetry in exchange gives the giver power over the recipient. The recipient is then expected to repay the giver in another way, often by providing services and loyalty. Asymmetries of exchange, which cause the differences in power within societies, are evident in the patrimonial systems of authority that prevail in most undemocratic countries. These countries are usually also technologically backward and have much inequality in wealth and education. One top authority, with relatives and cronies, provides the less powerful with protection and often some types of rights, goods, or services. In exchange, those in power demand subordination, goods, and labor.

Such patrimonial systems once predominated everywhere. Their purest form was feudalism, in which authority came by birth, and all persons swore fealty to those over them. But as money economies and democratic governments develop, Max Weber (1921/1978) noted, officials are increasingly limited in their distribution of favors by formal laws that require good financial records, written contracts, fair elections, and impartial adjudication. This change from purely patrimonial to more rational and law-based administration in business and government occurs slowly. As it does, gifts to persons in authority come to be condemned as bribery, but they rarely disappear completely. The danger is that decisions affected by such gifts or favors prevent maximum rationality and efficiency.

Bribes have different purposes. —Variance bribes" are payments for overlooking regulations, such as ignoring health or safety code violations (Reissman, 1979). —Outright purchase" bribes occur when an official is paid enough to be obligated primarily to the briber rather than to the employer. —Transaction bribes,— what others often call "lubrication" or money for "greasing palms," are the relatively small bribes that so often help get permits expedited, licenses issued, and favorable reports written.

Bribery is relatively uncommon in the United States as compared with some other countries, although charges of outright purchase bribes have occasionally been made by Congressional investigators against Department of Defense procurement officers. A slow decline also seems to have occurred in transaction bribes in business and, especially, in local government. Jacoby, Nehemkis, and Eels (1977) claim that the more a government regulates citizens' behavior, and the greater officials' discretion in granting permits, the greater is the prevalence of transaction bribery. They assert that Taiwan, by deregulating most of its industries, ended extensive bribery and thereby fostered phenomenal prosperity. In contrast, India's many required transaction fees promote corruption and impede its economy.

In the United States, a legal way to pay an elected official is to contribute to that person's campaign fund. More subtle gifts include free transportation on company planes and use of corporation resorts, as well as liberal speaking fees for talks to company employees. Perhaps the most obvious sort of bribery in U.S. official life surrounds campaign contributions. Although recipients commonly deny that it is so, large campaign contributions to an elected official obligate that person to the givers. Contributors expect, minimally, access to the official, and maximally, full compliance with any requests. To assure such benefit, many wealthy persons and organizations make regular payments to all leading candidates for offices that concern them.

It has been said that "people who give in larger sums or to more candidates than their fellow citizens are in effect voting more than once" (Nugent & Johannes, 1990, p. 10). Large contributions therefore seem unfair in a democracy. But to get elected to major U.S. political offices, many large contributions are needed, for the cost of campaigning increases with almost every election. The estimated total cost of all federal, state, and local election campaigns rose from $425 million in 1972 to $2.7 billion in 1988, a more than sixfold increase, and continues to rise. This increase is largely explained by growth in the total spent for political advertising— from $24.6 million in 1972 to $227.9 million in 1988, a more than ninefold increase (Alexander, 1992, pp. 82-84).

As deplorable as trends in campaign contribution patterns may be, bribery is probably much more extensive in business than in government today. Buyers for large corporations (e.g., manufacturers, department stores, or discount chains) often expect and receive gifts from those who seek orders from them. Wholesale sellers compete with each other in giving corporate officials lavish presents and entertainment, acts that would be crimes if doing business with a government official.

Prevention of Political Crime

The incidence of all types of bribery diminishes when a free press is actively exposing and criticizing wrongdoing by political figures and when independent legislatures and courts are actively punishing them. Also important historically in reducing bribery has been the change from the patrimonial system of appointing government employees through the political party in power to civil service appointment through competitive examinations, with job security largely independent of election results. These features have not made governments totally corruption free, but they make blatant bribes much less prevalent than they were formerly.

On January 1, 1996, the Lobbying Disclosure Act of 1995 took effect. It requires registration and semiannual reports from all persons who are employed for more than 20% of their time to influence federal legislators or other officials, or are paid more than $5,000 in 6 months by a single client for such activity. This law replaced a less strict 1946 law that was evaded by many—perhaps most—lobbyists, yet led to some prosecutions and penalties. It is too soon to assess the impact of the new law. Many cities, counties, and states also regulate lobbying, with diverse success, but many others do little or nothing to curtail it.

Much less regulated than campaign contributions by individuals or corporations have been those by Political Action Committees (PACs), which are established by businesses, unions, professional associations, foreign governments, or other interest groups to avoid limits on corporate and individual contributions to candidates. Since 1973, candidates for the U.S. presidency have been able to collect federal campaign funds in an amount that matches the total of individual contributions to their campaign of $250 or less. In return, candidates must accept limits on other donations. But there are no limits on independent campaigning for them by groups, including PACs, that are not part of their political organization. And although PACs may not contribute more than $5,000 annually to any candidate in a federal election, they can collect an unlimited amount of money to use in the process of campaigning. Many states are even less restrictive of PAC spending in nonfederal elections.

PACs contribute eight times as much to incumbents seeking reelection as to opposing candidates. This ratio prevails because those in office have already been able to favor contributors, their names have become familiar to the public, and about 90% of them seeking reelection win. One method that has been proposed for combating the advantage of incumbency has been to limit the number of successive terms that anyone can have in one office. However, term limits restrict the least corrupted officials as well as the most corrupted ones.

The main curbs to the power of "fat-cat" contributors have always been mass movements, such as Common Cause, Public Citizen, and other groups pushing for fairer elections, as well as the small contributors and volunteers who rally behind poorly funded but charismatic candidates or popular initiatives. These efforts may prevail against an opposition that is better funded, but most often the richest side wins.

Although many object to the idea of using tax money to pay for election campaigns, this method of funding can be much cheaper for the public than the favors that large contributors expect and receive from election winners. Phillip Stern (1992) has long proposed government campaign funding. He estimates that the cost of this support for both primary and general election campaigns for all House and Senate seats, plus the presidency, would total $400 million dollars, including $25 million to each of the two major parties for their national conventions. He points out that this cost is much less than the cost of the federal dairy subsidy, which was passed after dairy PACs contributed over $1 million to House and Senate campaigns; that subsidy costs consumers $2 billion annually in higher dairy prices. Many other public financial burdens are the result of legislation enacted as payback to campaign contributors.

Under Stern's plan, public funds would be given to all candidates in federal elections who collect at least a specified number of small contributions from a minimum number of different voters. Citizen-financed candidates would be permitted to buy radio, TV, or cable time at a reduced cost, such as half the station's lowest rate, up to a specified percentage of the station's for-sale time. To be eligible for this aid, however, candidates would have to appear in person for a minimum fraction of their broadcast time, and agree to be in a minimum number of broadcast debates with their opponents.

Quasi-bribery and extortion by large campaign contributors could also be reduced if we followed British and Australian models. These governments pay most election costs for candidates of the major parties, provide free television time, and limit the duration of campaigns to a relatively brief period, such as 4 weeks before election day. Several U.S. cities and states have begun some of these practices, and others are considering them, as have some federal legislators.

Profitable Penalties for Political Crime

Curbs on corporate contributions to presidential campaigns began with a 1907 law, and curbs were extended to labor unions in 1943 and 1947. The 1940 Hatch Act forbade individuals or businesses working for the federal government to contribute to federal elections. Controls increased with the 1972 legislation that created the Federal Election Commission for enforcement, and that limited an individual's campaign contributions to $1,000 to any candidate for federal office. This donation may be repeated in primary and general elections, but all federal election campaign contributions by one person may not exceed $25,000 per year. In addition, federal restrictions on gifts to senators and representatives keep growing.

State campaign contribution limits for individuals also tend to be shrinking but are very diverse (Alexander, 1992; Sorauf, 1992). Few states much restrict PAC contributions in state and local elections. However, most states require that PAC contributions be disclosed. State government agencies publish contribution data, but often only after the election.

Violators of limits on PAC gifts to a candidate for federal office often evade prosecution by creating several PACs with different names but that are funded by the same sources. News reports also show that many who make payments larger than the limits are not prosecuted. When convictions occur, appreciable fines and community service requirements with probation are the most profitable penalties, because these offenders are unlikely to be dangerous if unconfined.

Assuring Profits From
Punishments for Corporations

Crimes against the public, from pollution of the environment to illegal favors for elected officials, often become customary corporate practices. A firm's top-level officials are usually unaware of many lower-level decisions that create poisonous products, pollute factories, or fix prices by collusion to avoid competition. These crimes are committed by middle management personnel who perform specialized tasks and are rewarded or penalized for short-run changes in the production, sales, or costs of their units. Where illegal practices have long been routine, the risk of penalty is remote and guilt is minimal because co-workers share rationalizations for the illegal practices. Anthony Downs is credited with setting forth a Law of Diminishing Control that explains the way corporate crime becomes customary: The larger any organization becomes, the weaker is the control exercised by those at the top (Green, 1990, p. 99).

Even when a corporation is prosecuted, managers responsible for law violations are often unidentifiable or are no longer employed there. Furthermore, defense attorneys for corporations are skilled at keeping the government uninformed about their employers' culpability; getting continuances or filing appeals to delay the conclusion of hearings; and, if necessary, plea bargaining (Mann, 1985). Corporations can often negotiate settlement of cases in U.S. courts for very modest penalties and a plea of nolo contendere, which says that they do not contest the charges. This plea is attractive to corporations because it protects them against some civil suits and may confuse the public about their guilt. Largely analogous are "consent decrees" granted by some regulatory agencies, notably the SEC.

When a court or a regulatory agency finds a corporation guilty, the traditional penalty is a fine. A fine would be effective as a deterrent if it were appreciable and certain, but often the corporation considers the fine a business expense much lower than the profits from the original crime. In any case, Congressional funding of regulatory agencies dropped sharply in 1994, and thus a new low of only 250 federal prosecutions of businesses took place in that year (Burnham, 1995). In general, some other way of punishing corporate transgressions seems needed.

The accountability model, the Australian way of controlling workplace dangers, reformulated for many other types of offenses by Fisse and Braithwaite (1993), is a form of government-monitored corporate self-regulation. A regulatory agency begins most leniently, with advice, warnings, and persuasion. If these fail, fines may be imposed, and corporate remedial actions requested. When these methods do not suffice, court-ordered remedies are sought, and, if warranted, criminal sanctions. The severest criminal penalty, "corporate capital punishment," requires the firm's liquidation. Fisse and Braithwaite stress trying to avoid the "deterrence trap": punishing corporate offenses so severely as to force a firm into bankruptcy. Such an extreme outcome penalizes all the firm's employees and the communities in which it is established. Fisse and Braithwaite (1993) call for experimental and other research to enhance knowledge of what works best in various types of circumstances, and describe their accountability model as "a self-learning device" (p. 238).

Three distinct types of penalties for convicted corporations sometimes are more profitable to the public than money fines alone:

• *Equity fines*, proposed by John Coffee (1981) as an alternative to financial penalties, require that a convicted corporation give a state's victim compensation fund as many shares of its stock as have a current market value equal to a specified monetary fine. This sort of fine, he points out, can be worth much more than a fine in money, because the market value of a company's stock usually exceeds the cash it can raise. An equity fine also has a broader effect on the corporation's leaders: The declining value of a stock as a consequence of an equity fine makes this penalty a burden on stockholders and on top managers whose incentive payments are in stock options. Thus they will be motivated to monitor operations more closely to reduce the corporation's risk of punishment for its crimes. Top management also fears equity fines, Coffee claims, because diluted stock, being cheaper, is an easier target for hostile takeovers of the firm, which usually threaten management's jobs. But equity fines may not be as much of a threat as large cash fines, which may enhance a firm's chance of going bankrupt or getting a bad credit rating.

- *Independent monitors* are often appointed by a regulatory agency or a court to assure a corporation's conformity to its rulings. Convicted firms may be required to pay for such monitors, who represent the public and are independent of the company. Their task is to check that offenses cease and that restitution or other obligations imposed as penalties are fulfilled. These monitors send reports both to the firm and to concerned government agencies, and may recommend time limits for the company's correction of specified misconduct.

- *RICO* (The Racketeer Influenced and Corrupt Organizations Act of 1970) was intended to combat any organized crime that affects interstate commerce. It is applied especially to illegal drug distribution, but also to environmental pollution, bribery, illegal securities transactions, and other corporate offenses. Conviction under RICO requires proof that a pattern of racketeering or corrupt acts occurred, consisting of at least two distinctly different offenses within a 10-year period. This federal crime may be charged even for two similar acts, such as two illegal waste disposals or acceptance of bribes from two different people, and it may be charged even after state penalties have been imposed for the acts. RICO penalties can be severe, including forfeiture of all gains ascribed to the offenses, payment of triple damages to any victims, and up to 20 years in prison (Green, 1990, pp. 167-168, 223).

Such policies, pursued under dedicated leadership with adequate funding, can help agencies such as OSHA, FTC, and SEC effectively investigate corporations, adjudicate alleged violations, impose penalties, and order reforms successfully.

Preventing and Punishing Government Crime

A special category of criminality in legitimate occupations consists of acts by government officials in clear violation of criminal laws. For example, Congressional investigators and journalists have claimed that the CIA long supported smugglers of narcotics, arms, and other valuables who aided our military efforts in Vietnam and our attempts to control or subvert governments in Central America. Others are accused of profiteering through their government employment, notably for arms sales or shipping, mostly to nondemocratic forces. The CIA is also alleged to have recruited and paid assassins to murder politicians in nations with which we were not at war. Because of the Freedom of Information Act, it is now know that the FBI, for more than 40 years after World War II, had a deliberate policy of planting false reports to malign some civil rights and antiwar leaders. And the FBI, CIA, and military intelligence organizations opened mail and tapped telephones of thousands of American citizens in violation of the Fourth Amendment to the U.S. Constitution and various specific laws. Such crimes by intelligence agencies are common under dictatorships, but are also likely in a democracy whenever public opinion is polarized and government agencies are allowed much secrecy. Chambliss (1989) points out that

> state agencies whose activities can be hidden from scrutiny are more likely to engage in criminal acts than those whose record is public. . . . The more open the society, the less likely it is that state-organized crime will become institutionalized. (p. 284)

Zealots in these agencies, because they view themselves as on the right side in important issues, feel justified in using government resources illegally against those with whom they differ. A few are convicted and sentenced for such illegal activities, but most such crimes are unprosecuted, as they are committed with the tacit or overt approval of higher officials. The Watergate and Iran-Contra scandals were among the few revelations of state- organized crimes at the White House level in which several offenders were prosecuted and some got prison terms. How many such crimes occur at a lower level is unknown.

Government officials may be deterred from lawbreaking by the appointment and adequate funding of special prosecutors to investigate alleged crimes by government agencies, especially if such prosecutions actually lead to conviction and punishment of offenders. Use of special prosecutors increased during the 1990s, as did curbs on government secrecy. These measures enhance our system of checks and balances among the legislative, executive, and judicial branches of government.

Conclusion

Persons in legitimate occupations, because there are more of them, perpetrate more law violations than do people traditionally called criminals. Because most employees are not hardened criminals, the most profitable penalties reflect the offenders' prior offenses. Someone who has committed few prior crimes or none should pay fines and do community service, not be confined where her or his job-holding skills will wither away.

A corporation's criminal endangerment of its workforce is most spectacular when it leads to explosions or fires, but it is more frequently revealed as a gradual impairment of health through pollutants in the workplace. To prevent such insidious threats, more adequate funding of OSHA is needed for independent checking on workplace endangerment. Another profitable penalty may be enforced self-regulation, a system of rule making and monitoring by independent local boards with the government checking on these bodies, rather than formulating uniform rules for very diverse workplaces.

Crimes of legitimate businesses against the public are diverse, and some are extremely costly. As a rule, however, each dollar invested in such government regulatory agencies as OSHA, FTC, FDA, SEC, and EPA yields high profits because of the public benefits from preventing crimes as well as collecting fines. However, corporate lobbying efforts often succeed in cutting funds for these regulatory organizations, which is as unprofitable a policy as reducing tax collections by much more than budget cuts. A model for more profitable penalties may be the increasingly innovative penalties for corporations violating environmental protection laws. They are required not only to pay fines and restitution, but also to publicize their offenses and to invest in public education to prevent pollution.

Bribery is probably more persistent today in business than in government. But bribery of decision makers in both realms may be reduced by requiring fewer separate types of approvals from individual officials, plus more rigorous bookkeeping, clearer laws or rules, and objective tests for appointments and promotions. Mandated publicity, as well as fines and restitution, are likely to be profitable penalties for government and corporate officials alike.

Large political campaign contributions are today's most extensive form of bribery. They are often meant to promote public policies that favor businesses or special interest groups. PACs evade most regulation of large individual contributors. More complete government funding of advertising for major party candidates for important offices, plus limits on the lengths of campaigns, would be much less costly to the public than the favors that campaign contributors now get from government. Such reform is already well developed in Australia, Britain, and several other democracies; it has started in some of our states and should be expanded in federal elections.

Equity fines, which a convicted corporation pays to a state victim indemnity fund in shares of stock, provide one way to save the company while punishing top management for being lax about criminal actions by middle managers. A more severe penalty is requiring a convicted firm to pay for independent monitors to report to courts or regulatory agencies on its postconviction conformity with the law. RICO penalties, which may be very expensive and require long prison terms, are now our most severe way of suppressing corporate crimes.

Among government agencies, most criminal offenses seem to occur whenever the White House, the State or Defense Departments, the CIA, or other units of government long maintain secrecy. However, the Watergate and Iran-Contra scandals were exposed by our free press and investigated under our system of checks and balances, whereby Congress and the federal courts oversee executive agencies. A passion for maximum feasible responsibility and openness in government will set an example for those in business and thus further help to reduce crime by those in legitimate occupations.

9

Incapacitating
Professional, "Career,"
and Psychopathic Criminals

People from many lands, and all centuries, have told stories of full-time predators: thieves, bandits, highwaymen, pirates, brigands, or racketeers. Then and now, the professionals who devote themselves to crime enjoy fairly steady illegal incomes, with hardly any interruption by arrest. If they are caught, they present a difficult problem for those interested in profitable penalties. Normally, they can be punished for only one or a few of their many crimes.

Two other categories of offenders, with the imprecise labels "career criminal" and "psychopath," are often confused with professionals. This chapter explains the differences among them in methods and motivations and in the effectiveness of various penalties.

Pursuing Professional Criminals

Persons traditionally called professionals, such as lawyers and physicians, have several characteristics in common:

- They earn their livelihood by their expertise.
- They use esoteric terminology that is like a private language.
- They share standards of competence and ethics.

◆ Their field has formal entry requirements, such as schooling, examinations, internships, probationary periods, and state licensing.

◆ They form organizations (e.g., bar associations, medical associations)
   that promote their interests as well as build their pride, loyalty, and
   expertise.

Pride in occupation and commitment to its values motivate the work of
professionals. They want to impress colleagues favorably, apart from seeking an income from their activities.

Not only the most prestigeful occupations, but also many other types
of skilled labor—cooks, plumbers, and barbers, for example—have elements of professionalism. Those long in such trades are proud of their
competence, use distinctive terminology, and deride others in their line
of work who have less professional methods or values. Some quasi-
professional occupations maintain standards through trade organizations
and licensing.

Many master criminals share all these characteristics of professionals
except licensing. Professional criminals pursue lawbreaking as a primary
occupation. They differ from amateur offenders in their greater skill,
wisdom, and self-control, which enable them to commit crimes more
continuously without getting caught. Professional criminals identify with
others of similar ability and use a slang or argot unfamiliar to others. They
maintain "connections" with or knowledge about many persons who can
further their illegal enterprises—for example, potential partners in crime,
customers for the goods they steal, bail bondsmen, and defense lawyers.
They also study the police, prosecutors, and judges, sharing with one
another much lore on these officials and ways to deal with them. Sometimes professional criminals organize as teams, gangs, or syndicates that
maintain standards of ability, values, and loyalty.

Unlike other professionals, however, professional criminals have an
ideology that rationalizes predatory behavior—for example, that others
do worse things and go unpunished, that everyone has a price. They
regard all who moralize about crime as hypocrites. Tannenbaum's (1938,
chap. 7) classic analysis referred to the professional criminal's "warrior
psychosis," which is expressed in "ruthlessness towards enemies and
traitors" (p. 178) and an "all-pervading suspicion" that "is a natural
protective covering" (p. 183). Professional criminals transmit this lore in
gatherings at bars, restaurants, or other places that become their hangouts,
and in traveling and working together. In such settings, past successes and

failures are analyzed, and persons are informally rated by their performance in crimes.

Professional criminals make their illegal work stable by reducing its risks. Many drink and use drugs, but not as heavily and frantically as street addicts, chronic alcoholics, and childhood-transition offenders, who are more likely to commit crimes impulsively. Most professional offenders show caution, shrewdness, and skill.

The greater self-control of professional criminals shows even in their adolescent offenses. John Mack (1972) found that only a third of 102 British full-time "able criminals" had acquired juvenile records. Juvenile offenders develop into professional criminals when they capably carry out adolescent lawbreaking, favorably impressing the more mature and sophisticated criminals, who then ask the young offenders to assist in larger crimes. Young offenders are disdained by professionals unless they can show that they are "solid," meaning sophisticated in lawbreaking and mature in lifestyle (Letkemann, 1973, chap. 5).

All who persist in crime and become close associates of other criminals verbalize a code of ethics that may be summarized (largely following Inciardi, 1975) as

- Do not hold out on partners in crime.
- Deal honestly; "level" with partners in crime.
- If caught, try to fix cases—"put in a good word"—for partners.
- Never inform on partners or on any other criminal.

The most persistent moral theme in conversations among criminals is how evil it is to inform ("snitch," "fink," "sing," be a "stool pigeon"). Yet police and prison officials solve many crimes following tips from other offenders, usually provided in realistic expectation that the favor will be reciprocated by reduction of charges or of bail, or by greater comforts while confined. Many criminals who help each other while committing crimes, when caught will bargain for their own security at the expense of others. Some assert that their Golden Rule, learned "the hard way," is "Do unto others before they do it to you."

We learn about professional criminals from interviews with the probably atypical ones who are caught, and from a few in the community whom some investigators manage to know and write about, or who write autobiographies. We can only infer that professionals are numerous, mainly because of the many unsolved crimes that seem to be done by atypically skillful and careful offenders.

Varieties of Professional Crime

Professional crime is immensely varied, but it falls into four major categories: theft, burglary, and fencing; fraud; violent crime; and organized crime. It ranges from confidence games to truckload hijackings, from counterfeiting to gangland assassinations. It is not the types of offenses, but how they are perpetrated and the lifestyles of the perpetrators that identify professional crime.

Professional Theft, Burglary, and Fencing

Many professional criminals make a living by taking other people's property. Their methods change in reaction to changing economic conditions and changing technology for protecting property. The future will probably bring further innovations in stealing (or "larceny," the old English term that the law still uses), because all new valuable items and all new security initiatives challenge the ingenuity of thieves. Currently, however, the main forms of professional stealing are pickpocketing, auto theft, and burglary. Professional thieves are aided in their work by fences.

Pickpocketing is one of the oldest professions. Its devotees often work in teams, with two to four persons dividing the tasks:

- Identifying a potential victim or "mark"
- Distracting or "stalling" the mark—for example, by flattering and chatting, by asking for help in judging a garment in a store, or by bumping as though accidentally and either apologizing profusely or arguing angrily about the accident
- Removing the wallet
- Passing the wallet to another, who quietly slips away

Some pickpockets work with fewer people playing these separate roles. Others work alone.

Among the places that pickpockets work are football or other games, and race tracks, where exciting events—such as a long run or a close finish—bring the spectators to their feet with attention completely riveted. It is then that thieves, unnoticed by the fans, take previously targeted wallets, meanwhile carrying programs or other items to hide their hand movements and the loot (Inciardi, 1983). Crowded resorts where vacationers bring money, drink too much, and seek pleasure carelessly have also always attracted professional criminals.

Making a living as a professional pickpocket has become more difficult since people stopped going out so much at night. Television has made home entertainment more popular, and fear of crime keeps many people at home. In addition, increased use of credit cards and traveler's checks has somewhat discouraged pickpocketing by reducing the amount of cash that can be stolen. But pickpockets are now finding a market for stolen credit cards, and some thieves use them immediately, forging the signature.

Auto theft is changing as well. It was once mostly the teenage sport of joyriding until out of gas, then abandoning the vehicles; thus, the total losses to owners and insurance firms were only a small fraction of the high value of the cars. But increasingly, vehicles are taken by professionals or by youths recruited by professionals to steal and sell cars to them. The vehicles are then sold with different license plates and papers, or are stripped for salable parts and abandoned. Between 1983 and 1989, California's annual motor vehicle thefts rose by 57%, and vehicles recovered with parts removed increased by 250% (California Bureau of Criminal Statistics, 1990).

Many professional auto thieves specialize in stealing certain car parts or such stereo equipment as radios, tape decks, compact disc players, and speakers, removing these items in seconds. Professional vehicle thieves are expert at opening and starting cars, trucks, and motorcycles without keys, getting duplicate keys, altering serial numbers, creating false registration papers, repainting, and transporting their loot to places where it is unlikely to be identified as stolen. Many vehicles stolen in the Southwestern United States are taken to Mexico for alteration of registration and resale there. Professional auto thieves prefer luxury cars, but focus on makes and models that are common, hence inconspicuous.

Unlike auto theft, *burglary*—breaking into a locked place to commit a serious crime, usually theft—still is mostly done by "kids in the neighborhood," primarily at residences when no one is at home. Amateur burglars' median age at arrest is about 18, but many start at 13 or earlier. Contrastingly, professional burglars are adults who steal valuable goods from stores, wealthy homes, and banks or other financial institutions. Their team may include a tipster or "finger," who for a share of the loot or a cash fee locates "good scores" (valuable loot safely obtainable); a lookout, who may sit in the getaway car and listen to police radios; an expert in evading burglar alarms; a safecracker; and persons skilled in tunneling through walls or floors from adjacent buildings. Safes are now less often burglary targets than formerly, as checks and credit cards have replaced cash and armored trucks make frequent pick-ups at stores. Thus most professional burglars now steal merchandise in wholesale quantities for which they have procured an "order" in advance, often for shipment to a distant place.

To receive stolen goods knowingly is a crime, but "fences," those who regularly buy stolen goods, are among the most secure and prosperous professional criminals. Fences generally run what appear to be legitimate businesses, often selling wholesale and retail. Much of their merchandise comes from legal sources, but their largest profits are from buying stolen goods cheaply. They are wary about buying from strangers, but to those with whom they deal, they indicate what they will buy and at what price. For mutual safety, these suppliers and the fences do not tell each other much about their methods and sources (Klockars, 1974; Steffensmeier, 1986; Walsh, 1977).

Professional Fraud

Much criminal gain comes from persuading people to hand over their money or other valuables voluntarily, unaware of being cheated. Often the victims think that they are cheating others. Crimes of fraud, often called *swindling*, include forgery, computer fraud, counterfeiting, false insurance claims, and confidence games.

Amateur forgery is typically done by persons who run out of money while pursuing a vice, such as drinking, gambling, or seeking sex. These "naive forgers," as Edwin Lemert (1967, chap. 7) called them, write small checks to continue their activities. They overdraw their own account or use checks or credit cards of friends or relatives. Their bank, or the person whose account is used, usually does not press criminal charges if restitution occurs or seems likely. This pattern is persistent because it is linked to chronic vices, especially drinking, but is not professional. In recent years it has increasingly occurred among women. In contrast, "systematic forgers," again Lemert's (1967, chaps. 8 & 9) label, are professional criminals who use stolen or counterfeit credit cards, checks, driver's licenses, and sometimes passports to make many purchases in one area, then move elsewhere, often with another set of documents. Sometimes they work alone, but often in couples or larger teams of both sexes. Professional forgery is a very stressful life, Lemert notes, especially if done alone, because the person is rarely in one place long enough to form relationships with other people.

A more recent crime linked to forgery is computer fraud, which has grown rapidly as electronic transfer of money and titles has increased. Criminals make unauthorized computer entries to steal funds or other property. Some estimate that the annual cost of such offenses totals billions. These crimes are punishable under theft and fraud laws, but in the 1980s California pioneered legislation specifically on computer crimes, and other states have followed.

Counterfeiting of currency or of other negotiable documents has been a type of professional fraud since ancient times. It has repeatedly prompted innovations in printing and detection, which then evoke new criminal techniques. Only experts can recognize professional counterfeiting. Faked currency of nations with strong economies, such as Switzerland or the United States, is often smuggled into poor countries, where it is in greatest demand and can most profitably be spent. Revolutionary and terrorist groups do much counterfeiting of currency and passports. Not until the 1950s did the United States become very active in Interpol, a world association of police forces created in 1923 to combat these and other professional crimes.

Insurance companies are frequent victims of fraud, some of it professional. One prevalent insurance swindle in older cities, especially in the slums, is for owners of buildings that could more profitably be converted to another use to hire arsonists and then collect the insurance benefits. The destruction reduces the cost of dismantling buildings and eliminates the obligation to pay tenants for relocation. It is often done only after the buildings have long been neglected and have begun to incur citations and repair orders that the owner ignores. Not only does this swindle hurt the insurance companies that pay the claims; it also causes tenant losses of shelter and possessions, and even horrible deaths by fire (Simon & Witte, 1982; Slade, 1978).

The most democratic, colorful sort of swindle, which is achieved by persuading persons to trust someone and then violating this trust, is called a "confidence game," "bunco," "scam," or "larceny by trick." It has existed throughout history, often as a full-time job. David Maurer's (1940) classic analysis of these swindles distinguished up to 10 steps:

1. Locating the victim or "mark" by opening a temporary office, sometimes in a hotel, and advertising in local newspapers, radio, and television about "investment opportunities"; or on a smaller scale,

through word of mouth by confidence men or women who attend conventions, take tours, or go to resorts where they are likely to meet gullible small business operators, widows and widowers, and retirees.

2. Gaining the victim's confidence by a team member called the "roper" or "shill," who impresses the mark as a prosperous person accustomed to making money cleverly, hence one whom the mark feels flattered to know.

3. Introducing the mark to the "insider" through the roper (sometimes assisted by other shills), who refers to the insider as a source of profitable deals.

4. Explaining or verifying, in which the insider confirms her or his success in the course of leisurely conversations in which the mark is flattered.

5. Issuing the come-on, in which the mark is invited to join in an investment or two, and makes some easy money.

6. Sizing up the mark, in which the insider or the roper boasts about large investments and transactions to elicit the mark's financial disclosures.

7. Sending the mark for the largest feasible sum when the mark has the idea that all are eager to invest lavishly and wants "to get in on it" too.

8. Fleecing the mark by involving her or him in a large but "losing" investment, while conveying the impression that all in the group are losing.

9. Separating from the mark either abruptly, or often by one or more ropers or the insider staying to "cool the mark out."

10. Forestalling prosecution by creating the impression that the mark is an accomplice in a crime, by hiding or destroying the evidence, or by shifting the loot to new accounts.

Erving Goffman (1952) pointed out that the mark's problem of coping with failure is common in everyday life, and is due more to losing face than to anger over losing money. Typically the mark believes "that he is a pretty shrewd person when it comes to making a deal and that he is not the sort of person who is taken in by anything" (p. 452). Wily swindlers may fleece the mark repeatedly, with "come-on" gains between losses. Marks may even thank the swindler for explaining their ostensibly shared loss.

Confidence games may be perpetrated on any scale. Maurer (1940) distinguished as "Big cons" the games that last for days, weeks, or months, often involving numerous persons and sham offices or stores. "Short cons" are completed in a few hours and have amazing success, despite their wide use for decades.

One well-used short con is the "pigeon drop." Every small town and all big-city neighborhoods repeatedly suffer it, despite assumptions that "no one is dumb enough to fall for it." The swindlers often choose a victim at a savings bank, whom they then follow. One of them, when near the mark, pretends to find a package with a large amount of money. An accomplice also happens to be there. The finder pretends that they all found it, and should share. Loot from this short con is gained when the money finder or the accomplice suggests that each of them advance several hundred or even a thousand dollars to show that they are used to handling large sums, and the other agrees. This makes the mark, from pride and greed, feel similarly obligated. Sometimes one of these swindlers asserts that the found money is probably from a drug dealer and can rightfully be kept. Often one of them feigns calling an attorney for advice, and is told that they must deposit "good faith money" with the attorney and wait a specified period to see if the found money is claimed. At some point the mark deposits the found money, and the new "partners" all vanish. The mark, from shame over being duped, often does not notify the police, but the Los Angeles Police Department reports more than a half million dollars is lost annually to this game in that city. It is frequent nationwide, in communities of all sizes.

Swindlers also perpetrate innumerable varieties of real estate frauds. For instance, they often advertise vacation or retirement homes or land but depart with deposits and contracts before many customers realize that they were duped. Home repair or remodeling scams encourage owners to believe that a firm will do needed major rebuilding of their residences on easy credit. The owners sign a contract for the work, which is often not described precisely in writing, and title to the home serves as collateral until many years of monthly payments have been completed. But the firm fails to do the kind of work orally promised and correctly points out that it is not clearly indicated in the contract. If payments are delinquent, the firm claims title to the home and often has the occupants evicted.

The variety of scams is amazing. For instance, there is much fraud in sale of vocational and other types of instruction. Applicants are told that their entrance exams or trial lessons show great talent. After payment in full in advance, the lessons become more difficult, and few complete the course. In video or audio piracy, criminals copy recordings without paying royalties and sell them very profitably as originals. Immigrants, especially those who enter the country illegally, are often duped by swindlers of their own nationality who are more fluent in English than they. The swindlers claim to be able to handle government or business problems for them.

Frequently these persons collect large sums for services that are free from the government, or claim that they need money for expenses, often for alleged bribes, that actually are neither needed nor paid. Carnivals, circuses, county fairs, boardwalks, and amusement parks have a large variety of "grift" games in which mechanical devices or card games are manipulated to let the victims and shills make some easy money before the victims bet more and lose.

The only prerequisite for most confidence games is the mark's eagerness for "easy money" or "bargains," legal or not. Typical con artists are skilled thespians, egocentric and proud of their shrewdness, especially when they hoodwink persons of superior education or wealth.

Professional Violent Crime

Most of the violent offenders who are professionals engage in robbery, kidnapping, or extortion. The common element is the use of force or the threat of force to obtain money or some other valuable.

Robbery is taking another's property by force or threat of force. Robberies are often associated with guns, but a gun may or may not be used. Most unarmed robberies, or "muggings," are committed by adolescent and young adult offenders who beat up weaker or outnumbered victims. Professionals, on the other hand, favor armed robberies, but guns are becoming so numerous among children that impulsive armed robberies by juveniles have increased. Because victims surrender possessions readily if confronted by a gun, injury rates are actually higher in unarmed robberies than in armed robberies.

Specialized robbers emerge among childhood-transition offenders, according to Jack Katz (1988), by acquiring roles as "hard men" in delinquent or criminal circles. They take pride in dominating a robbery situation by loud threats while seizing valuables from cowed victims. To hesitate or flee after this bravado would be humiliating to their self-image, so the novices often stay too long after an alarm has sounded and are caught. A few learn to maintain self-control and leave in time to escape with the goods. Despite the danger, they develop a strong motivation to commit robbery. Its "seduction," Katz says, is the reputation it gives them as hard men.

Bank robbery is one of the best-known forms of this crime. A fair amount of it is amateur, committed by financially strapped adults who out of desperation take a gun to a bank or other place with money. Haran and Martin (1984) classified 22% of 500 bank robbers convicted in Brooklyn, New York, as "amateurs" with no or only one prior property-crime conviction, 25% as "casual" with two or three prior convictions, 24% as "compulsives" seeking funds for alcohol or drugs, and only 29% as the most professional "Heavy-Career" bank robbers. Presumably career robbers are the ones who most often evade arrest, but bank robbery is less safe than most professional crime because witnesses and hidden cameras see the offenders, and explosive dye packages are hidden in bundles of money that cashiers keep on hand to give bank robbers (often with only the outside bills real). In addition, bank robberies mobilize the FBI, our most resourceful police agency. Clarke (1992, pp. 21, 66) claims that preventive measures instituted in banks in many nations have eliminated regular success at this offense.

Yet professional robbery persists wherever teams of specialists, with much planning, can get highly concentrated wealth from banks, jewelry stores, and armored vans. Roles may include an outside lookout, the driver of a getaway car, one or more inside lookouts, and one or more who collect the loot. Many professional robbers remain calm but deliberately keep potential witnesses confused by startling and intimidating their victims, threatening to kill, and yelling loud profanity. Disguises reduce risks of later identification, and the getaway vehicle is a stolen car that will be abandoned where another vehicle has been parked (Conklin, 1972; Haran & Martin, 1984).

One specialized form of robbery on the rise is carjacking—taking a vehicle by force or, more often, by threat of force, as by waving a gun at the person with the keys. In the 1990s, as guns proliferated, both juveniles and professionals in car theft shifted to carjacking. Carjacking accounts for only about 2% of the nearly 2 million cars stolen annually in the United States, but has been increasing. Most such robberies occur in parking lots or garages (Rand, 1994).

In less technologically developed parts of the world, professional robber gangs may also commit much violence. Many are deserters or veterans of armed forces, usually those that lost wars, and often from guerrilla forces that "lived off the land" by pillaging. After the revolt fails, the rebels tend to persist in robbery and forget politics. Throughout history, these robbers have been called "bandits," "brigands," or, if at sea, "pirates." They have been much celebrated, from Robin Hood to the stagecoach and bank robbers of the American West, many of whom were Civil War veterans, mainly from the Confederacy. Eric Hobsbawm (1981) shows that banditry has had a very uniform history in many countries. It remains prominent in less stable nations of Latin America, Africa, Asia, and Eastern Europe.

Kidnapping and extortion are two other professional crimes of violence. Intensive FBI reactions to alleged interstate kidnappings seem to have deterred them in the United States, but they are frequent elsewhere, notably in Italy, Latin America, and the Philippines. *Extortion*, the use of threats to force compliance with some criminal request, is often linked to confidence games. Criminals ferret out damaging information about wealthy persons, or tempt them into embarrassing situations where they photograph them, then demand money for keeping photos or information confidential.

Similarly, organized criminals employ professional "hit men" to extort cooperation and eliminate competition in order to acquire a local monopoly in a legal or illegal business. Limited research on professional hit men indicates that at first they are robbers who kill a victim or witness and are not caught. Then they are offered large sums for assassinations, and become more efficient and dispassionate at their work (Dietz, 1983).

Professionally Organized Crime

So many crimes are perpetrated by two or more accomplices, that the phrase *organized crime* can fit most lawbreaking, but here, as in Chapter 5, this label has its customary connotation. It refers to relatively stable groups that collaborate in large criminal enterprises such as selling protection, making usurious loans, or selling drugs or gambling services. Crime organizations use threat, violence, or bribery to control participants; would-be competitors; complainers; and, in many areas, unions, trade associations, or local politicians.

In some areas, conflict between organized crime gangs often becomes deadly warfare for dominance. Earlier in this century, Italian American gangs won in our largest Northeast and Midwest cities, then feuded with each other. Several times annually for decades (although less often in recent years), organized crime leaders were assassinated. These homicides were presumably committed by professionals contracted for each killing. In a period when three out of four murders were cleared by arrest and conviction, less than one in a hundred gangland murders had this outcome.

In the 1920s, as Chapter 5 indicated, when Prohibition made the alcoholic beverage industry accessible only to those willing to violate the law, Italian immigrants had advantages in urban bootlegging. They came mostly from Southern Italy, where bandit groups such as the Mafia in Sicily and the Camorra in the Naples area had arisen centuries earlier to resist foreign conquerors and absentee landlords and then engaged in local crime and politics. Cultures in these areas greatly value loyalty to kin, repayment of favors, and secrecy about crimes by relatives and friends. Violence and vandalism are commonly employed to enforce these values and to extort money, especially from outsiders (Hess, 1973; Nelli, 1976; Servadio, 1976). The best validated accounts of the Mafia show that it has consisted primarily of autonomous local "family" organizations rather than tightly controlled national or international hierarchies, as is often alleged. Yet loose alliances among these families, varying in duration, frequently are formed for business or warfare.

After the 1933 repeal of Prohibition, and aided by resources accumulated from prior bootlegging, many Mafiosos prospered in other illegal enterprises (e.g., selling stolen securities, corrupting the building and trash-collection industries, and hijacking trucks). But as Italian Americans prospered and left the slums, they also advanced in legitimate businesses, professions, and politics.

Our knowledge of Mafia operations in the United States comes mainly from Senate investigations, mostly in the 1950s, and from the federal prosecutions of Cosa Nostra between 1978 and 1988, plus the corrupt Teamster union locals that they controlled (Jacobs, 1994). Newspaper and magazine headlines probably exaggerate current Italian and Mafia dominance of national and worldwide organized crime.

The Italians have been largely replaced in organized crime by newer migrants to our urban slums, notably African Americans, Latinos, and, most recently, Asians. Many in each ethnic and racial group, when new immigrants, initiate professional crime by maintaining native customs of lending money at usurious rates to those unable to get loans from banks. They then organize to serve their group's illegal vices, such as gambling and drugs, but gradually recruit customers and accomplices of other ethnicities. Much collaboration of foreign and U.S. organized crime groups occurs now in smuggling drugs and illegal immigrants into our country.

Loan sharking is well established not only in ethnic communities, but at many large employment places, especially where paydays are monthly. Typically, these offenders offer loans to be repaid at payday with 20% or more interest per week. If the principal is not repaid on time, only the interest must be paid weekly, and partial repayments of the principal are not accepted. Payments are encouraged by threats that hired "goons" will injure a defaulting debtor or the debtor's family. In practice, violence is rare, most loans are repaid, and the convenience of this money source is appreciated when its recipients are fearful about going to legal loan sources.

Racketeering and corruption by criminal organizations have long prevailed in much large-scale urban construction. Crime groups often control some firms and unions, and they corrupt government agencies through bribery, adding billions to building costs (Goldstock, Marcus, Thacher, & Jacobs, 1990). They also have come to dominate commercial garbage and other waste disposal businesses in several areas by vandalizing and terrorizing competitors, then allocating customers to their several small firms, in restraint of trade (Reuter, 1993).

Many professional criminal groups commit scams by gaining control of a legitimate firm. From it they take high salaries or large loans, or they have the company make credit purchases for their benefit, before leaving it in bankruptcy.

Profitable Penalties for Professional Criminals

Catching professional criminals is difficult. Al Capone and other Prohibition-era gangsters were ultimately imprisoned only because their reported income could not have supported their lavish lifestyles. To prevent the authorities from detecting even such indirect signs of criminality, professional criminals now often hide their illegal income as well as their large purchases, aided by Swiss and Caribbean bank accounts immune to prosecutor examination. They also "launder" their money by disguising its sources and ownership or by reporting illegal income as legal and paying taxes on it.

Another tool in the hands of those pursuing professional criminals is the wiretap. Congress in 1968 permitted federal courts to give police 30-day authorizations to tap telephones. Yet this long-sought weapon proved helpful in only a few high-level cases, as it costs thousands of dollars for much monitoring, and it is still controversial in the courts.

Organized crime is especially difficult to prosecute. Witnesses are often threatened and sometimes killed. The federal "witness protection program," which gives some witnesses a guarded hideout during a trial plus a new location and identity thereafter, is too expensive and imperfect for most cases. Furthermore, as Peter Reuter (1983) depicts well in his aptly titled *Disorganized Crime*, the provision of illegal goods and services is loosely organized. Many "legitimate" businesspeople cheat their associates, change their affiliations, lose customers to competitors, and take or keep customers by threat or intimidation.

Relatively infrequently, professional criminals are brought to justice. It seems reasonable to punish by long confinement those who are finally caught after years or decades in full-time, professional crime against many victims. A severe penalty is warranted both to obtain just deserts and to protect the public from further offenses. But when a professional criminal is arrested, this type of incapacitation is unlikely, often because most of the offender's crimes are unknown to the police. To help uncover punishable crimes whenever lawbreaking is done in a very professional manner, police and prosecution should investigate whether the offender's apparent cost of living has been compatible with his or her legitimate income. If not, a search for evidence of other crimes should have high priority.

To prevent a highly successful professional predator from again victimizing others when released, the maximum legal period of restraint is likely to be needed. Long incarceration plus heavy fines is incapacitating and may also be deterrent. RICO (Racketeer Influenced and Corrupt Organization) statutes (discussed in Chapter 8) permit severe federal penalties for organized criminals convicted of two or more offenses in a decade, regardless of their prior state penalties for these crimes.

Yet if former professional offenders are released from confinement while still capable of earning a living legally, efforts to get them into legitimate roles can be successful (Glaser, 1964, chap. 4 and 1969, chap. 3; Sampson & Laub, 1993; Shover, 1985). They may be most successful if released under close supervision. Many of these persons have good verbal skills and high intelligence, which is useful in sales or other legal occupations, and frequently they have experience at types of conventional employment to which they can return. Indeed, many have funds or family that help them get a business started. For example, a man known as one of the nation's most successful fences for 20 years before getting a federal prison term for interstate transport of stolen merchandise, when released on parole respectably operated his own mobile-home lot (Glaser, 1964, p. 60 and 1969, p. 36).

Curbing "Career Criminals"

A few decades ago, leaders of our "war on crime" began to demand long imprisonment for those they called "career criminals." Prompted by evidence that a few percentages of our male population is charged with about half the serious crimes cleared by arrest, the Justice Department subsidized research to identify these "high-rate" offenders. It also called for special prosecution procedures to assure their getting long prison terms.

To understand these career criminals better, Rand Corporation researchers developed apparently reliable ways of asking prisoners about the usual frequency of their crimes, both those for which they were caught and others, as well as their legal sources of income and their vices during their last periods of freedom. The first Rand study showed that in a California prison, males convicted of armed robbery could be divided into "intermittents" and "intensives." The average annual crime rate of intensives when free was 10 times as high as that of the intermittents. Although intensives committed five times as many offenses per arrest as the intermittents, they engaged in one crime after another so rapidly that they were twice as likely to be arrested in any month in which they were free (Petersilia, Greenwood, & Lavin, 1977). Neither group showed a high level of planning, sophistication, or specialization in their lawbreaking.

The largest Rand study of career criminals sampled all male prisoners received in every prison and in the major jails of California, Texas, and Michigan. Resembling the intensives of the first study were 15% whom the researchers initially called "versatile predators" and later "violent predators." These criminals robbed, assaulted, sold drugs, and committed other crimes of many types, including more burglaries than those specializing in that offense. They started crime when younger, had more arrests, more juvenile confinement, and less legitimate work than inmates with other crime patterns. Most also spent an average of $50 a day on heroin, and used much alcohol and other drugs (Chaiken & Chaiken, 1982). These violent predators were so reckless and impulsive in their crimes and intoxications that few were long out of prison. They wanted careers as professional criminals, but their high rate of drug use and adolescent lifestyles in lawbreaking made them career prisoners instead (Collins, Hubbard, & Rachal, 1985).

One of the most thorough studies of incarcerated high-rate offenders is Malin Åkerström's (1985) *Crooks and Squares*. It was based on interviews and questionnaire surveys of Swedish male prisoners and of law-abiding male Swedes of about the same ages. Her findings, and her review of such studies elsewhere, make it evident that those imprisoned in many nations are quite similarly high-rate lawbreakers trying in vain to be professional criminals. Åkerström found that these lawbreakers commit many more offenses than those for which they are caught, and crime was more rewarding to them than any legitimate jobs they ever held.

Åkerström's subjects were proud of their successful offenses, and rationalized their failures. Their egos were also enhanced by their ability to dupe authorities and exploit rehabilitation programs while planning further crimes, but they generally were soon back in prison. Such persistent property offenders have a commercial orientation, Åkerström found, and a larger percentage of them than of the comparison sample had actually operated businesses. The prisoners viewed themselves favorably as risk takers, emphasizing as their rewards in lawbreaking not only the money, but also the independence and excitement.

The carelessness these persons showed in their crimes seemed due to personality traits also evident in their noncriminal activities, traits that produced high failure rates in both. For example, 58% of the prisoners but only 14% of the others who filled out Åkerström's questionnaires disagreed with the statement "When I am going by car, I always fasten the seat belt"; 64% of the inmates but only 33% of the comparison group disagreed with "Before I go out shopping, I make a shopping list." Unlike professional criminals, Åkerström's wanna-bes were persistently impulsive and had been addiction-prone since childhood.

These traits make career criminals poor risks for release. Thus they can most profitably be punished by incapacitation for the full just-desert limits of the offenses for which they were convicted. While confined, efforts should be made to give them better habits of self-discipline, optimally by training and experience in skilled work, and in relationships with ex-offenders or other law-abiding persons to whom they can relate positively. Release should be gradual, with close monitoring and assistance to assure and facilitate their psychological maturation and their integration into acceptable social roles and relationships.

Protecting the Public From Psychopaths

One unanswered issue about those most persistent in lawbreaking is whether they represent a distinct biological type. Darwin's theory of evolution inspired many to ascribe the affinity for crime to biological differences between criminals and the rest of us, postulating that offenders are throwbacks to a more primitive stage in development of the human species. These ideas motivated 19th-century research on biological traits of criminals. Widely cited reports by the Italian prison physician Cesar Lombroso described ape-like or Neanderthal features in the skulls and skeletons of individual convicts. British statistical research by Charles

Goring, however, showed that these traits were as common in soldiers and police officers as in prisoners.

Some lawbreaking is committed by almost everyone at one time or another, so Gabor (1994) is certainly justified in contending that "criminality is most accurately viewed as a matter of degree, rather than as an attribute that we either possess or lack" (p. xiii). Yet, as detailed in Chapter 6, many statistically significant differences between those with delinquent and criminal records and those without them are demonstrable. In particular, offenders more frequently have both biological and other handicaps.

Several investigators have found that frequent offenders have sluggish nervous systems and thus are less likely than other persons to respond to pain. Lykken (1957) showed that convicts tend to be slower than presumably noncriminal college students in learning to avoid painful electric shocks for making errors in a finger-maze puzzle. Lykken (1982) later concluded that exceptionally fearless persons in motor racing and aviation have similarly low emotional arousal under stress. Raine (1993) also found that offenders tend to have slow heart beats and sluggish arousal of their autonomic nervous systems, both in response to pain and in returning to a normal state after arousal.

Schachter (1971) and his assistants pretended to give adrenalin to some prisoners to arouse their nervous systems, but actually gave a placebo to a random fraction of them. They found that those with the stimulant significantly exceeded those with the placebo in learning to avoid electric shocks in a finger maze. In another experiment, they pretended to give everyone in a class the tranquilizer chlorpromazine, to depress their nervous systems and reduce anxiety, but gave a random portion of them a placebo. They then had the students sit, ostensibly for another experiment, in walled booths from which each could see the blackboard without being seen by the others. But first, the experimenters said that because they had not had time to grade a recent class test, they would return the papers to have the students grade their own from answers on the board. Actually, the experimenters had copied the students' test sheets before returning them. They found that those with the tranquilizer (and thus, ostensibly, lower sensitivity to stress) cheated significantly more by changing their answers than did those with the placebo.

These studies suggest that sluggish nervous systems create what psychiatrists call "psychopathic personalities," lacking both conscience and fear of punishment. This personality aberration can be ascribed not only to criminals but also, as Herbert Cleckley (1976) influentially noted, to some respected and powerful "pillars of society" who have what he called a "mask of sanity." After World War II, writers often ascribed psychopathy to extreme deprivation of love in childhood, and thus replaced this term by "sociopathy." From statistical evidence that many sociopaths differ biologically from other persons, however, "psychopath" returned to preferred usage.

One major limitation of the concept "psychopath" is its unreliability when used. Psychiatrists and psychologists who work with prisoners use this term only for the few who impress them as the worst, but those who work mainly with noncriminal patients apply it to almost every convicted criminal they encounter. During World War II, psychiatrists examining draftees could reject them from military service by any of four diagnoses: severely psychoneurotic, psychotic, psychopathic, or other serious psychological defect. Among those found psychologically unfit, the percentage diagnosed as "psychopathic" at different induction centers varied from 0 to 100, and through most numbers in between (Stouffer et al., 1950, pp. 553-554).

Some psychologists now assert that "primary" or "true" psychopaths are "antisocial individuals with a long history of criminal behavior" who differ biologically from "sociopaths" (Bartol & Bartol, 1986). The so-called career criminals, on whom federal programs focus, seem to fit the conception of primary psychopath, because they start lawbreaking at an earlier age and are more active at it than other childhood-transition offenders. Yet their criminality may not be due to biology as much as to social learning through early delinquency and parental neglect in high-crime-rate neighborhoods. Such experience would tend to associate them closely with other offenders, handicap them in school, and cause their rejection by law-abiding persons.

Research has long shown that many high-rate lawbreakers lack the biological attributes ascribed to psychopaths, and that some noncriminals have them (Hare, 1977). And psychometric tests and clinical diagnoses to identify psychopaths do not predict recidivism better than prior crime record alone (Andrews & Bonta, 1994, pp. 215-220). So far, biological correlates of criminality have not been definitively determined.

At this point, then, we should be careful about labeling certain criminals "psychopaths." Specific policies for curbing psychopaths cannot be applied with confidence unless the traits implied by the term are more reliably denoted. For example, we may more reliably identify biologically different "career criminals" if we objectively measure offenders and nonoffenders of similar age and background for speed and strength of auto-

nomic nervous system arousal in response to a standardized source of
stress (e.g., an unexpected electric shock) and speed of return to normal
thereafter. We also need better information about the origin and possible
development of these traits. Ideally, both the traits and rates of misconduct
would be measured in large samples of young children, and periodically
remeasured in them well into adulthood. Such studies could show the
stability of these traits and their correlates, as well as their relationship to
lawbreaking and to effective penalties.

Conclusion

Professional criminals share with persons in legitimate professions an
esoteric expertise, gradual development of the qualifications for their
occupational status, and pride in this competence. They pursue almost all
kinds of predation that can safely yield an appreciable income. The main
problem in trying to restrain and reform such accomplished criminals is
the difficulty of catching and convicting them.

    Therefore, for the offenses that may be pursued with a high level of
professionalism, hence a relatively low rate of failure, the most effective
public protection may be only to reduce the opportunities for crime.
Counterfeiting, pickpocketing, bank robbery, and forgery are diminished
by better monitoring and guarding. Fraud is forestalled by educating and
warning the public and lobbying for more government assistance, as such
diverse organizations as Better Business Bureaus, Consumers Union,
Public Citizen, and Common Cause do. The best protection for all of us
who may be potential marks for swindlers is simply continual wariness.
Nations will probably have to bear the great expense and limited success
of efforts to suppress the professional violence and corruption of organized crime as long as they rely more on their criminal justice system than
on health and education programs to diminish addictive vices.

    When professional criminals, high-rate "career" offenders, or ostensi-
ble "psychopaths" are caught, restraint for as long as their proven offenses
warrant is the most demonstrably effective way of protecting the public
from them. Yet their recidivism rates can be reduced by extensively retraining them for new vocations during confinement, plus closely monitoring them after release. A good job or legitimate business and law-abiding
associates—especially spouses—may finally help releasees achieve law-
abiding lives following careers as persistent thieves, fences, or other types
of habitual criminal.

10

Optimum Investments to Reduce Crime Rates

This book has been mainly about using criminal punishments to reduce recidivism by convicted lawbreakers and to deter others from following their example. The underlying assumption has been that the most cost-effective way to maintain a peaceful, secure society is to prefer penalties that minimize our investment in law-enforcement, criminal justice, and corrections resources, as long as the other objectives of punishment are being met. But punishments for convicted criminals are not the only way to keep crime rates down. In fact, punishments are only one of four broad ways to lower crime rates:

- Reduce opportunities to commit crimes
- Keep people from wanting to break the law
- Increase the certainty that offenders are caught and convicted
- Sentence those convicted in ways that profitably diminish their recidivism rates

These approaches are the subject of this chapter.

Making Crime Targets Unappealing to Lawbreakers

One of the best ways to reduce opportunities to commit crimes is to make the surroundings unappealing and inhospitable to predators. Architect

Oscar Newman's (1973) landmark book on this topic, *Defensible Space*, described the design features of places resistant to surreptitious criminal activity:

> A defensible space is . . . employed by inhabitants for the enhancement of their lives, while providing security for their families, neighbors, and friends. The public areas of a multi-family residential environment devoid of defensible space can make the act of going from street to apartment equivalent to running the gauntlet. . . . On the other hand, by grouping dwelling units to reinforce associations of mutual benefit; by delineating paths of movement; by defining areas of activity for particular users through their juxtaposition with internal living areas; and by providing for natural opportunities for visual surveillance, architects can create a clear understanding of the function of a space, and who its users are and ought to be. This . . . can lead residents of all income levels to adopt extremely potent territorial attitudes and policing measures, which act as strong deterrents to potential criminals. (pp. 3-4)

Newman offered many comparisons to demonstrate the importance of such design features. Among them were two large adjacent housing projects in New York City with about the same number of residents per acre. One had 17-story buildings; the other had low walk-up apartments in circular groups, each with 6 to 12 family units. All entrances in the low groups faced a central courtyard. Crime was long rampant in the high-rise buildings, as gangs took over and vandalized elevators and stairways. They extorted protection money from residents and terrorized anyone who spoke to the police. But in the low buildings, residents soon knew each other, readily saw intruders, and were more likely to call the police if serious crimes occurred.

In the 1990s, at Newman's urging, other architects and urban planners have designed more defensible spaces for law-abiding citizens. Iron fences divide sprawling housing projects, with most streets dead-ended so that only residents and persons with business there normally enter. Front- and backyards are marked by low walls to identify them as belonging only to the adjacent housing units. In some, porches are added to facilitate residents' watch over their yards (Cisneros, 1995).

Other preventives to criminal activity are extremely diverse: improved locks and alarms in all types of buildings and vehicles; bars or burglar-proof screens on windows and doors (or solid steel doors); removal of thick shrubs or trees from windows or entrances; prompt repair of graffiti or other vandalism, to discourage their repetition; and recording of serial numbers and etching of names on personal property. Alarm inserts in book bindings have drastically reduced theft from libraries and book-stores, and those in plastic tags on clothing sharply cut shoplifting of apparel. Small glass windows on parking meters to show the last coin inserted greatly reduced use of slugs in New York City (Decker, 1992).

Because youths have particularly high crime rates, crime prevention includes keeping them away from unguarded targets. Young people's preference for fast foods may explain the report that crime rates increase the closer one is to a McDonald's restaurant. To minimize youth crime, Felson (1994) suggests uniform school schedules, so that the community knows when youths on the street are truant; after-school activities that keep juveniles under adult supervision until parents arrive from work; organized weekend activities for children with adults; lunches eaten in school only, to keep students from shopping areas in midday; a low limit on the amount of cash students are permitted to bring to school, so that they are neither targets for crime nor tempted to make illegal purchases; construction of high schools away from shopping areas and shopping areas away from high schools.

Building social bonds among neighbors also reduces crime opportunities. When people know or at least recognize their neighbors, they are more likely to notice someone or something that doesn't belong.

Stunting Early Criminality

Building social bonds helps most in the second approach to reduction of lawbreaking. Because criminality develops most readily among young people who are not well integrated into society, it pays to help juveniles and law-abiding adults form trusting relationships.

How is "normal" early misconduct kept from evolving into serious later criminality? A child's misbehavior tends to diminish if it promptly has negative consequences, especially if approved alternative conduct is gratifying. If a youngster's arrest brings no punishment, not even a formal reprimand, rearrest soon on new charges is more likely.

In addition, research (cited in Chapter 4) shows that most children who persist in theft or other misconduct are punished for "badness" only about as much as other youngsters and are less often praised for any of their good acts. At any age, people want favorable feelings about themselves, and children's self-concepts in particular come mainly from other persons' reactions. Children's need for self-esteem is intensified if unabated reprimands and other derogations seem to be all they can expect from adults.

Then the only favorable view of themselves may come from delinquent peers who applaud their misconduct and share rationalizations for it. A good self-conception is more likely to be retained by youths if those who react negatively to their misbehavior convey feelings of affection even when reprimanding, and praise their subsequent improvement. Reinforcement of good conduct, combined with what Braithwaite (1989) called *reintegrative shame,* as opposed to *stigmatizing shame,* is what most effectively stops misbehavior, but adults angered by a child tend to be too slow to end their purely hostile reactions.

Deficiency in building good character and competent decision making is found with either *authoritarian* parenting, which insists that children give absolute obedience to rules without asking questions, or *permissive* parenting, which imposes few restrictions. These extremes are less effective, Chapter 4 pointed out, than *maturative* parenting (often called "authoritative"), which emphasizes discussion of the undesirable acts rather than derogation of the actor. Maturative parents intervene physically when necessary to stop a child from doing something seriously wrong or dangerous, but explain why they do so, and discuss the morality and consequences of misconduct. Maturative parenting, plus exemplary conduct by the reprimander and associates, are the best ways of teaching children how to behave.

Education in parenting techniques cuts delinquency rates in the children, Chapter 4 showed. However, delinquency is promoted by the fact that children are away from adults for more hours per day than ever before in our history. About a quarter of children now live with only one parent, and only about half are always in a two-parent household while growing up. Ninety percent of homes on welfare are headed by single women. But also, in most other homes where a married couple with one or more children reside, both parents have jobs. In addition, for some decades there has been a decline of membership in churches, scouts, clubs, and other organizations that bring adults and children together. These conditions, and often long journeys to school and to work, cause children to live primarily in the company of peers.

Preventing children from becoming persistent delinquents requires their early, frequent, and intimate association with anticriminal persons, preferably of diverse ages. Adult supervision and assistance for children when school is out can somewhat compensate for absence of parents.

Many of our social policies have worked against children's need for supervision and attention from caring adults. In many states, if the father earns even a low income and remains in the home, the family may be ineligible for larger or more secure AFDC payments. However, reformed welfare systems in many states now provide more secure stipends for dependent children when total household income is low, thus encouraging low-earning fathers to stay at home.

In workfare programs, mothers are required to work—in subsidized jobs if necessary—in order to receive benefits, but child care is provided if needed. Workfare may also offer academic or vocational education, and drug therapy or other treatment if needed, to increase the mothers' ability to compete in the regular job market. Such programs can both reduce poverty and keep more juveniles under adult supervision when not in school, thus profitably reducing delinquency and crime.

Education and economic advancement also help keep people from wanting to break the law. But individuals today need more and better education to keep up. Longer school years, longer school days, and briefer summer vacations serve this purpose. They also reduce crime rates by keeping youngsters occupied and away from delinquent influences. Head Start preschool instruction, as well as breakfast and lunch aid in school, plus Follow Through tutoring where needed, compensate for educational and economic deficiencies of children's homes. They offset nutritional handicaps and improve school attendance. They also increase the gratifying and instructive association of children with anticriminal adults. In high schools, Ohio's Scholarship in Escrow program, described in Chapter 4, deposits money in a college fund for each favorable grade, and adds other rewards for further schooling, thus getting students to look forward to an attractive and law-abiding future. Democratic youth clubs of all types, aided by adults who are maturity-promoting rather than either too authoritarian or too permissive, prepare youngsters of all ages for success in adult organizations of work and leisure. Magnet schools for students with specialized interests, as well as computers and teaching machines, plus tutoring—especially for those too slow or too rapid in regular classes—enhance academic achievement.

Those who still do poorly in school and impede the progress of others, may best be served by trade-training classes, combination work and study programs, or apprenticeships, all of which facilitate their transition to self-sufficient full-time employment. Lowering the upper age limit of compulsory education seems to reduce crime rates if school dropouts get jobs and then marry nondelinquents. These role changes propel those who are most maladjusted in school into legitimate adulthoods.

If vocational training, as well as GED tutoring and tests, are available for anyone at any age, many high school dropouts and others correct their educational handicaps later. Education of every legitimate type for which there is significant demand should be available for all who qualify for it. Much of this instruction increases national productivity, and most of it tends to reduce crime rates.

During the Great Depression of the 1930s, federal employment at minimum wage as a last resort prevented a major crime wave. State and federally funded Youth Corps programs now keep many youngsters out of crime while preparing them for adult roles. Such programs should be funded to accept all jobless youths who apply and perform satisfactorily.

It is also important to keep neighborhoods from deteriorating physically. Once this process starts, it tends to accelerate, and resulting slum conditions promote delinquent gangs and street crime. Civic leadership in organizing residents for neighborhood watch, cleaning up graffiti, and undertaking other mixed-age collaborative activities, helps give generations a shared morality while maintaining a good neighborhood.

The police can lower delinquency rates not only by intercepting truants, but also by giving classroom instruction on the law. The police are especially effective, research cited in Chapter 4 shows, if trained to promote participation in discussion by students who do not readily volunteer to speak. The consequent police acquaintance with neighborhood schools and students also helps them in the third approach to crime prevention, which is usually considered their primary function.

Catching and Convicting Lawbreakers

The third way to lower crime rates is to do a better job of intercepting those who have committed a crime. That job falls to the police. Wilson's (1968) classic discernment of three policing styles can usefully be revived for analysis of the history of U.S. policing in the past century. The *watchman* style prevailed at first, fusing the police with local political machines. It was widely replaced after World War II by a *militaristic* (or legalistic) style. Later a *service* style developed, mostly in suburbs, to emphasize courtesy and extra services to middle- and upper-class residents. The service style is now reborn as "community" policing, with added emphasis on neighborhood meetings, resident volunteers, and anticrime education. Whichever style of policing prevails, however, the police cannot be considered effective unless those they arrest for crime are actually convicted.

Historical Policing Styles

The watchman style of policing was popular during the first half of this century and remains popular in some business and skid-row areas of metropolises today. It is epitomized by the "cop on the beat." Beat cops, almost always males, got their jobs by sponsorship from a precinct or ward committeeman of the political party in power. Typically they were former high school athletes hired to work in that part of the city where they went to school, and were mostly employed there for foot patrol. Such officers generally knew and were known by all the small business owners and politicians, many residents, and all the persistent juvenile and adult offenders in their area. They were usually granted much discretion to overlook misdemeanors and juvenile offenses, so their practices would reflect the values and prejudices of the local residents and politicians.

Replacement of watchman-type by militaristic style policing accelerated during reform movements and when cities grew rapidly, especially in the West. Militaristic policing accompanied changes in local government agencies from political party fiefs to civil service bureaucracies, with competitive examinations rather than political sponsorship as the basis for employment and promotion. These police recruits were mostly armed forces veterans, accustomed to modern equipment and methods. Higher education requirements for new officers made it necessary to pay larger salaries, to recruit from wide areas of the state or nation, and to expand pay differences between higher and lower ranks.

In comparison to the watchman-style officers, militaristic police are impersonal and incorruptible. They get initial training in police academies run like Marine Corps boot camps that stress command authority and group drills. At these indoctrination academies, as in Los Angeles during the 1980s, police cadets were required to do everything in unison on barked-out commands, even in going to their desks, sitting down, and picking up pencils and pads before a lecture. The message in several weeks of this initial training, and in frequent rituals thereafter, is that they are an elite and quasi-military force, superior to ordinary humans, and heroically fighting criminals.

Militaristic police officers are expected to know the law, to enforce it inflexibly, and to bring as many offenders as possible to the courts. Individual merit ratings, made regularly, emphasize such tangible features of their performance as number of arrests. However, many large city police forces became unionized, and unions usually favor seniority as the basis for automatic promotions to supervisory positions. As a result, some police forces have over 40% of their officers in a supervisory rank (Bouza, 1990, p. 239).

The transition from watchman to militaristic styles generated what Reuss-Ianni (1993) called "the two cultures of policing," that of "street cops" and of "management cops." The street cops, reflecting the watchman style, promote a code among patrol officers of watching out for each other, not implicating other officers if they are caught in improper conduct, not backing down from civilians, working neither too little nor too much, not intruding in the areas or tasks of other officers, not "making waves," and "checking out" new officers to be sure that they can be depended upon.

The service style developed in more affluent suburbs, which usually had small police forces, a large per capita tax base, and many influential citizens who could effectively convey their complaints to elected officials. They wanted well-trained and incorruptible officers who were always available for any kind of emergency. Obligated for their appointments to community political leaders, the chiefs encouraged officers to take initiative in pleasing residents and to build friendships with community leaders, as had prevailed with the watchman style. The service style officers were also granted the discretion of the watchman "cop on the beat" in their arrest practices. Residents' complaints or minor offenses were to be dealt with informally to everyone's satisfaction, if possible; arrest and prosecution were focused on crimes by strangers.

Militaristic policing was jolted by the urban riots that began in the Watts area of Los Angeles in 1965, then recurred intermittently in urban areas throughout the nation. A major complaint of the rioters was the racism of the predominantly white male police, who aggressively patrolled poor minority neighborhoods to impress superiors by their arrest rates. They would often emerge from squad cars to stop persons or autos there, question, and search without probable cause. They would speak harshly, rough up objectors, and arrest on minor charges. These "aggressive patrol" practices persisted throughout the 1980s and into the 1990s, despite efforts after urban riots to develop "community relations" in police forces, and despite affirmative action laws that spurred police employment of ethnic minorities. Militaristic police resisted the service approach; they belittled efforts to "make social workers out of cops," preferring their warrior image of being always in battle with crime.

The most dramatic setback to militaristic policing began in 1991, in reaction to a civilian's chance videotaping of three white Los Angeles police officers long and savagely beating an arrested black speeder after he was on the ground. Their sergeant, and eventually a dozen other officers, stood around watching rather than handcuffing the arrestee. This "Rodney King Incident," named after the severely beaten arrestee, occurred in a police force that epitomized the militaristic style. Controversy raged on whether the incident was merely an "aberration," as the chief claimed, or reflected police customs of reaction to any driver who leads them on a chase instead of obeying an order to stop, especially if the driver appears to be of low status. The video stirred up the city, and an independent commission recommended major changes in its policing. The three officers and sergeant who were present at the beating were indicted for illegal assault, but their defense lawyers convinced a judge that they could not get an unbiased jury in Los Angeles. In 1992 they were acquitted by an all-white jury in a suburban and predominantly white adjoining county, where many of the residents were commuting Los Angeles police officers. Los Angeles then erupted in the most destructive riot in U.S. history. The militaristic police chief was replaced by an African American with a good community policing record in Philadelphia. In 1993, a federal court convicted King's principal police beater and the sergeant in charge at the incident of denying King his civil rights. All these events got national attention that prompted federal subsidies for expanded community policing.

Community Policing

Community policing evolved from the service style, as a reaction to the discrediting of militaristic police forces by riots. It also reflected experimental research that questioned the effectiveness of primary reliance on intensive auto patrols. Friedman (1992), from studies in four nations, concludes,

> Community policing is . . . aimed at achieving more effective and efficient crime control, reduced fear of crime, improved quality of life, improved police service and police legitimacy, through a proactive reliance on community resources that seeks to change crime-causing conditions. It assumes a need for greater accountability of police, greater public share in decision making, and greater concern for civil rights and liberties. (p. 4)

Changes in police practices with community policing include a shift from auto to foot patrol in densely populated areas, and to horseback, bicycle, or scooter patrols in park and beach areas.

Research findings differ on whether these alternatives reduce crime rates, but studies regularly find that placing officers where they interact more readily with pedestrians, residents, and merchants reduces fear of crime and makes attitudes toward the police more favorable (Kelling, 1983). Officers find non-auto patrolling, which renews aspects of watchman and service styles, less boring than squad car duty (Friedman, 1992, pp. 1-2).

What was at first often called "team policing" has evolved through community policing. In its initial format, a few officers are responsible for almost all services in a very small segment of the city. They have both patrol and investigative duties and are not to be sent outside their area except in emergencies. They are urged to try to know and be known by as many of the residents in their sector as possible. This objective involves them in meeting with local business people, residents' associations, and schools, and in organizing neighborhood watch groups for separate blocks or other small areas. However, a neighborhood watch group generally does not attract many residents unless it acquires functions in addition to surveillance, such as social activities, mutual aid in child supervision, or lobbying for other government service such as street-crossing signals or better sewers. In some cities, notably Los Angeles, team policing worked poorly because officers were too often given duties outside their area, and their own homes were usually in distant suburbs.

With community policing, small storefront police stations are established in high-crime areas to foster more contacts between area residents and officers and to reduce public fear of crime. Questionnaire responses showed that fear declined and attitudes toward the police improved greatly where officers systematically knocked on doors to introduce themselves, ask residents about their problems in the neighborhood, and offer advice and assistance in crime-proofing their homes. The police at first resisted such assignment, but soon liked it, and said that they learned much from the residents. In Houston, a police officer with 12 years of prior service said: "For the first time in my career, it has given me a chance to be nice to people" (Brown & Wycoff, 1987, p. 88). Similar reports on community policing experiences have come from officers in Newark and elsewhere (Williams & Pate, 1987).

Efficient Policing

For police resources to be used cost-effectively, the work they do to detect and apprehend criminals should bear maximum results at minimum cost. One profitable way of increasing police efficiency is to use summons or citations instead of arrests, if the officer can assume with much confidence that the accused will appear in court as scheduled. This practice saves time for the police; reduces crowding and expense in jails and police lockups; eliminates the need for court hearings regarding bail; and lets the accused avoid indignities, loss of time from work, and possibly criminalizing effects of being locked up. If conviction subsequently occurs, fines are more likely to be imposed than is confinement; the result is lower recidivism rates (Glaser & Gordon, 1990b; Gordon & Glaser, 1991). We now issue summons or citations for most traffic violations, but in Britain, Japan, and other countries with less mobile populations than ours, this method is also used in most theft, fraud, and assault cases. We could most appropriately use citation instead of arrest in the United States when the accused is employed, is a homeowner, or has other evidence of a stake in conformity that makes flight unlikely, or when the prospective penalty for the crime is less severe than that for flight to avoid prosecution.

Another way to increase the efficiency of police resources is to convict more of those the police arrest. Yet about half of adult arrestees and most juveniles are released after arrest without even being prosecuted. These proportions differ greatly from one city to the next, even within one county, and are unrelated to the race, age, or poverty within a city's population. Rather, they vary with the police costs per arrest (the total a city spends on police, divided by the number of arrests its police make). The greater the police costs per arrest, the more likely the arrests are to stand up in court (Petersilia, Abrahamse, & Wilson, 1990). To convert more arrests to convictions, therefore, police need adequate funding.

But the problem is not just a lack of funding; sometimes police make arrests that they cannot justify well in court. Police grade their crime-fighting success by the percentage of offenses they think they have cleared by arrest, rather than by the percentage of crimes for which someone is convicted and sentenced. This practice exists because most felony convictions occur months or years after the arrest, and are settled by plea bargaining that does not involve the arresting officers, to whom the case outcomes are unlikely to be communicated. Loose coupling of police with prosecution is clearly a major source of delays, uncertainties, and waste in our criminal justice system.

The problem is now being attacked through "vertical prosecution," in which teams of police and prosecutor personnel regularly work together on major offense cases. Their percentage of convictions then increases.

Such "vertical" prosecution has grown in popularity and now is used for most major crimes in large cities (Dawson, Smith, & DeFrancis, 1993).

It seems clearly profitable to cease to assess police work quality by percentage of crimes cleared by arrest, rather than percentage cleared by a conviction. But simply knowing the percentage of arrests leading to convictions is an elusive goal at this point. It requires more integration of police, prosecution, and court records, which can be done efficiently with modern computer systems. The ultimate source of profit in this area is better research on the relative effectiveness of arrests, citations, and summons for particular types of offenses, offenders, or circumstances.

Using the Most Profitable Penalties

Public anger at deaths, injuries, or property losses from crimes, and frustration in trying to end illegal vices, lead to demands for harsher punishments. Politicians who oppose severer penalties are often charged by their opponents with "being soft on crime." Yet simply increasing a penalty may not serve the public interest if it

- ◆ Does not deter the defendant or others from crime
- ◆ Does not reduce recidivism
- ◆ Increases the offender's criminality by instilling attitudes conducive to committing more crimes
- ◆ Reduces the offender's ability to get and hold a legitimate job and have law-abiding associates
- ◆ Is excessively severe, hence unfair, in relation to the damage caused by the offense
- ◆ Costs more than its benefits are worth

These six considerations must all be investigated and taken into account if a decision on any offender's penalty is to maximize the net public benefit. The most profitable reactions to any lawbreaking are those that most cost-effectively reduce the probability of further offenses. This book has shown which penalties work best for different types of offenders and the state of scientific knowledge about them.

Penalties for Young Offenders

The transition from childhood to adulthood is the period of life most conducive to serious criminal behavior, as pointed out in Chapter 4. How lawbreaking by adolescents is treated greatly affects a society's rates of serious crimes. Punishments that closely associate young offenders with each other and isolate them from law-abiding adults promote subsequent criminality and impede the effectiveness of education and vocational training efforts. Conversely, penalties that involve the offenders with respectable adults in restitutive and legitimately instructive activities in which they can be gratified, as well as restrict their delinquent or criminal activities, are most likely to be reformative. Correctional programs are especially profitable for all involved when they lead offenders to legitimate and satisfying employment.

With persons convicted for crimes they committed when just over 18 years old (or a few years younger in some states), an obstacle to deciding on optimum penalties is that they are tried in a criminal court for adults that lacks access to juvenile court records. Without the prior record, the judge does not know if the person to be sentenced is a first offender or has had many years of continuous, serious lawbreaking. The earliness, frequency, and recency of prior crimes in a defendant's life history best predict that person's subsequent crime rate.

A way to provide more adequate information for a rational sentencing decision, yet avoid permanently stigmatizing adults for their juvenile offenses, is practiced in Canada and many other nations. Canada lets courts know about minor juvenile offenses for a period of 2 years after they occur, and about serious offenses for 5 years. If no further offenses occur in this period, records on them are expunged. Many other countries clear the past record for most offenses at any age, after a specified span of crime-free years. We could well follow these reintegrative policies.

Penalties for Participants in Illegal Vices

For illegal vices—such as alcohol abuse, gambling, prostitution, and drug abuse—no type of prohibition effort has been very successful, Chapter 5 showed. These activities are easily hidden, and all participants usually engage in them voluntarily, so that only a minute percentage are reported to the police. These vices produce at least fleeting expectations or sensations of intense pleasure, hence are compulsively pursued, especially when associates support and assist each other in them. Few who are addicted to a vice are deterred even by extreme penalties; they usually do not think of themselves either as victimized by the vice or as morally wrong in pursuing it, and they usually are not caught and punished for it.

Neither widespread moral outrage, disgust with participants, nor illegality has much reduced the prevalence of prostitution, gambling, or drug abuse in democratic countries. Yet fines, supplemented after the first offense by brief jailing, probation, or house arrest, when applied with increased certainty, seem to reduce the visibility of these vices.

No developed countries now try to prohibit use of alcoholic beverages, but all try in other ways to reduce their physical, mental health, and public safety hazards, and the times and places where they are used. Similar focus on reducing the damages and visibility of other vices, but not prohibiting them, prevail in most of Western Europe for prostitution and in Britain, the Netherlands, and Switzerland for drug use. Treatment of those much addicted to a vice, and anti-vice education, though far from perfectly successful, apparently yield benefits in excess of costs—profits—more than do highly punitive vice prohibition laws.

In this country, a nonpunitive approach has worked for close to 100,000 heroin addicts, and many more in Western Europe and elsewhere. They get methadone, a synthetic opiate, prescribed for them in therapy programs. This legal drug maintains their addiction but permits them to live an otherwise normal life. The AIDS epidemic, which is partly due to drug addicts' sharing of hypodermic needles, has accelerated a medical over a criminal justice approach to drug control. How far the medical approach will go remains to be seen.

Penalties for the Passionate

Crimes expressing the passion of anger are most common where close relationships have existed, as between spouses, lovers, and parents or stepparents and children. Wife battering is especially damaging to close relationships. As detailed in Chapter 6, experimental research on penalties for wife battering greatly increased rates of police arrest in these cases after 1985, because the first results indicated that arrest would curtail repetition of this offense more than did police attempts at mediation. Subsequent experiments indicated, however, that arrests deterred only those with a stake in conformity, such as employed persons without prior criminal records; violence by batterers who were unemployed increased after their arrests. Different types of penalties for different kinds of arrested spouse batterers have rarely been evaluated. Most arrestees are released in a few hours without prosecution, but many get longer detention, court hearings, fines, and jail terms. The most apparently profitable punishments range from fines for unadvanced offenders to long confinement for habitual severe assaulters, plus a requirement on release that they deposit money as peace bonds, usually as a condition of parole or probation, to be forfeited if further offenses occur.

If a person's habits and experience in reaction to frustration or loss of face in inter-personal relationships are only to act violently, any training that increases the ability to handle such situations nonviolently will use-fully supplement punishment. However, counseling has generally proved ineffective if involuntary, and if nondirective in groups of similar offend-ers. Well-trained ex-offenders or professional counselors may be prefer-able, either in leading groups or in giving individual treatment. Courses in parenting are reported to be effective in preventing mistreatment of children; but again, their value if mandated as penalties rather than pursued voluntary is less certain. Experiments are also needed to assess the requirement that arrestees study until they have satisfactory scores on tests that ask about optimum parent behavior in simulated provocative situations, much like current requirements for a driver's license. In gen-eral, more research is needed on ways to make marriage counseling, instruction on parenting, and training in nonviolent resolution of conflicts more extensive and effective.

For homicide, Chapter 6 pointed out, ending or restoring the death penalty does not significantly affect offense rates. Where capital punish-ment is permitted, it is applied to less than 1% of murderers, for there are too many inhibitions about executing persons who might be innocent or who were understandably provoked in their crime. Also, selection of the minute proportion who are executed from those who are instead impris-oned shows no consistency, except for the tendency to use capital punish-ment mainly for low status persons who kill higher status victims. In addition, government costs for extra court sessions and services in trials and appeals of death penalty cases usually far exceed those of life impris-onment.

Penalties for rape, sexual molestation, and other sex offenses, Chapter 7 indicated, have included programs in which offenders, generally all males, meet with women, sometimes even with victims of these crimes. Usually the sessions are held in penal or mental institutions. Emphasis is placed on role training in interaction with the opposite sex, a type of behavior at which these criminals have usually been inept. They frequently have misconceptions of female mentality. Research has not evaluated the effectiveness of role training well, but it shows that the effectiveness of ordinary penalties, such as fines, is appreciable with first offenders but not with persons having much prior criminality of any type.

Especially in crimes of passion, questions are raised about the defendant's sanity at the time of the offense or mental competence at time of trial. Research indicates that alternative legal definitions of *sanity* have no clear effect on jury conclusions on whether an accused was "crazy," and that doubt about competence to stand trial sometimes leads to long mental hospital confinement following arrest for only a petty offense. The most profitable public policy for these types of defendants seems to be to conduct court hearings to determine as fairly as feasible whether the defendant actually did the alleged crimes; if so, to assess whether the offender was sane when doing them, and competent at hearings or trials on them; if sane and competent, to impose penalties no more severe than the law permits for these offenses; to provide mental health treatment if needed, whether the offender is imprisoned or in the community; and at any time when officials deem it warranted, to arrange a civil court hearing on justifications for the offender's involuntary mental hospitalization.

Penalties for Criminals in Legitimate Occupations

Employees' crimes against their employers range from petty pilfering to immense embezzling. Usually, the crime is discovered by a supervisor or the employer before the police are informed, and often it is in the firm's best financial interest to seek restitution without prosecution or publicity. Penalties for large-scale embezzlements often include restitution agreements, sometimes with the offenders continuing employment, but with pay deductions until losses are repaid. Because these lawbreakers are unlikely to recidivate, especially if they have no close association with other criminals of any type, such dispositions are profitable for the offenders, the victims, and the public.

Illegally dangerous conditions creating risk of explosion, fire, or other costly interruption of the work process are likely to be prosecuted vigorously if they can be blamed on a particular supervisor or other employee. However, the rates of such accidents have decreased markedly, mainly because of safety engineering. Conditions of greater risk to employees today, detailed in Chapter 8, are those that produce gradual, long-term damage to health (e.g., from working with or breathing toxic substances).

Such situations tend to persist unless prosecuted, especially if they cost less than safer working conditions.

Dangerous working conditions are often so long established that no individual is culpable for them, and they are so diverse from one employment place to another that it is hard to prescribe optimum rules and penalties to eliminate them. In addition, they are so widespread in comparison with the resources of government agencies—such as OSHA—assigned to identify and punish them, that only lenient penalties are imposed. Litigation, which would have greater deterrent value, is too expensive and time-consuming for the overwhelmed agencies.

"Enforced self-regulation," promoted by John Braithwaite in Australia, copes with variability of dangerous working conditions by creating local committees of employer, employee, and community representatives to draft worker-protection rules for large establishments and to monitor compliance. The local inspection board notifies employers, employees, and the government of rule violations, and negotiates correction. The government intervenes and punishes transgressors for both inadequate inspections and the failure to correct violations. This idea of enforced self-regulation has been elaborated as "the accountability model" for dealing with many corporate offenses, especially poisoning of the environment and of workers.

The greatest diversity in criminal activities, and the largest total damage and loot, is in offenses against the public by ostensibly legitimate occupations and businesses. Profitable penalties to control them, however, can only be legislated by overcoming the powerful political opposition of vested business interests. An important remedy is reform of political campaign financing. For every million dollars that various industries, such as dairying, pay to elect their Congressional supporters, they gain tens of millions of dollars in higher market prices, higher subsidies, and higher profits at the public's expense. Greatly increased limits to financial contributions by Political Action Committees and others, with severe fines or other penalties for violations and free media access for all leading candidates during the last month before an election, could make many government agencies more responsive to the public.

Better regulation of all businesses entrusted with other people's money might have saved current and future U.S. taxpayers the thousands of dollars each will eventually pay for fraud in the 1980s by savings and loan officials. Also shown effective in deterring illegal financial transactions are the penalties that the Securities and Exchange Commission can impose for stock transaction illegalities and investment mismanagement.

When long-established criminal practices at corporations are not trace-able to any individual, the firms should be held strictly liable for their actions as organizations. Perhaps the most deterrent penalty then is man-datory publicity for their crimes, which may discredit the corporations with current and potential customers and investors. Also, independent monitors, paid for by the convicted corporation but appointed by courts or regulatory agencies, help to assure compliance with government laws or rules, and reduce a firm's freedom to recidivate. RICO prosecutions in federal courts increase the severity of penalties for both legal and illegal organizations that repeatedly commit serious crimes, even crimes for which they have already received state punishments.

An especially profitable penalty for corporate wrongdoing is the equity fine, proposed by John Coffee (1981), whereby corporations committing crimes transfer shares of their stock to a government victim compensation fund. Equity fines levy a larger dollar penalty than could be collected in cash, reduce the value of stock options paid to top executives, and make hostile takeovers by other firms more feasible—all significant punish-ments to corporate decision makers. But they do not cause a bankruptcy and thereby destroy jobs and local economies as readily as do large cash fines.

Penalties for Habitual Offenders

For persons whose commitment to a life of crime we judge to be high and difficult to change, Chapter 9 argued, physical restraints that incapaci-tate are the only way to protect the public. Lengthy incarceration therefore seems logical as the penalty for professional criminals who have long supported themselves by crime with rare interruption by arrest, as well as for so-called career criminals and "psychopaths" who persist in criminal-ity even if often caught and punished.

"Habitual offender" statutes permit longer confinement after convic-tion for repeated serious offenses, and ultimate release, if any, only on long parole that facilitates monitoring the releasee. Yet these laws sometimes seem too severe for repetition of relatively minor crimes by persons who generally are quite law-abiding. Prosecutors thus tend to use such laws mainly as bargaining devices to obtain quick guilty pleas for new offenses in exchange for dropping the "habitual offender" charge.

Our major limitation in dealing with the most successful criminals is what makes them professional: our difficulty in catching and convicting them. More police vigilance will always be needed against cunning confidence persons and professional hit men. It is for them that the "three-strike" laws are most appropriate. What proportion of such persons will be sentenced under three-strike laws, however, is still uncertain, as is the number of less dangerous offenders sentenced under such laws who will be costly geriatric cases for several decades before their death in prison.

Conclusion

As appealing as "getting tough on crime" may be, severity of punishment has not always guaranteed the results we seek: justice and efficient crime reduction. For example, although the death penalty most completely prevents recidivism, death is deemed an unjust punishment for all but those who commit the most heinous murders, and some persons have moral objections to its use even for them. Only a fraction of 1% of murderers are actually executed. Also, in practice, the legal appeals and delays before a death sentence is applied cost the government several times as much as would confinement for life. Death is clearly an unprofitable penalty.

Imprisonment is a more customary punishment, and, like the death penalty, it is highly effective in controlling the behavior of criminals, especially with maximum security. However, imprisonment is by far the most costly of customary punishments. Furthermore, only about 2% of those sentenced to prison are there for life; the rest are released at some point. Therefore, it is appropriate to invest in reducing the probability of prisoners' postrelease recidivism. Remedial academic education, vocational training, and realistic work experience while confined increase the prospects of releasees achieving economic self-sufficiency in legitimate employment. Visiting and correspondence by law-abiding persons, especially relatives, and by reformative organizations such as Alcoholics Anonymous and religious groups, usually enhance the prospects that releasees will abandon criminal pursuits and costly vices. Profits from confinement penalties vary immensely, depending on the success with which prisoners can be guided toward a noncriminal lifestyle.

The most widely imposed sentence is probation, but it varies greatly in the intensity of the surveillance and assistance it provides, and hence in its cost. However, probation is almost always cheaper than punishment by confinement. Similar to probation, and often supervised by the same personnel, is parole during the last part of a confinement sentence. The profits of these forms of conditional release may be increased in diverse ways, although the costs increase as well. Halfway houses, group homes, day-reporting centers, and periodic detention (e.g., on weekends) provide controls of or assistance to releasees as well as costs that are intermediate between those of confinement and ordinary probation or parole. Also, house arrest with electronic monitoring or paging lets supervising officers know more promptly if a probationer or parolee leaves home at an unauthorized time; this punishment has been shown to reduce recidivism rates by persons with poor work records and mild vices. Drug testing reveals illegal narcotics use by releasees. Also, judges and parole boards can impose special rules for individual releasees, such as avoiding specified persons or places, obtaining particular types of therapy, or completing education or training.

Clearly the most profitable penalty for the government is to impose fines on offenders who can pay them, as this punishment yields income to the state that may be much above the cost of its administration. Fines have also been shown to reduce recidivism to a greater extent than jail terms for similar offenders. Day fines, which are based on the earnings of the person fined, less a reasonable allowance for cost of living and support of dependents, make such penalties fairer. Finally, community service penalties permit indigent offenders or other lawbreakers to contribute their labor to the government instead of, or in addition to, fines.

For a punishment to be just, it must be suitably severe given the heinousness of the crime that evokes it. This moral issue is addressed by legislators who enact and amend criminal law, prescribing lighter penalties for lesser offenses and severer ones for more serious crimes. The range of severity of punishment that the law permits should be appreciable, and not only to take into account the variations in crimes that have the same label (e.g., assault or theft). Punishments must also be flexible to fit the criminal.

With a wide range of choices in punishments, the most profitable penalties can be tailored to individual offenders. A large range of variation in severity permits judges and parole boards to study the life histories, recent conduct, and current circumstances of each offender; to impose the punishment that will most profitably reform and control that individual; and to modify the initial penalty on the basis of the offender's subsequent conduct. Continuous scientific research is essential to evaluate past experience so as to create sentencing, parole, and supervision guidelines that maximize society's profits from its penalties.

References

Ageton, S. (1983). *Sexual assaults among adolescents*. Lexington, MA: Lexington Books.

Åkerström, M. (1985). *Crooks and squares*. New Brunswick, NJ: Transaction Books.

Alexander, H. (1992). *Financing politics: Money, elections, and political reform* (4th ed.). Washington, DC: Congressional Quarterly Press.

Allan, E., & Steffensmeier, D. (1989). Youth, underemployment, and property crime. *American Sociological Review, 54*(1), 107-123.

Allison, J., & Wrightsman, L. (1993). *Rape: The misunderstood crime*. Newbury Park, CA: Sage.

Andrews, D., & Bonta, J. (1994). *The psychology of criminal conduct*. Cincinnati, OH: Anderson.

Anglin, M., Brecht, M., & Maddahian, E. (1989). Pretreatment characteristics and treatment performance of legally coerced versus voluntary methadone maintenance admissions. *Criminology, 27*(3), 537-557.

Anglin, M., & Speckart, G. (1988). Narcotics use and crime. *Criminology, 26*(2), 197-233.

Archer, D., Gartner, R., & Beittel, M. (1983). Homicide and the death penalty. *Journal of Criminal Law and Criminology, 74*(3), 991-1013.

Armentaro, D. (1982). *Antitrust and monopoly*. New York: John Wiley.

Avison, W., & Loring, P. (1986). Population diversity and cross-national homicide: The effects of inequality and heterogeneity. *Criminology, 24*(4), 733-749.

Bakalar, J., & Grinspoon, L. (1984). *Drug control in a free society*. New York: Cambridge University Press.

Ball, J. (1965). Two patterns of narcotic addiction in the United States. *Journal of Criminal Law, Criminology and Police Science, 56*(2), 203-211.

Ball, R., Huff, C., & Lilly, J. (1988). *House arrest and correctional policy*. Newbury Park, CA: Sage.

Bankston, W., Floyd, H., Jr., & McSeveny, D. (1977). Social structural contingencies in the decision of criminal courts to commit defendants as incompetent to stand trial or criminally insane. *Criminal Justice Review, 2*(10), 111-130.

Barak, G. (1991). *Gimme shelter: A social history of homelessness in contemporary America*. New York: Praeger.

Bard, M. (1970). *Training police in family crisis intervention*. Washington, DC: Government Printing Office.

Barlow, S. (1968). Patterns of arrests for misdemeanor narcotics possession: Manhattan police practices 1960-62. *Criminal Law Bulletin, 4*(10), 549-582.

Barnett, O., & LaViolette, A. (1993). *It could happen to anyone: Why battered women stay*. Newbury Park, CA: Sage.

Barry, K. (1995). *The prostitution of sexuality*. New York: New York University Press.

Bartol, C., with Bartol, A. (1986). *Criminal behavior* (2nd ed.). Englewood Cliffs, NJ: Prentice Hall.

Baumer, T., & Mendelsohn, R. (1992). Electronically monitored home confinement: Does it work? In J. M. Byrne, A. Lurigio, & J. Petersilia (Eds.), *Smart sentencing*. Thousand Oaks, CA: Sage.

Baumrind, D. (1978). Parental disciplinary patterns and social competence in children. *Youth and Society, 9*(2), 239-276.

Beck, A., & Gilliard, D. (1995). *Prisoners in 1994*. Washington, DC: Bureau of Justice Statistics.

Becker, H. (1964). *Outsiders*. New York: Free Press.

Bedau, H. (1982). *The death penalty in America* (3rd ed.). Garden City, NY: Doubleday.

Berk, R., Cambell, A., Klap, R., & Western, B. (1992). A Bayesian analysis of the Colorado Springs Spouse Abuse Experiment. *Journal of Criminal Law and Criminology, 83*(1), 170-200.

Berns, W. (1979). *For capital punishment*. New York: Basic Books.

Berrueta-Clement, J., Schweinhart, L., Barnett, W., & Weikhard, D. (1987). The effects of early educational intervention on crime and delinquency in adolescence and early adulthood. In J. Burchard & S. Burchard (Eds.), *Prevention of delinquent behavior*. Newbury Park, CA: Sage.

Biernacki, P. (1986). *Pathways from heroin addiction*. Philadelphia: Temple University Press.

Black, C., Jr. (1981). *Capital punishment: The inevitability of caprice and mistake* (2nd ed.). New York: Norton.

Blau, J. (1992). *The visible poor*. New York: Oxford University Press.

Blau, J., & Blau, P. (1982). Metropolitan structure and violent crime. *American Sociological Review, 47*(1), 114-129.

Blau, P. (1964). *Exchange and power in social life*. New York: John Wiley.

Block, C., & van der Werff, C. (1990). *Initiation and continuation of a criminal career*. The Hague: Netherlands Ministry of Justice, Research and Documentation Centre.

Blumer, H. (1939). Collective behavior. In A. McL. Lee (Ed.), *Principles of sociology*. New York: Barnes and Noble.

Blumstein, A. (1995). Youth, violence, guns, and the illicit drug industry. *Journal of Criminal Law and Criminology, 86*(1), 10-36.

Blumstein, A., Cohen, J., Roth, J., & Visher, C. (Eds.). (1986). *Criminal careers and "career criminals"* (2 vols.). Washington, DC: National Academy Press.

Blumstein, A., Farrington, D., & Moitra, S. (1985). Delinquency careers: Innocents, desisters, and persisters. In M. Tonry & N. Morris (Eds.), *Crime and justice: Vol. 6.* Chicago: University of Chicago Press.

Bondeson, U. (1989). *Prisoners in prison societies.* New Brunswick, NJ: Transaction Books.

Bornheimer, J. (1996, May 18). Clinton calls on youth to help curb crime. *Los Angeles Times*, p. A12.

Booth, W. (1995, December 25-31). Rattling chains to make a point. *Washington Post National Weekly Edition.* (reprinted in *Los Angeles Times*, January 8, 1996)

Bourque, B., Han, M., & Klein, S. (1996). *A national survey of boot camp graduates.* Washington, DC: National Institute of Justice.

Bouza, A. (1990). *The police mystique.* New York: Plenum.

Bowker, L., & Klein, M. (1983). The etiology of female delinquency and gang membership. *Adolescence, 18*(72), 739-751.

Bowman, G., Haim, S., & Seidenstat, P. (Eds.). (1993). *Privatizing correctional institutions.* New Brunswick, NJ: Transaction Books.

Braff, J., Arvantes, T., & Steadman, H. (1983). Detention patterns of successful and unsuccessful insanity defendants. *Criminology, 21*(3), 439-448.

Braithwaite, J. (1985). *To punish or persuade: Enforcement of coal mining safety.* Albany: State University of New York Press.

Braithwaite, J. (1989). *Crime, shame, and reintegration.* Cambridge, UK: Cambridge University Press.

Braithwaite, J. (1992). Poverty, power, and white collar crime. In K. Schlegel & D. Weisburd (Eds.), *White collar crime reconsidered.* Boston: Northeastern University Press.

Brecher, E. (1978). *Treatment programs for sex offenders.* Washington, DC: U.S. Department of Justice.

Brennan, P., & Mednick, S. (1994). A learning theory approach to the deterrence of criminal recidivism. *Journal of Abnormal Psychology, 103*(3), 430-440.

Brennan, P., Mednick, S., & John, R. (1989). Specialization in violence. *Criminology, 27*(3), 437-453.

Brennan, T., Huizinga, D., & Elliott, D. (1978). *The social psychology of runaways.* Lexington, MA: Lexington Books.

Brown, J., Gilliard, D., Snell, T., Stephan J., & Wilson, D. (1996). *Correctional populations in the United States, 1994.* Washington, DC: Bureau of Justice Statistics.

Brown, L., & Wycoff, M. (1987). Policing Houston: Reducing fear and improving services. *Crime and Delinquency, 33*(1), 71-89.

Brown, W., Miller, T., & Jenkins, R. (1988). The favorable effect of juvenile court adjudication of delinquent youth on first contact with the juvenile justice system. In R. Jenkins & W. Brown (Eds.), *The abandonment of delinquent behavior.* New York: Praeger.

Browne, A., & Williams, K. (1989). Exploring the effects of resource availability and likelihood of female-perpetrated homicide. *Law and Society Review, 23*(1), 75-94.

Browne, J., Gilliard, D., Snell, T., Stephan, J., & Wilson, D. (1996). *Correctional populations in the United States, 1994*. Washington, DC: Bureau of Justice Statistics.

Buchwald, A. (1982, May 11). *Los Angeles Times*, Section V, p. 3.

Bureau of Justice Statistics. (1991). *Criminal victimization in the United States: 1973-88 trends*. Washington, DC: U.S. Department of Justice.

Bureau of Justice Statistics. (1994). *Violence between intimates*. Washington, DC: U.S. Department of Justice.

Burnham, D. (1995, December 29). The feeble war on corporate America. *Los Angeles Times*.

Burton, W., & Butts, J. (1990). Viable options: Intensive supervision programs for juvenile delinquents. *Crime and Delinquency, 36*(2), 238-256.

"Busting books." (1994, February 28). *Massachusetts Lawyers Weekly*, p. 1.

Byrne, J., Lurigio, A., & Petersilia, J. (Eds.). (1992). *Smart sentencing*. Thousand Oaks, CA: Sage.

Buzawa, E., & Buzawa, C. (1996. *Domestic violence* (2nd ed.). Thousand Oaks, CA: Sage.

Calavita, K., & Pontell, H. (1990). Heads I win, tails you lose: Deregulation, crime, and crises in the savings and loan industry. *Crime and Delinquency, 36*(3), 309-344.

California Bureau of Criminal Statistics. (1990). Motor vehicle theft recovery data, 1983-89. *Outlook* (Sacramento: Department of Justice).

Caplan, G. (1984). The facts of life about teenage prostitution. *Crime and Delinquency, 30*(1), 69-74.

Chaiken, J., & Chaiken, M. (1982). *Varieties of criminal behavior*. Santa Monica, CA: Rand Corporation.

Chambliss, W. (1989). State-organized crime. *Criminology, 27*(2), 183-208.

Chappell, D., & Strang, H. (1992). Violence and the prevention of violent crime in Australia. *Studies on Crime and Crime Prevention, 1*(1), 52-60.

Cisneros, H. (1995). *Defensible space: Deterring crime and building communities*. Washington, DC: U.S. Department of Housing and Urban Development.

Clarke, R. (Ed.). (1992). *Situational crime prevention: Successful case studies*. New York: Harow and Heston.

Cleckley, H. (1976). *The mask of sanity* (5th ed.). St. Louis, MO: C. V. Mosby.

Clinard, M. (1978). *Cities with little crime: The case of Switzerland*. Cambridge, UK: Cambridge University Press.

Clinton, H. (1996). *It takes a village*. New York: Simon and Schuster.

Clotfelder, C., & Cook, P. (1989). *Selling hope: State lotteries in America*. Cambridge, MA: Harvard University Press.

Cochran, J., Chamlin, M., & Seth, M. (1994). Deterrence or brutalization: An impact assessment of Oklahoma's return to capital punishment. *Criminology, 21*(1), 107-134.

Cocks, J. (1968). From "Whisp" to "Rodeo," *Youth Authority Quarterly, 21*(4), 7-11.

Coffee, J., Jr. (1981). "No soul to damn, no body to kick": An unscandalized inquiry into the problem of corporate punishment. *Michigan Law Review, 79*(3), 386-459.

Cohen, R. (1992). *Drunk driving.* Washington, DC: Bureau of Justice Statistics.

Coleman, J. (1982). Summer learning and school achievement. *Public Interest, 66,* 140-144.

Collins, J., Hubbard, L., & Rachal, J. (1985). Expensive drug use and illegal income. *Criminology, 23*(4), 743-764.

Conklin, J. (1972). *Robbery and the criminal justice system.* Philadelphia: J. B. Lippincott.

Conrad, J. (1981). Who needs a doorbell pusher? In J. Conrad, *Justice and consequences.* Lexington, MA: Lexington Books. (Reprinted from *Prison Journal, 59*[2], [1979], pp. 17-26)

Cook, P. (1991). The technology of personal violence. In M. Tonry (Ed.). *Crime and justice: Vol. 14.* Chicago: University of Chicago Press.

Cordelia, A. (1983). *The making of an inmate.* Cambridge, MA: Schenkman.

Cox, D. (1980). Exhibitionism: An overview. In D. Cox & R. Daitzman (Eds.), *Exhibitionism.* New York: Garland STPM.

Craddock, A. (1996). Classification systems. In M. McShane & F. Williams III (Eds.), *Encyclopedia of American prisons.* New York: Garland.

Cressey, D. (1971). *Other people's money.* Belmont, CA: Wadsworth. (Original work published 1953)

Csikszentmihalyi, M., & Larson, R. (1984). *Being adolescent: Conflict and growth in the teenage years.* New York: Basic Books.

Cullen, F. (1994). Social support as an organizational concept for criminology. *Justice Quarterly, 11*(4), 527-559.

Currie, I., & Thomas, D. (1995). Does Head Start make a difference? *American Economics Review, 85*(3), 341-363.

Curtis, L. (1974). *Criminal violence.* Lexington, MA: Lexington Books.

Cusson, M. (1983). *Why delinquency?* Toronto: University of Toronto Press.

Davis, S. (1978). The influence of an untoward public act on conception of self. *Symbolic Interaction, 1*(2), 106-123.

Dawson, J., & Langan, P. (1994). *Murder in families.* Washington, DC: Bureau of Justice Statistics.

Dawson, J., Smith, S., & DeFrancis, C. (1993). *Prosecutors in state courts, 1992.* Washington, DC: Bureau of Justice Statistics.

Decker, J. (1992). Curbside deterrence? In R. V. Clarke (Ed.), *Situational crime prevention.* New York: Harow and Heston.

DeJong, W. (1995). *Building the peace: The Resolving Conflict Creatively Program.* Washington, DC: National Institute of Justice.

Dennison, M. (1994). *OSHA and EPA process safety management requirements.* New York: Van Nostrand Reinhold.

DETC teaches an old television new tricks. (1996). *Corrections Alert, 3*(7), 1-2.

Dietz, M. (1983). *Killing for profit.* Chicago: Nelson-Hall.

Diggs, D., & Pieper, S. (1994). Using day reporting centers as an alternative to jail. *Federal Probation, 58*(1), 9-12.

DiIulio, J. (1991). *No escape.* New York: Basic Books.

Ditton, J. (1977). *Part-time crime.* London: Macmillan.

Dixon, J., & Lizotte, A. (1987). Gun ownership and the Southern subculture of violence. *American Journal of Sociology, 93*(2), 383-405.

Durkheim, E. (1947). *The division of labor in society* (G. Simpson, Trans.). New York: Free Press. (Original work published 1893; see also a 1984 edition, translated by W. Halls, Free Press)

Dwyer, D., & McNally, R. (1993). Public policy, prison industries, and business. *Federal Probation, 57*(2), 30-36.

Earle, R. (1995). *Helping to prevent child abuse—and future criminal consequences: Hawaii's healthy start.* Washington, DC: National Institute of Justice.

Edin, K., & Lein, L. (1996). *Making ends meet: How single mothers survive welfare and low-wage work.* New York: Russell Sage.

Eichenlaub, L. (1992). Furloughs and recidivism. *Federal Bureau of Prisons Research Forum, 1,* 1-5.

Eisenberg, M., & Markley, G. (1987). Something works in community supervision. *Federal Probation, 51*(4), 28-32.

Elliott, D. (1994). Serious violent offenders: Onset, developmental course, and termination. *Criminology, 32*(1), 1-21.

Elliott, D., Huizinga, D., & Menard, S. (1989). *Multiple problem youth.* New York: Springer.

Ellis, D., Grasmick, H., & Gilman, B. (1974). Violence in prisons. *American Journal of Sociology, 80*(1), 16-43.

Engbersen, G., Schayt, K., Timmer, J., & van Wearden, F. (1993). *Cultures of unemployment.* Boulder, CO: Westview.

Entwisle, D., & Alexander, K. (1992). Summer setback: Race, poverty, school composition, and achievement. *American Sociological Review, 57*(1), 72-84.

Eskridge, C., & Newbold, G. (1993). Corrections in New Zealand. *Federal Probation, 57*(3), 59-66.

Fagan, J. (1993). Cessation of family violence: Deterrence and dissuasion. In L. Ohlin & M. Tonry (Eds.), *Crime and justice: Vol. 11. Family violence.* Chicago: University of Chicago Press.

Farrington, D. (1986). Age and crime. In M. Tonry & N. Morris (Eds.), *Crime and justice: Vol. 7.* Chicago: University of Chicago Press.

Farrington, D. (1993). Understanding and preventing bullying. In M. Tonry (Ed.), *Crime and justice: Vol. 17.* Chicago: University of Chicago Press.

Farrington, D. (1995). The development of offending and anti-social behavior from childhood. *Journal of Child Psychology and Psychiatry, 36*(6), 929-964.

Farrington, D., Gallaher, B., Morley, L., St. Ledger, R., & West, D. (1986). Unemployment, school leaving, and crime. *British Journal of Criminology, 26*(4), 335-356.

Federal Bureau of Investigation. (various dates). *Crime in the United States.* Washington, DC: Government Printing Office.

Feld, B. (1989). The right to counsel in juvenile court. *Journal of Criminal Law and Criminology, 79*(4), 1185-1346.

Feld, B. (1993). *Justice for children: The right to counsel and the juvenile court.* Boston: Northeastern University Press.

Felson, M. (1994). *Crime and everyday life.* Thousand Oaks, CA: Pine Forge Press.

Felson, M., & Gottfredson, M. (1984). Social indicators of adolescent activities near peers and parents. *Journal of Marriage and the Family, 46*(4), 709-714.

Felson, R., & Steadman, H. (1983). Situational factors in disputes leading to criminal violence. *Criminology, 21*(1), 59-74.

Ferrell, J. (1993). *Crimes of style.* New York: Garland.

Finestone, H. (1957). Cats, kicks, and color. *Social Problems, 5*(1), 3-13.

Finkelhor, D., Hotaling, G., & Sedlak, A. (1990). *Missing, abducted, runaway, and throwaway children in America.* Washington, DC: U.S. Department of Justice.

Finn, P., & Parent, D. (1993). Texas collects substantial revenues from probation fees. *Federal Probation, 57*(2), 17-22.

Finn, P., & Newlyn, A. (1993). *Miami's drug court: A different approach.* Washington, DC: National Institutes of Justice.

Firestone, D., & Reed, F. (1983). *Environment and the law for non-lawyers.* Ann Arbor, MI: Ann Arbor Science Publishers.

Fisse, B., & Braithwaite, J. (1993). *Corporations, crime, and accountability.* New York: Oxford University Press.

Fleisher, M. (1989). *Warehousing violence.* Newbury Park, CA: Sage.

Ford, D., & Regoli, M. (1993). The criminal prosecution of wife assaulters. In N. Hilton (Ed.), *Legal responses to wife assault.* Newbury Park, CA: Sage.

Forst, B. (1977). The deterrent effect of capital punishment. *Minnesota Law Review, 61,* 743-767.

Freburger, C., & Almon, M. (1994). Intensive supervision: A new way to connect with offenders. *Federal Probation, 58*(3), 23-28.

Friedman, R. (1992). *Community policing.* New York: St. Martin's.

Frieze, I., & Browne, A. (1989). Violence in marriage. In L. Ohlin & M. Tonry (Eds.), *Crime and justice: Vol. 11. Family violence.* Chicago: University of Chicago Press.

Gabor, T. (1994). *Everybody does it: Crime by the public.* Toronto: University of Toronto Press.

Gamoran, A., & Mare, R. (1989). Secondary school tracking and educational inequality. *American Journal of Sociology, 94*(5), 1146-1183.

Garfinkel, H. (1956). Conditions of successful degradation ceremonies. *American Journal of Sociology, 61*(5), 420-424.

Garrett, C. (1985). Effects of residential treatment on adjudicated delinquents. *Journal of Research in Crime and Delinquency, 22*(2), 287-308.

Gerber, J., & Fritsch, E. (1995). Adult academic and vocational correctional education programs. *Journal of Offender Rehabilitation, 22*(1/2), 119-142.

Ghodse, H. (1989). *Drugs and addictive behavior.* London: Blackwell.

Gilbert, D. (1988). *Compendium of American public opinion.* New York: Facts on File.

Giles-Sims, J. (1983). *Wife battering.* New York: Guilford.

Glaser, D. (1964). *The effectiveness of a prison and parole system.* Indianapolis, IN: Bobbs-Merrill.

Glaser, D. (1969). *The effectiveness of a prison and parole system* (Abridged ed.). Indianapolis, IN: Bobbs-Merrill.

Glaser, D. (1978). *Crime in our changing society.* New York: Holt, Rinehart & Winston.

Glaser, D. (1979. Capital punishment—Deterrent or stimulus to murder? *University of Toledo Law Review, 10*(2), 317-333.

Glaser, D. (1985). Who gets probation and parole? Case-study versus actuarial decisionmaking. *Crime and Delinquency, 31*(3), 367-378.

Glaser, D. (1995). *Preparing convicts for law-abiding lives: The pioneering penology of Richard A. McGee.* Albany: State University of New York Press.

Glaser, D. (1996). Indeterminate sentences. In L. McShane & F. Williams III (Eds.), *Encyclopedia of American Prisons.* New York: Garland.

Glaser, D., Lander, B., & Abbott, W. (1971). Opiate-addicted and non-addicted siblings in a slum area. *Social Problems, 18*(4), 510-521.

Glaser, D., & Gordon, M. A. (1990a). Exposing: Indecent exposure crimes and their adjudication. *Sociology and Social Research, 74*(2), 150-157.

Glaser, D., & Gordon, M. A. (1990b). Profitable penalties for lower-level courts. *Judicature, 73*(5), 248-252.

Glaser, D., & Watts, R. (1992). Electronic monitoring for drug offenders on probation. *Judicature, 76*(3), 112-117.

Glassner, B., & Loughlin, J. (1987). *Drugs in adolescent worlds.* New York: St. Martin's.

Goetting, A. (1982). Conjugal association in prison. *Crime and Delinquency, 28*(1), 52-82.

Goffman, E. (1952). On cooling the mark out. *Psychiatry, 15*, 451-463.

Goffman, E. (1963). *Behavior in public places.* New York: Free Press.

Goffman, E. (1967). *Interaction ritual.* Garden City, NY: Doubleday.

Goldstein, A. (1983). Excuse: Insanity. In S. Kadish (Ed.), *Encyclopedia of crime and justice.* New York: Free Press.

Goldstock, R., Marcus, T., Thacher, I., & Jacobs, J. B. (1990). *Corruption and racketeering in the New York City construction industry*. New York: New York University Press.

Goleman, D. (1995). *Emotional intelligence*. New York: Bantam.

Gordon, M., & Glaser, D. (1991). The use and effects of financial penalties in municipal courts. *Criminology, 29*(4), 651-676.

Gordon, M., & Riger, S. (1989). *The female fear*. New York: Free Press.

Gottfredson, D. (1985). Youth employment, crime, and schooling. *Developmental Psychology, 21*, 419-432.

Gottfredson, G., & Gottfredson, D. (1985). *Victimization in schools*. New York: Plenum.

Gottfredson, M., & Hirschi, T. (1990). *A general theory of crime*. Stanford, CA: Stanford University Press.

Gouldner, A. (1954). *Wildcat strike*. Yellow Springs, OH: Antioch University Press.

Gouldner, A. (1960). The norm of reciprocity. *American Sociological Review, 25*(2), 161-178.

Gowen, D., & Speyerer, J. (1995). Compulsive gambling and the criminal offender. *Federal Probation, 59*(3), 36-39.

Grasmick, H., Bursik, Jr., R., & Arneklen, B. (1993). Reduction in drunk driving as a response to increased threats of shame, embarrassment, and legal sanctions. *Criminology, 31*(1), 41-67.

Green, G. (1990). *Occupational crime*. Chicago: Nelson Green.

Greenawalt, K. (1983). Punishment. In S. Kadish (Ed.), *Encyclopedia of crime and justice*. New York: Free Press.

Greenfield, L. (1996). *Child victimizers*. Washington, DC: Bureau of Justice Statistics.

Greenwood, P. (1986). *Intervention strategies for chronic juvenile offenders*. Westport, CT: Greenwood.

Greenwood, P. (1987). *The VisionQuest Program*. Santa Monica, CA: Rand.

Greenwood, P., Model, K., Rydell, C., & Chiesa, J. (1996). *Diverting children from a life of crime*. Santa Monica, CA: Rand.

Greer, J., & Stuart, I. (1983). *The sexual aggressor*. New York: Van Nostrand Reinhold.

Gross, J. (1996, August 4). For many on welfare, obstacles to jobs abound. *Los Angeles Times*, Part B, p. 1.

Gross, S., & Mauro, R. (1989). *Death and discrimination*. Boston: Northeastern University Press.

Gueron, J., & Pauly, E., with Lougy, C. (1991). *From welfare to work*. New York: Russell Sage.

Gurnani, P., & Dwyer, M. (1986). Serum testosterone levels in sex offenders. *Journal of Offender Counseling, Services, and Rehabilitation, 11*(1), 39-45.

Gusfield, J. (1963). *Symbolic crusade*. Urbana: University of Illinois Press.

Haaga, J., & Reuter, P. (1990). The limits of the czar's ukase: Drug policy at the local level. *Yale Law and Policy Review, 8*(1), 36-74

Hackler, J., & Hagan, J. (1975). Work and teaching machines as delinquency prevention tools. *The Social Service Review, 49*(1), 92-106.

Hagan, J., & Peterson, R. (Eds.). (1995). *Crime and inequality.* Stanford, CA: Stanford University Press.

Halbrook, S. (1984). *That every man be armed.* Albuquerque: University of New Mexico Press.

Hamm, M. (1993). Reforming juvenile corrections [Book Review]. *Justice Quarterly, 10*(4), 697-708.

Hamberger, L., & Hastings, J. (1993). Court-mandated treatment of men who assault their partner. In N. Hilton (Ed.), *Legal responses to wife assault.* Newbury Park, CA: Sage.

Haran, J., & Martin, J. (1984). The armed bank robber. *Federal Probation, 48*(4), 47-53.

Hare, R. (1977). Electrodermal and cardiovascular correlates of psychopathy. In R. Hare & D. Schalling (Eds.), *Psychopathic behavior.* New York: John Wiley.

Harland, A. (Ed.). (1996). *Choosing correctional options that work.* Thousand Oaks, CA: Sage.

Harris, K. (1993). Work and welfare among single mothers in poverty. *American Journal of Sociology, 99*(2), 317-352.

Harris, P. (1994). Client-management classification and prediction of probation outcome. *Crime and Delinquency, 40*(2), 154-174.

Harris, R. (1993, August 25). One state gives juveniles a hand instead of a cell. *Los Angeles Times,* A1.

Hawkins, D., Catalano, R., Jones, G., & Fine, D. (1987). Delinquency prevention through parental training. In J. Wilson & G. Lowry (Eds.), *From Children to citizens: Vol. 3.* New York: Springer.

Hawkins, J., Von Cleve, E., & Catalano, R. (1991). Reducing early childhood aggression: Results of a primary prevention program. *Journal of the American Academy of Child and Adolescent Psychiatry, 30*(2), 208-217.

Hemenway, D., Solnick, J., & Azrael, D. (1995). Firearms and community feelings of safety. *Journal of Criminal Law and Criminology, 86*(1), 121-132.

Henry, S. (1978). *The hidden economy.* London: Martin Robinson.

Hepburn, J. (1989). Prison guards as agents of social control. In L. Goodstein & D. MacKenzie (Eds.), *The American prisoner.* New York: Plenum.

Hess, H. (1973). *Mafia and mafioso.* Lexington, MA: Lexington Books.

Hester, R., & Smith, R. (1973). Effects of a mandatory death penalty on the decisions of simulated jurors as a function of the heinousness of the crime. *Journal of Criminal Justice, 1*(4), 319-326.

Hillsman, S. (1992). Fines and day fines. In M. Tonry & N. Morris (Eds.), *Crime and justice: A review of research* (Vol. 12). Chicago: University of Chicago Press.

Hirschi, T. (1969). *Causes of delinquency.* Berkeley: University of California Press.

Hobsbawm, E. (1981). *Bandits* (Rev. ed.). New York: Random House.

Hobson, B. (1987). *Uneasy virtue.* New York: Basic Books.

Hochstedler, E. (1986). Criminal prosecution of the mentally disturbed. *Law and Society Review, 20*(2), 279-292.

Hollinger, R., & Clark, J. (1983). *Theft by employees.* Lexington, MA: Lexington Books.

Holmes, R., & Holmes, S. (1994). *Murder in America.* Newbury Park, CA: Sage.

Holt, N. (1995). California's determinate sentencing law: What when wrong? *Perspectives* [the American Probation and Parole Association journal], *19*(3), 19-23.

Hombs, M. (1994). *American homelessness* (2nd ed.). Santa Barbara, CA: ABC-CLIO.

Homel, R. (1988). *Policing and punishing the drinking driver.* New York: Springer.

Homel, R. (1990). Random breath testing and random stopping programs in Australia. In R. Wilson & R. Mann (Eds.), *Drinking and driving.* New York: Guilford.

Hong, P. (1996, August 13). Court's war on drugs. *Los Angeles Times,* B2.

Horney, J., Osgood, D., & Marshall, I. (1995). Criminal careers in the short term. *American Sociological Review, 60*(5), 655-673.

Horning, D. (1983). Employee theft. In S. Kadish (Ed.), *Encyclopedia of crime and justice.* New York: Free Press.

Howitt, D. (1995). *Paedophiles and sexual offenses against children.* New York: John Wiley.

Hubbard, R., Marsden, M., Rachal, J., Harwood, J., Cavanaugh, E., & Ginnsburg, H. (1989). *Drug abuse treatment.* Chapel Hill: University of North Carolina Press.

Huff, C., Rattner, A., & Sagarin, E. (1986). Guilty until proved innocent. *Crime and Delinquency, 32*(4), 518-544.

Huff, R. (1989). Youth gangs and public policy. *Crime and Delinquency, 35*(4), 524-537.

Hughes, W., & Brewin, R. (1979). *The tranquilizing of America.* New York: Harcourt Brace Jovanovich.

Hser, Y., Anglin, M., & Powers, K. (1993). A 24-year follow-up of California narcotic addicts. *Archives of General Psychiatry, 50*(17), 577-584.

Ianni, F. (1972). *A family business.* New York: Russell Sage.

Ianni, F. (1974). *Black Mafia.* New York: Simon & Schuster.

In brief. (1995). *Juvenile Justice* (U.S. Department of Justice), *2*(2), 25-28.

Inciardi, J. (1975). *Careers in crime.* Chicago: Rand McNally.

Inciardi, J. (1983). On grift at the Superbowl. In G. Waldo (Ed.), *Career criminals.* Newbury Park, CA: Sage.

Inciardi, J., Horowitz, R., & Pottieger, A. (1993). *Street kids, street drugs, street crime.* Belmont, CA: Wadsworth.

Jacobs, J., with Parasella, C., & Worthington, J. (1994). *Busting the mob: U.S. and Costa Nostra.* New York: New York University Press.

Jacobs, M. (1990). *Screwing the system and making it work.* Chicago: University of Chicago Press.

Jacoby, N., Nehemkis, P., & Eels, R. (1977). *Bribery and extortion in world business.* New York: Macmillan.

Jacoby, S. (1983). *Wild justice: The evolution of revenge*. New York: Harper & Row.

Jamieson, K. (1994). *The organization of corporate crime: Dynamics of antitrust violation*. Thousand Oaks, CA: Sage.

Jencks, C. (1994, June 23). Really cheap housing on the bottom rung. *Los Angeles Times*, B7.

Jenkins, R., & Brown, W. (Eds.). (1988). *The abandonment of delinquent behavior: Promoting the turnaround*. New York: Praeger.

Jensen, C. (1976). Race, achievement and delinquency. *American Journal of Sociology, 82*(2), 379-387.

Johnson, B., Golub, B., & Fagan, J. (1995). Careers in crack, drug use, drug distribution, and nondrug criminality. *Crime and Delinquency, 41*(3), 275-295.

Johnson, J. (1996, April 27). A new side to domestic violence. *Los Angeles Times*, A1.

Johnson, R. (1996). *Hard time* (2nd ed.). Monterrey, CA: Brooks/Cole.

Joint Committee on New York's Drug Law. (1977). *The nation's toughest drug law: Evaluating the New York experience*. New York: Association of the Bar of the City of New York.

Jolin, A., & Stipack, B. (1992). Drug treatment and electronically monitored home confinement. *Crime and Delinquency, 38*(2), 158-170.

Kandel, E., & Mednick, S. (1991). Perinatal complications predict violent offending. *Criminology, 29*(3), 519-529.

Karmel, R. (1982). *Regulation by prosecution*. New York: Simon & Schuster.

Katz, J. (1988). *Seductions of crime*. New York: Basic Books.

Katz, S., & Mazur, M. A. (1979). *Understanding the rape victim*. New York: John Wiley.

Kelling, G. (1983). On the accomplishments of the police. In M. Punch (Ed.), *Control in the police organization*. Cambridge: MIT Press.

Kempe, H., Silverman, F., Steele, B., Droegemueller, W., & Silver, H. (1962). The battered child syndrome. *Journal of the American Medical Association, 181*, 17-24.

Kemper, T. (1987). How many emotions are there? *American Journal of Sociology, 93*(2), 263-289.

Kimbrough, J. (1986). School-based strategies for delinquency prevention. In *The rehabilitation reader*. Washington, DC: OJJDP.

Kitchener, H., Schmidt, A., & Glaser, D. (1977). How persistent is post-prison success? *Federal Probation, 41*(1), 9-15.

Kleck, G. (1979). Capital punishment, gun ownership, and homicide. *American Journal of Sociology, 84*(4), 882-910.

Kleck, G. (1991). *Point blank: Guns and violence in America*. New York: Aldine de Gruyter.

Kleck, G., & Gertz, M. (1995). Armed resistance to crime. *Journal of Criminal Law and Criminology, 86*(1), 150-187.

Klein, L., Forst, B., & Filator, V. (1978). The deterrent effect of capital punishment. In A. Blumstein, J. Cohen, & D. Nagin (Eds.), *Deterrence and incapacitation.* Washington, DC: National Academy of Science.

Klein, M. (1984). *Western systems of juvenile justice.* Newbury Park, CA: Sage.

Klein, M. (1995). *The American street gang.* New York: Oxford University Press.

Klockars, C. (1974). *The professional fence.* New York: Free Press.

Klofas, J., & Weisheit, R. (1987). Guilty but mentally ill. *Justice Quarterly, 4*(1), 39-50.

Kowalski, G., & Petee, T. (1991). Sunbelt effects on homicide rates. *Sociology and Social Research, 75*(2), 73-79.

Krahn, H., Hartnagel, T., & Gartrell, J. (1986). Income inequality and homicide rates. *Criminology, 24*(2), 269-295.

Krisberg, B., & Austin, J. (1993). *Reinventing juvenile justice.* Newbury Park, CA: Sage.

Kunen, J. (1995, July 10). Teaching prisoners a lesson. *New Yorker,* pp. 34-39.

Langan, P., & Innes, C. (1986). *Preventing domestic violence against women.* Washington, DC: Bureau of Justice Statistics.

Larzelere, R., & Patterson, G. (1990). Parental management: Mediator of the effect of socioeconomic status on early delinquency. *Criminology, 28*(2), 301-323.

Laws, D. (1989). *Relapse prevention with sex offenders.* New York: Guilford.

LeBlanc, M., & Frechette, M. (1989). *Male criminal activity from childhood through youth.* New York: Springer.

LeClair, D., & Guarino-Ghezzi, S. (1991). Does incapacitation guarantee public safety? Lessons from the Massachusetts furlough and prerelease programs. *Justice Quarterly, 8*(1), 9-36.

Lefkowitz, M., Eron, L., Welder, L., & Huesemann, L. (1977). *Growing up to be violent.* Elmsdale, NY: Pergamon.

Lemert, E. (1967). *Human deviance, social problems, and social control.* Englewood Cliffs, NJ: Prentice Hall.

Lerman, P. (1991). Counting youth in trouble in institutions. *Crime and Delinquency, 37*(4), 465-480.

Lester, D. (1987). Availability of guns and the likelihood of suicide. *Sociology and Social Research, 71,* 287-288.

Letkemann, P. (1973). *Crime as work.* Englewood Cliffs, NJ: Prentice Hall.

Levinson, B. (1980). TC or not TC? That is the question. In H. Toch (Ed.), *Therapeutic communities in corrections.* New York: Praeger.

Lilly, J., Ball, R., Curry, G., & Smith, R. (1992). The Pride, Inc., program: An evaluation of five years of electronic monitoring. *Federal Probation, 56*(4), 42-47.

Lindner, C. (1993, March 29). Cost of death: A billion dollars and counting. *Los Angeles Times,* M1.

Lipsey, M. (1984). Is delinquency prevention a cost-effective strategy? *Journal of Research in Crime and Delinquency, 21*(2), 279-302.

Lipton, D. (1996). Prison-based therapeutic communities: Their success with drug-abusing offenders. *NIJ Journal, 230,* 12-20.

Liska, A., & Bellair, P. (1995). Violent crime rates and racial composition: Convergence over time. *American Journal of Sociology, 101*(3), 578-610.

Loeb, R. (1973). Adolescent groups. *Sociology and Social Research, 58*(1), 13-22.

Loeber, R., & Southamer-Loeber, M. (1986). Family factors as correlates and predictors of juvenile conduct problems and delinquency. In M. Tonry & N. Morris (Eds.), *Crime and justice* (Vol. 7). Chicago: University of Chicago Press.

Loftin, C., & Hill, R. (1974). Regional subculture and homicide. *American Sociological Review, 39*(5), 714-724.

Loftin, C., Heumann, M., & McDowall, D. (1983). Mandatory sentencing and firearm violence. *Law and Society Review, 17*(2), 287-318.

Logan, C. (1990). *Private prisons: Cons and pros.* New York: Oxford University Press.

Luckenbill, D. (1977). Criminal homicide as a situated transaction. *Social Problems, 25*(4), 176-186.

Lunde, D. (1976). *Murder and madness.* San Francisco: San Francisco Book Co.

Lundsgaarde, H. (1977). *Murder in Space City.* New York: Oxford University Press.

Lykken, D. (1957). A study of anxiety in the psychopathic personality. *Journal of Abnormal and Social Psychology, 55*(1), 6-10.

Lykken, D. (1982). Fearlessness. *Psychology Today, 16*(1), 20-28.

MacCoun, R., & Reuter, P. (1992). Are the wages of sin $30 an hour? Economic aspects of street-level drug dealing. *Crime and Delinquency, 38*(4), 477-491.

Mack, J. (1972). The able criminal. *British Journal of Criminology, 12*(1), 44-54.

Mackenzie, D., Brame, R., McDowall, D., & Souryall, C. (1995). Boot camp prisons and technical violations in eight states. *Criminology, 33*(3), 327-357.

Maguin, E., & Loeber, R. (1996). Academic performance and delinquency. In M. Tonry (Ed.), *Crime and justice* (Vol. 20). Chicago: University of Chicago Press.

Maguire, K., & Pastore, A. (1995). *Sourcebook of criminal justice statistics, 1994.* Washington, DC: Bureau of Justice Statistics.

Mair, G., Lloyd, C., New, C., & Sibbit, R. (1995). Intensive probation in England and Wales: An evaluation. *Home Office Research Findings,* No. 15 (London).

Makkai, T., & Braithwaite, J. (1994). Reintegrative shaming and compliance with regulatory standards. *Criminology, 32*(3), 361-383.

Mann, K. (1985). *Defending white collar crime.* New Haven, CT: Yale University Press.

Mare, R., Winship, C., & Kubitschek, W. (1984). The transition from youth to adult: Understanding the age pattern of unemployment. *American Journal of Sociology, 90*(2), 326-358.

Martin, P., DiNitto, D., Maxwell, S., & Norton, D. (1985). Controversies surrounding the rape kit exam in the 1980s. *Crime and Delinquency, 31*(2), 223-246.

Maurer, D. (1940). *The big con.* Indianapolis, IN: Bobbs-Merrill.

Mayer, A. (1985). *Sexual abuse.* Holmes Beach, FL: Learning Publications.

Mayer, G., & Butterworth, T. (1981). Evaluating a preventive approach to reducing school vandalism. *Phi Delta Kappan, 62*(3), 498-499.

McCaffery, D. (1982). *OSHA and the politics of health regulation.* New York: Plenum.

McCarthy, B., & Hagan, J. (1992). Mean streets: The theoretical significance of situational delinquency among homeless youths. *American Journal of Sociology, 98*(3), 597-627.

McCord, J. (1983). A longitudinal study of aggression and antisocial behavior. In K. van Dusen & S. Mednick (Eds.), *Prospective studies in crime and delinquency.* Boston: Kluwer-Nijhoff.

McCord, J. (1985). Deterrence and the light touch of the law. In D. Farrington & J. Gunn (Eds.), *Reactions to crime.* New York: John Wiley.

McDonald, C. (Ed.). (1990). *Private prisons and the public interest.* New Brunswick, NJ: Rutgers University Press.

McDowall, D., Loftin, C., & Wiersema, B. (1995). Easing concealed firearm laws: Effects on homicide in three states. *Journal of Criminal Law and Criminology, 86*(1), 193-206.

McGillis, D. (1996). *Beacons of hope: New York City's school-based community centers.* Washington, DC: National Institute of Justice.

McKee, G. (1972). *A cost-benefit analysis of vocational training in the California prison system.* Unpublished doctoral dissertation, Claremont Graduate School. (University Microfilms Dissertation No. 72-26)

McKee, G. (1978). Cost effectiveness and vocational training. In N. Johnston & L. Savitz (Eds.), *Crime and justice* (3rd ed.). New York: John Wiley.

McKee, G. (1985). Cost-benefits analysis of vocational training. In R. Carter, D. Glaser, & L. Wilkins (Eds.), *Correctional institutions* (3rd ed.). New York: Harper & Row.

McKissack, I. (1967). The peak age for property crimes. *British Journal of Criminology, 7*(2), 184-194.

McKissack, I. (1973). The peak age for property crimes: Further data. *British Journal of Criminology, 13*(3), 253-261.

McWilliams, J. (1994). *Then throw away the key: Past and present perspectives on the impact of mandatory minimum sentences on drug offenders.* Unpublished paper, History Department, Pennsylvania State University.

Messner, S. (1982). Poverty, inequality, and the urban homicide rate. *Criminology, 20*(1), 103-114.

Messner, S. (1989). Economic discrimination and societal homicide rates. *American Sociological Review, 54*(4), 597-611.

Messner, S., & Tardiff, K. (1986). Economic inequality and levels of homicide: An analysis of urban neighborhoods. *Criminology, 24*(2), 297-317.

Meyer, R. (1992). *Abnormal behavior and the criminal justice system.* Lexington, MA: Lexington Books.

Mieczkowski, T. (1996). The prevalence of drug use in the U.S. In M. Tonry (Ed.), *Crime and justice* (Vol. 20). Chicago: University of Chicago Press.

Mignon, S., & Holmes, W. (1995). Police response to mandatory arrest laws. *Crime and Delinquency, 41*(4), 430-442.

Miller, A. (1995, August 20). '94 prison rolls at record high, study shows. *Los Angeles Times*, A5.

Miller, J. (1991). *Last one over the wall: The Massachusetts experiment in closing reform schools*. Columbus: Ohio State University Press.

Mock, L. (1994). Young people, violence, and guns. *National Institute of Justice Journal, 228*, November, 42-46.

Model, K. (1993). The effect of marijuana decriminalization on hospital emergency room drug episodes: 1975-1978. *Journal of the American Statistical Association, 88*(423), 737-747.

Moffitt, T. (1993). Adolescence-limited and life-course persistent anti-social behavior: A developmental typology. *Psychological Bulletin, 100*(4), 674-701.

Monk-Turner, E. (1989). Effects of high school delinquency on educational attainment and adult occupational status. *Sociological Perspectives, 32*, 413-418.

Moran, R. (1995, Spring). Crimes against tourists in Florida. *American Sociological Association, Crime and Deviance Newsletter*, p. 9.

Morris, N. (1982). *Madness and the criminal law*. Chicago: University of Chicago Press.

Morse, B., & Elliott, D. (1992). Effects of ignition interlock devices on DUI recidivism. *Crime and Delinquency, 38*(2), 131-157.

Musto, D. (1987). *The American disease: Origins of narcotic control* (Expanded ed.). New York: Oxford University Press.

Nadelmann, E. (1995, September). Beyond Needle Park: The Swiss maintenance trial. *The Drug Policy Letter, 27*, 12-14.

Nader, R. (1965). *Unsafe at any speed*. New York: Grossman.

Nagin, D., Farrington, D., & Moffitt, T. (1995). Life course trajectories of different types of offenders. *Criminology, 33*(1), 111-139.

National Institute of Justice. (1994). *Environmental crime prosecution: Results of a national survey*. Washington, DC: Author.

National Institute of Justice. (1995a). *Drug use forecasting: 1994: A report on adults and juvenile arrestees*. Washington, DC: Author.

National Institute of Justice. (1995b). *Youth violence, guns, and drug markets: Research review*. Washington, DC: Author.

Nelli, H., (1976). *The business of crime*. New York: Oxford University Press.

Nettler, G. (1984). *Explaining crime* (3rd ed.). New York: McGraw-Hill.

Newman, L. (1973). *Defensible space*. New York: Macmillan.

Newton, G., & Zimring, F. (1969). *Firearms and violence in American life* (Staff Report to the National Commission on the Causes and Prevention of Violence). Washington, DC: Government Printing Office.

Noble, C. (1986). *Liberalism at work: Rise and fall of OSHA*. Philadelphia: Temple University Press.

Nugent, M., & Johannes, J. (1990). *Money, elections, and democracy: Reforming Congressional campaign finance*. Boulder, CO: Westview.

Oakes, J. (1985). *Keeping track: How schools structure inequality*. New Haven, CT: Yale University Press.

Oakes, J. (1990). *Multiplying inequalities: The effects of race, social class, and tracking on opportunities to learn math and science*. Santa Monica, CA: Rand.

Office of Juvenile Justice and Delinquency Prevention (OJJDP). (1985). *Law-related education*. Washington, DC: U.S. Department of Justice.

Office of Juvenile Justice and Delinquency Prevention (OJJDP). (1995). *Delinquency prevention works*. Washington, DC: U.S. Department of Justice.

Office of Juvenile Justice and Delinquency Prevention (OJJDP). (1996). *Curfew*. Washington, DC: U.S. Department of Justice.

O'Keefe, M. (in press). *Predictors of dating violence among high school students. Journal of Interpersonal Violence*.

O'Keefe, M., & Treister, L. (in press). *Victims of dating violence among high school students: Are the predictors different for males and females. Journal of Interpersonal Violence*.

Okun, L. (1986). *Women abuse*. Albany: State University of New York Press.

Olweus, D., Block, J., & Raske-Yarrow, M. (Eds.). (1986). *Development of antisocial and prosocial behavior*. Orlando, FL: Academic Press.

Ostrow, R. (1995, October 5). Sentencing study sees race disparity. *Los Angeles Times*, pp. A1, A17.

Otto, L. (1976). Social integration and status attainment. *American Journal of Sociology, 81*(6), 1360-1383.

Pagelow, M. (1981). *Women battering*. Newbury Park, CA: Sage.

Palmer, T. (1994). *A profile of correctional effectiveness and new directions for research*. Albany: State University of New York Press.

Pandiani, J. (1982). The crime control corps: An invisible New Deal program. *British Journal of Sociology, 32,*), 238-258.

Parent, D., Byrne, J., Tsarfaty, V., Valade, L., & Esselman, J. (1995). *Day reporting centers* (Vol. 1). Washington, DC: National Institute of Justice, Office of Justice Programs.

Parker, R., & Smith, M. (1979). Deterrence, poverty, and type of homicide. *American Journal of Sociology, 85*(3), 614-624.

Passas, N. (1995). The mirror of global evil: A review essay on the BCCI affair. *Justice Quarterly, 12*(2), 377-405.

Paternoster, R. (1989). Decisions to participate in and desist from four types of common delinquency: Deterrence and the rational choice perspective. *Law and Society Review, 23*(1), 7-40.

Paternoster, R. (1991). *Capital punishment in America*. Boston: Lexington Books.

Patterson, G. (1980). Children who steal. In T. Hirschi & M. Gottfredson (Eds.), *Understanding crime*. Newbury Park, CA: Sage.

Pearl, J. (1987). The highest paying customers. *Hastings Law Journal, 38*(2), 769-800.

Petersilia, J. (1996). The state of probation in America. In M. Tonry (Ed.), *Crime and justice* (Vol. 23). Chicago: University of Chicago Press.

Petersilia, J., Abrahamse, A., & Wilson, J. (1990). A summary of RAND's research on police performance, community characteristics, and case attrition. *Journal of Police Science and Administration, 17*, 219-226.

Petersilia, J., Greenwood, P., & Lavin, M. (1977). *Criminal careers of habitual felons.* Santa Monica, CA: Rand.

Petersilia, J., & Turner, S. (1993). Intensive probation and parole. In M. Tonry (Ed.), *Crime and justice* (Vol. 17). Chicago: University of Chicago Press.

Pittman, D., & Handy, W. (1964). Patterns in criminal aggravated assault. *Journal of Criminal Law, Criminology and Police Science, 55*(4), 462-470.

Podkopacz, M., & Feld, M. (1996). The end of the line. *Journal of Criminal Law and Criminology, 86*(2), 449-492.

Polk, K. (1985). Rape reform and criminal justice processing. *Crime and Delinquency, 31*(2), 191-205.

Prejean, Sister H. (1994). *Dead man walking.* New York: Random House.

Rada, R. (1978). *Clinical aspects of the rapist.* New York: Grune & Stratton.

Raine, A. (1993). *The psychopathology of crime.* New York: Academic Press.

Rand, M. (1994). *Carjacking.* Washington, DC: Bureau of Justice Statistics.

Rank, M. (1994). *Living on the edge: The realities of welfare in America.* New York: Columbia University Press.

Rauma, D., & Berk, R. (1987). Remuneration and recidivism. *Journal of Quantitative Criminology, 3*(3), 3-27.

Reese, C. (1983). *Deregulation and environmental quality.* Westport, CT: Quorum.

Reiss, A., Jr. (1961). The social integration of peers and queers. *Social Problems, 9*(1), 102-120.

Reiss, A., Jr., & Farrington, D. (1991). Advancing knowledge about co-offending: Results from a prospective longitudinal survey of London males. *Journal of Criminal Law and Criminology, 82*(2), 360-395.

Reissman, W. (1979). *Folded lies.* New York: Free Press.

Renzema, M. (1992). Home confinement programs. In J. M. Byrne, A. Lurigio, & J. Petersilia (Eds.), *Smart sentencing.* Thousand Oaks, CA: Sage.

Reuss-Ianni, E. (1993). *The two cultures of policing.* New Brunswick, NJ: Transaction Books.

Reuter, P. (1983). *Disorganized crime.* Cambridge: MIT Press.

Reuter, P. (1992). The limits and consequences of U.S. foreign drug control efforts. *Annals of the Academy of Political and Social Science, 521*, 151-162.

Reuter, P. (1993). The cartage industry in New York. In M. Tonry & A. Reiss, Jr. (Eds.), *Crime and justice: Vol. 18. Beyond the law: Crime in complex organizations.* Chicago: University of Chicago Press.

Reuter, P., Falco, M., & MacCoun, R. (1993). *Comparing Western European and North American drug policies.* Santa Monica, CA: RAND.

Riley, D. (1987). Time and crime. *Journal of Quantitative Criminology, 3*(4), 339-354.

Robinson, R. (1992). Intermediate sanctions and the female offender. In J. M. Byrne, A. Lurigio, & J. Petersilia (Eds.), *Smart sentencing*. Thousand Oaks, CA: Sage.

Romero, J., & Williams, L. (1985). Recidivism among convicted sex offenders. *Federal Probation, 49*(1), 58-64.

Rosenbaum, J. (1989). Family dysfunction and female delinquency. *Crime and Delinquency, 35*(1), 31-44.

Ross, H. (1992). *Confronting drunk driving*. New Haven, CT: Yale University Press.

Rossel, H. (1990). *The carrot or the stick for school desegregation policy: Magnet schools or forced busing*. Philadelphia: Temple University Press.

Roth, J. (1994a). *Firearms and violence*. Washington, DC: National Institute of Justice.

Roth, J. (1994b). *Psychoactive substances and violence*. Washington, DC: National Institute of Justice.

Rushen, R., & Hunter, E. (1970). *The RODEO model*. Los Angeles: County of Los Angeles Probation Department.

Russell, D. (1994). *Rape in marriage* (2nd ed.). Bloomington: Indiana University Press.

Rutter, M., Maughan, B., Mortimore, P., & Ouston, J. (1979). *Fifteen thousand hours: Secondary schools and their effects on children*. Somerset, UK: Open Books Publishing.

Rydell, C., & Everingham, S. (1994). *Controlling cocaine: Supply versus demand programs*. Santa Monica, CA: RAND.

Sampson, R. (1987). Urban black violence. *American Journal of Sociology, 93*(2), 348-382.

Sampson, R., & Groves, W. (1989). Community structure and crime. *American Journal of Sociology, 94*(4), 774-802.

Sampson, R., & Laub, J. (1990). Stability and change in crime and deviance over the life course: The salience of adult social bonds. *American Sociological Review, 55*(5), 609-627.

Sampson, R., & Laub, J. (1993). *Crime in the making*. Cambridge, MA: Harvard University Press.

Sampson, R., & Laub, J. (1996). The military as a turning point in the lives of disadvantaged men. *American Sociological Review, 61*(3), 347-367.

Sampson, R., & Wilson, W. (1995). Toward a theory of race, crime, and urban inequality. In J. Hagan & R. Peterson (Eds.), *Crime and inequality*. Stanford, CA: Stanford University Press.

Sanday, P. (1990). *Fraternity gang rape*. New York: New York University Press.

Sarason, I. (1978). A cognitive social learning approach to juvenile delinquency. In R. D. Hare & D. Schalling (Eds.), *Psychopathic behavior*. New York: John Wiley.

Saunders, D., & Azar, S. (1992). Treatment programs for family violence. In L. Ohlin & M. Tonry (Eds.), *Crime and violence: Vol. 11. Family violence*. Chicago: University of Chicago Press.

Saylor, W., & Gaes, G. (1992, January 8). *PREP study links UNICOR work experience with successful post-release outcome.* Washington, DC: Federal Bureau of Prisons, Office of Research and Evaluation.

Schachter, S. (1971). *Emotion, obesity, and crime.* New York: Academic Press.

Schlossman, S., Zellman, G., Shavelson, R., Sedlak, M., & Cobb, J. (1984). *Delinquency prevention in South Chicago: A fifty-year assessment of the Chicago Area Project.* Santa Monica, CA: Rand.

Schneider, A. (1984). Diverting status offenses from juvenile court jurisdiction. *Crime and Delinquency, 30*(3), 347-370.

Schneider, P., Griffith, W., & Schneider, A. (1982). Juvenile restitution as a sole sanction or condition of probation. *Journal of Research in Crime and Delinquency, 19*(1), 47-65.

Schuerman, L., & Kobrin, S. (1986). Community careers in crime. In A. Reiss, Jr., & M. Tonry (Eds.), *Crime and justice: Vol. 8. Communities and crime.* Chicago: University of Chicago Press.

Schutt, R., & Garrett, G. (1992). *Responding to the homeless.* New York: Plenum.

Schwartz, I., Jackson-Beeck, M., & Anderson, R. (1984). The "Hidden" system of juvenile control. *Crime and Delinquency, 30*(3), 371-385.

Seashore, M., Haberfield, S., Irwin, J., & Baker, K. (1976). *Prisoner education.* New York: Praeger.

Seligman, J. (1985). *The SEC and the future of finance.* New York: Praeger.

Seltser, B., & Miller, D. (1993). *Homeless families: The struggle for dignity.* Urbana: University of Illinois Press.

Servadio, G. (1976). *Mafioso.* New York: Stein & Day.

Sexton, G. (1995). *Work in American prisons: Joint ventures with the private sector.* Washington, DC: National Institute of Justice.

Shapiro, S. (1984). *Wayward capitalists.* New Haven, CT: Yale University Press.

Sheldon, J., & Zweibel, G. (1978). *Survey of consumer fraud law.* Washington, DC: U.S. Department of Justice.

Sheley, J., McGee, Z., & Wright, J. (1992). Gun-related violence in and around city schools. *American Journal of Diseases of Children, 146*(6), 677-682.

Sherman, L. (1992a). The influence of criminology on criminal law: Evaluating arrests for misdemeanor domestic violence. *Journal of Criminal Law and Criminology, 83*(1), 1-72.

Sherman, L. (1992b). *Policing domestic violence: Experiments and dilemmas.* New York: Free Press.

Sherman, L., & Berk, R. (1984). The specific deterrent effect of arrest for domestic assault. *American Sociological Review, 49*(2), 261-272.

Sherman, L., & Cohn, E. (1989). The impact of research on legal policy. *Law and Society Review, 23*(1), 117-144.

Sherman, L., Smith, D., Schmidt, W., & Rogan, P. (1992). Crime, punishment, and stake in conformity: Legal and informal control of domestic violence. *American Sociological Review, 57*(5), 680-690.

Sherman, L., Shaw, J., & Rogan, D. (1995). *The Kansas City gun experiment*. Washington, DC: National Institute of Justice.

Shichor, D. (1995). *Punishment for profit*. Thousand Oaks, CA: Sage.

Shogren, E. (1995, December 4). Population in U.S. prisons is up record 8.8% *Los Angeles Times*, pp. A1, A12.

Shover, N. (1985). *Aging criminals*. Newbury Park, CA: Sage.

Shuster, B. (1996, June 14). Part dad . . . part cop . . . all business. *Los Angeles Times*, B1.

Siegel, R. (1989). *Intoxication*. New York: E. P. Dutton.

Simon, C., & Witte, A. (1982). *Beating the system: The underground economy*. Boston: Auburn House.

Simon, D., & Eitzen, D. (1982). *Elite deviance*. New York: Allyn & Bacon.

Simon, R. (1967). *The jury and the defense of insanity*. Boston: Little, Brown.

Singer, R. (1979). *Just deserts*. Cambridge, MA: Ballinger.

Skinner, B. (1953). *Science and human behavior*. New York: Macmillan.

Skogan, W. (1990. *Disorder and decline*. New York: Free Press.

Skoll, G. (1992). *Walk the walk and talk the talk: An ethnography of a drug abuse treatment facility*. Philadelphia: Temple University Press.

Skolnick, J. (1978). *House of cards*. Boston: Little, Brown.

Slade, S. (1978, March 18). Arson: Business by other means. *Nation*, pp. 307-309.

Smith, A. (1937). *An inquiry into the nature and causes of the wealth of nations*. New York: Random House. (Original work published 1776)

Smith, C., & Thornberry, T. (1995). The relationship between childhood maltreatment and adolescent involvement in delinquency. *Criminology, 33*(4), 451-481.

Smith, D., & Gartin, P. (1989). Specifying specific deterrence: The influence of arrest on future criminal activity. *American Sociological Review, 54*(1), 94-105.

Snell, T. (1995). *Correctional population of the United States, 1993*. Washington, DC: Bureau of Justice Statistics.

Snider, L. (1990). Cooperative models and corporation crime. *Crime and Delinquency, 36*(3), 373-390.

Snyder, H., & Sickmund, M. (1995). *Juvenile offenders*. Washington, DC: Office of Juvenile Justice and Delinquency Prevention.

Sorauf, F. (1992). *Inside campaign finance*. New Haven, CT: Yale University Press.

Stark, R. (1987). Deviant places. *Criminology, 25*(4), 893-909.

Stark, R., Kent, L., & Doyle, D. (1982). Religion and delinquency. *Journal of Research in Crime and Delinquency, 19*(1), 4-24.

Steadman, H. (1979). *Beating a rap*. Chicago: University of Chicago Press.

Steadman, H., & Cocozza, J. (1974). *Careers of the criminally insane*. Lexington, MA: Lexington Books.

Steenhuis, D., Tigges, L., & Essers, J. (1983). The penal climate in the Netherlands. *British Journal of Criminology, 23*(1), 1-16.

Steffensmeier, D. (1986). *The fence*. Totowa, NJ: Rowman & Littlefield.

Steffensmeier, D., & Allan, E. (1995). Age-inequality and property crime. In J. Hagan & R. Peterson (Eds.), *Crime and inequality*. Stanford, CA: Stanford University Press.

Steffensmeier, D., Allan, E., Harer, M., & Streifel, C. (1989). Age and the distribution of crime. *American Journal of Sociology, 94*(4), 803-841.

Steinman, M. (1988). Anticipating rank and file police reactions to arrest policies regarding spouse abuse. *Criminal Justice Research Bulletin, 4*(3), 1-5.

Stephan, J., & Snell, T. (1996). *Capital punishment 1994*. Washington, DC: Bureau of Justice Statistics.

Stern, P. (1992). *Still the best Congress money can buy* (2nd ed. of *The Best Congress Money Can Buy*, 1988). New York: Pantheon.

Stinchcombe, A. (1969). *Rebellion in a high school*. Chicago: Quadrangle.

Stouffer, S., Guttman, L., Suchman, E., Lazarsfeld, P., Star, S., & Clausen, J. (1950). *Measurement and prediction: Vol. 4. Studies in social psychology in World War II*. Princeton, NJ: Princeton University Press.

Strauss, M., & Gelles, R. (1990). *Physical violence in American families*. New Brunswick, NJ: Transaction Books.

Sutherland, E., & Cressey, D. (1978). *Criminology* (10th ed.). Philadelphia: J. B. Lippincott.

Tanioka, I., & Glaser, D. (1991). School uniforms, routine activities, and the social control of delinquency in Japan. *Youth and Society, 23*(3), 50-75.

Tannenbaum, F. (1938). *Crime and the community*. New York: Ginn.

Thornberry, T., & Christenson, R. (1984). Unemployment and criminal involvement. *American Sociological Review, 49*(3), 398-411.

Thornberry, T., & Jacoby, J. (1979). *The criminally insane*. Chicago: University of Chicago Press.

Thornberry, T., Krohn, M., Lizotte, A., & Chard-Wierschein, D. (1993). The role of juvenile gangs in facilitating delinquent behavior. *Journal of Research in Crime and Delinquency, 30*(1), 55-87.

"Three strikes": Serious flaws and a huge price tag. (1995). *RAND Research Review, 19*(1), 1-2.

Tifft, L. (1993). *Battering of women*. Boulder, CO: Westview.

Timmer, D., Eitzen, D., & Talley, K. (1994). *Paths to homelessness*. Boulder, CO: Westview.

Titus, A., Heinzelmann, F., & Boyle, J. (1995). Victimization of persons by fraud. *Crime and Delinquency, 41*(1), 54-72.

Toby, J. (1983). Crime in the schools. In J. Wilson (Ed.), *Crime and public policy*. New Brunswick, NJ: Transaction Books.

Toby, J., & Armor, D. (1992). Carrots or sticks for high school dropouts? *The Public Interest, 106*, 76-90.

Toch, H. (1977). *Living in prison*. New York: Free Press.

Tonry, M. (1995a). *Malign neglect*. New York: Oxford University Press.

Tonry, M. (1995b). Twenty years of sentencing reform: Steps forward, steps backward. *Judicature, 78*(4), 169-172.

Tonry, M., & Hamilton, V. (1995). *Intermediate sanctions in overcrowded times.* Boston: Northeastern University Press.

Uelman, G. (1983, July 27). The death penalty costs too much. *Los Angeles Times,* Part II, p. 5.

U.S. Department of Health, Education and Welfare (U.S.H.E.W.). (1978). *Violent schools—safe schools: The safe school study report to the Congress* (Report WMCP:99-8). Washington, DC: Government Printing Office.

U.S. Department of Health and Human Services (USHHS). (1995a). *National Household Survey on Drug Abuse: Population estimates, 1994.* Washington, DC: Government Printing Office.

U.S. Department of Health and Human Services (USHHS). (1995b). *Preliminary estimates from the 1994 National Household Survey on Drug Abuse.* Washington, DC: Government Printing Office.

Vaillant, G. (1983). *The natural history of alcoholism.* Cambridge, MA: Harvard University Press.

van der Laan, P. (1993). Alternative sanctions for juveniles in the Netherlands. *Dutch Penal Law and Policy* (08/02). The Hague: Ministry of Justice, Research and Documentation Centre.

van Dijk, J., & Mayhew, P. (1993). Criminal victimisation in the industrialised world. In A. del Frate, U. Zvekic, & J. van Dijk (Eds.), *Understanding crime, experiences of crime and crime control.* Rome: United Nations Interregional Crime and Justice Research Institute.

van Swaaningen, R., & de Jonge, G. (1995). The Dutch penal system in the 1990s. In J. Ruggiero, M. Ryan, & J. Sims (Eds.), *Western European penal systems.* Thousand Oaks, CA: Sage.

Viscusi, W. (1983). *Risk by choice.* Cambridge, MA: Harvard University Press.

von Hirsch, A. (1986). *Doing justice.* Boston: Northeastern University Press. (Original work published 1976)

von Hirsch, A. (1993). *Censure and sanctions.* Oxford, UK: Clarendon Press.

Voss, H., & Hepburn, J. (1968). Patterns in criminal homicide in Chicago. *Journal of Criminal Law, Criminology and Police Science, 59*(4), 499-508.

Waldorf, D., Reinarman, C., & Murphy, S. (1991). *Cocaine changes: The experience of using and quitting.* Philadelphia: Temple University Press.

Walker, L. (1984). *The battered woman syndrome.* New York: Springer.

Walker, N. (1971). *Sentencing in a rational society.* New York: Basic Books.

Walsh, A. (1994). Twice labeled: The effect of psychiatric labeling on the sentencing of sex offenders. In D. West (Ed.), *Sex crimes.* Aldershot, UK: Dartmouth.

Walsh, M. (1977). *The fence.* Westport, CT: Greenwood Press.

Walters, L. (1990, December 25). Parents put to the test before kids start school. *Los Angeles Times,* E19.

Warr, M. (1993). Age, peers, and delinquency. *Criminology, 31*(1), 17-40.

Weber, M. (1978). *Economy and society*. Berkeley: University of California Press. (Original work published 1921)

Webber, R. (1989). The OSH act and state criminal law: A prosecutor's brief. *Criminal Law Bulletin, 25,* 234-256.

Weitzman, L. (1985). *The divorce revolution*. New York: Free Press.

Wells, L., & Rankin, H. (1988). Direct parental controls and delinquency. *Criminology, 26*(2), 263-285.

White, J., Moffitt, T., Earls, F., Robins, L., & Silva, P. (1990). How early can we tell? Predictions of childhood conduct disorder and adolescent delinquency. *Criminology, 28*(4), 507-533.

Wiatrowski, M., Griswold, D., & Roberts, M. (1981). Social control theory and delinquency. *American Sociological Review, 46*(5), 525-541.

Widom, C. (1995). *Victims of childhood sexual abuse—Later criminal consequences*. Washington, DC: National Institute of Justice.

Wiederanders, M. (1981). Some myths about the employment problems of young offenders. *Federal Probation, 45*(4), 9-11.

Williams, H., & Pate, A. (1987). Returning to first principles: Reducing the fear of crime in Newark. *Crime and Delinquency, 33*(1), 31-52.

Williams, K. (1984). Economic sources of homicide. *American Sociological Review, 49*(2), 283-289.

Williams, T., & Kornblum, W. (1985). *Growing up poor*. Lexington, MA: Lexington Books.

Williamson, D., Chalk, M., & Knepper, P. (1993). Teen court: Juvenile justice for the 21st century. *Federal Probation, 57*(2), 54-58.

Wilson, J. (1968). *Varieties of police behavior*. Cambridge, MA: Harvard University Press.

Wilson, W. (1987). *The truly disadvantaged*. Chicago: University of Chicago Press.

Wojtkiewicz, R. (1993). Duration in parental structures and high school graduation. *Sociological Perspectives, 36*(4), 393-414.

Wolfgang, M. (1958). *Patterns of criminal homicide*. Philadelphia: University of Pennsylvania Press.

Wolfgang, M., Thornberry, T., & Figlio, R. (1987). *From boy to man, from delinquency to crime*. Chicago: University of Chicago Press.

Wooldredge, J. (1988). Differentiating the effects of juvenile court sentences on eliminating recidivism. *Journal of Research in Crime and Delinquency, 25*(3), 264-300.

Worth, R. (1995, November). A model prison. *Atlantic Monthly*, pp. 38-44.

Woychuk, D. (1996). *Attorney for the damned*. New York: Free Press.

Wright, J., & Rossi, P. (1986). *Armed and considered dangerous*. Hawthorne, NY: Aldine.

Wright, J., Sheley, J., & Smith, M. (1992). Kids, guns and killing fields. *Society, 30*(6), 84-89.

Wright, K. N., & Wright, K. W. (1995). *Family life, delinquency, and crime.* Washington, DC: OJJD.

Yeager, P. (1993). Industrial water pollution. In M. Tonry & A. Reiss, Jr. (Eds.), *Crime and justice: Vol. 18. Beyond the law: Crime in complex organizations.* Chicago: University of Chicago Press.

Yoshikawa, H. (1994). Prevention as cumulative protection: Effects of early family support and education on chronic delinquency and its risks. *Psychological Bulletin, 115*(1), 28-54.

Young, R., McDowall, D., & Loftin, C. (1987). Collective security and the ownership of firearms for protection. *Criminology, 25*(1), 47-62.

Zaragoza, M., Graham, J. R., Hall, G., Hirschan, R., & Ben Porath, Y. (Eds.). (1995). *Memory and testimony in the child witness.* Thousand Oaks, CA: Sage.

Zawitz, M. (1995). *Guns used in crime.* Washington, DC: Bureau of Justice Statistics.

Zietz, D. (1981). *Women who embezzle or defraud.* New York: Praeger.

Zillman, D. (1979). *Hostility and aggression.* Hillsdale, NJ: Lawrence Erlbaum.

Zimring, F., & Hawkins, G. (1986). *Capital punishment and the American agenda.* New York: Cambridge University Press.

Zimring, F., & Hawkins, G. (1993). Crime, justice, and the savings and loan crisis. In M. Tonry & J. Reiss, Jr. (Eds.), *Crime and justice: Vol. 18. Beyond the law: Crime in complex organizations.* Chicago: University of Chicago Press.

Zimring, F., & Hawkins, G. (1995). *Incapacitation.* New York: Oxford University Press.

Index